STAGING AGE

STAGING AGE

THE PERFORMANCE OF AGE
IN THEATRE, DANCE, AND FILM

Edited by

Valerie Barnes Lipscomb and
Leni Marshall

palgrave
macmillan

STAGING AGE

Copyright © Valerie Barnes Lipscomb and Leni Marshall, 2010.

First published in 2010 by
PALGRAVE MACMILLAN®
in the United States—a division of St. Martin's Press LLC,
175 Fifth Avenue, New York, NY 10010.

Where this book is distributed in the UK, Europe and the rest of the world,
this is by Palgrave Macmillan, a division of Macmillan Publishers Limited,
registered in England, company number 785998, of Houndmills,
Basingstoke, Hampshire RG21 6XS.

Palgrave Macmillan is the global academic imprint of the above companies
and has companies and representatives throughout the world.

Palgrave® and Macmillan® are registered trademarks in the United States,
the United Kingdom, Europe and other countries.

ISBN: 978–0–230–62365–1

Library of Congress Cataloging-in-Publication Data

Staging age : the performance of age in theatre, dance, and film /
edited by Valerie Barnes Lipscomb and Leni Marshall.
     p. cm.
ISBN 978–0–230–62365–1 (hardback)
1. Age in the performing arts. 2. Ability, Influence of age on.
I. Lipscomb, Valerie Barnes, 1960– II. Marshall, Leni, 1969–

PN1590.A34S73 2010
700'.454—dc22   2010001961

A catalogue record of the book is available from the British Library.

Design by Newgen Imaging Systems (P) Ltd., Chennai, India.

First edition: August 2010

10 9 8 7 6 5 4 3 2 1

Printed in the United States of America.

CONTENTS

Section III: Dance

FOREWORD

Anne Davis Basting

A long time ago, when I was a much younger scholar, I remember my dissertation adviser staging an intervention of sorts. As I remember it, he sat me down at an outdoor café on the West Bank of the University of Minnesota, ordered us a drink, and proceeded to try to convince me not to write about aging. "There's no field of aging in the humanities," he lobbied. "Your committee is concerned that you won't be able to get a job." He urged me to consider broadening my focus. Why not write about gender? With a little aging mixed in? He was right, of course. But I was guided onward by my stubbornness and by the shining example of Kathleen Woodward's *Aging and Its Discontents*, which had come out the year before, and which I devoured as though it were ice cream. Really smart, provocative ice cream.

In 1998, that dissertation became a book, *The Stages of Age: Performing Age in Contemporary American Culture*. I was fortunate to find a scholarly home in an English department that was excited for me to teach undergraduates about generational identity in narratives ranging from film and theatre to literature. But it has indeed been an ongoing struggle to establish a *field* of aging studies. A handful of scholars have published lively, interdisciplinary work in subsequent years, but unlike disability studies, aging studies has not found a departmental or curricular foothold in the humanities. In addition to Woodward, Margaret Morganroth Gullette, Stephen Katz, Thomas Cole, and Ruth Ray are just a few of the scholars whose books provide the foundation for the growth of a field. They come from English, theatre, sociology, and history. Like aging, aging studies is at once everywhere and nowhere. Perhaps because we're all aging (if we're lucky) and because "gerontology" is so interdisciplinary, aging studies has not yet taken firm hold in the humanities.

But momentum is building. In 2007, the Gerontological Society of America launched, at long last, the field's first dedicated journal—the *Journal of Aging, Humanities, and the Arts*, a huge milestone for an organization in which the humanities is still a "committee" rather than a section.

The book you hold in your hand is another milestone. Editors Valerie Lipscomb and Leni Marshall—who has nurtured interest in aging studies with her list-serve born of the Modern Language Association interest group—have gathered a fascinating blend of essays on a range of representations of aging. From Cecil B. DeMille to Moliere, from Shakespeare to Al Pacino, from tap dancing to Beckett—this volume of essays demonstrates the rich breadth of aging studies. Here, Marshall and Lipscomb offer us new angles and new voices in aging studies, from cultural studies to psychoanalysis and qualitative interviews.

I am inspired anew by this volume and the blend of voices, approaches, and disciplines it represents. The aging process changes whom we understand ourselves to be, how we see the world, and how the world sees us. It has been, and continues to be, a rich area of research, one I encourage a new generation of students to pursue (and with this volume, it will be easier). A toast, then, to my adviser and to Kathleen Woodward for inspiring me (and so many others) to enter this field, and to the editors and authors here for their insightful essays and for continuing to form the field of aging studies.

PREFACE

From Valerie: My interest in age studies stems from a graduate seminar on Shakespeare. I was convinced that I had no chance of making any critical room for myself in Shakespeare studies, that every possible avenue had been explored. Then, the age difference between Othello and Desdemona jumped out at me, and my mentors encouraged me to shape an article that became my first publication. If age had gone relatively unexplored in Shakespeare's works, I thought, there must be room for me in age studies elsewhere in dramatic literature. I set off in search of the group of like-minded literary critics who had to be out there applying age studies theory with gusto to a broad range of texts. When I did not immediately find them, I figured that I was not searching hard enough. Eventually, I concluded that age studies was relatively unexplored in all of literature, which was both exciting and unnerving. I was (and remain) convinced that increased attention to age is essential to the advancement not only of scholarship, but also of Western culture. My initial reading in the field led me almost immediately to view age as a performance and examine its performative elements; it seemed so obvious to me, yet so absent in the scholarship, that I assumed I was missing something.

Participating in a Modern Language Association (MLA) session that Leni organized to honor Kathleen Woodward's work was a turning point for me, as scholars attending the panel enthusiastically shared interests, and Woodward welcomed us into the conversation so graciously. Leni particularly stood out as an organized, fearless advocate for age studies in literature. When she later proposed a session focusing on the performance of age, I was delighted to see a colleague taking up the cause. Without Leni, I would not have attempted assembling this volume—I am eternally grateful for her initiative and expertise.

From Leni: Valerie and I both were returning scholars in graduate school. I had been out of academia for seven years, managing a senior care home and then working for a managed health care consulting firm. I knew absolutely nothing about contemporary critical works. In the time between my undergraduate and graduate work, for example, Judith Butler had gone from being an unknown scholar to having published three books and being "old hat" feminist scholarship. Much like when I encountered Butler's writing, when I started reading about age studies, I assumed that the ideas I found were accepted critical works, probably older than Butler's—after all, people were arguing with Butler and other feminist scholars writing about bodies and identity, but no one was arguing with the age studies scholars. From Kathleen Woodward's exploration of méconnaissance, I learned that age was a mask; reading Margaret Gullette, I came to understand that cosmetics and narratives affected people's performances of age; Stephen Katz was most generous in sharing his thoughts about performances of age in advertising images; Peg Cruikshank challenged me to describe an old person's physical and mental attributes using positive language. For the MLA's 2003 conference, I proposed a session in tribute to the foundational work of Kathleen Woodward, and the MLA accepted it. To me, this seemed confirmation these ideas were well established. On that tribute panel, Valerie gave an illuminating presentation about theatre and age; afterward, when she started talking about age as a performative, I assumed that all of this scholarship had been around forever.

Three years later, a looming deadline for submitting a call for papers for the upcoming conference of the MLA was mere hours away. In a fit of late-night desperation, I borrowed Valerie's topic. She was quite gracious about it, really, and that generous spirit continued as we turned those conference proposals into this book. This is her turf, and when I tromped in uninvited, she did the academic equivalent of offering me high tea on her best china. As a coauthor, Valerie's gracious spirit and writing skills are unparalleled.

Together: Each of us feels fortunate to be working in the field of age and aging studies, and to have been able to create this collection of essays. This volume is a contribution, a tribute, and an invitation. We view this book first as a valuable addition to the field—a collection of writings to advance the collected understandings and parameters of age and aging studies. Many of the people whose ideas we found so relevant and engaging at the beginning of our studies have generously mentored our scholarship. Thus, *Staging Age* also serves as a tribute to those people who made it possible for the two of us to be involved in this scholarly arena. Furthermore, we hope that the essays' ideas will engage a broad audience, and we invite artists and critics to join this conversation. We look forward to future developments in age and aging studies, knowing that there is an expanding circle of colleagues who will be there with us, taking on the challenge.

ACKNOWLEDGMENTS

The editors wish to thank the contributing authors, the staff at Palgrave Macmillan, and the many other people who have provided encouragement and support during the creation of *Staging Age*. We gratefully acknowledge colleagues at the University of South Florida, the University of Minnesota, and the University of Wisconsin–Stout, as well as our students, who inspire us daily. Among individuals who should be singled out for thanks are Sara Munson Deats, Lagretta Tallent Lenker, Donald Ross, Mike Levy, Michael Misfeldt, and Jan Hare. Finally, we are forever grateful for the patience, love, and support of our family members: Kevin, Vanessa, Natalie, Mara, Sylvia, Meghan, and Julie.

INTRODUCTION

In preparation for a theatre performance as a 285-year-old woman, Phylicia Rashād[1] says this: "I began to watch elderly women more carefully, and I fell in love with what I saw. . . . My sensibilities about growing older changed because of performing this role. I began to feel like, if this is what it means, growing older, bring it on. *Bring it on!*" Performing the role of Aunt Ester in the Broadway production of August Wilson's drama *Gem of the Ocean* profoundly affected Rashād. She says that Aunt Ester "is the most beautiful woman I have ever been." For Rashād, the conscious performance of advanced age held a transformative power.

Rashād is not alone in experiencing a new understanding of age via performance. The chapters in this volume demonstrate the many ways in which audience members as well as performers alter their perceptions of age, aging, and old age through staged performances. The concept of using non-embodied experiences such as drama and literature to access a broader range of bodily experiences than any one individual can have is not new.[2] Performances of age can similarly transport audience members to new enactments, conceptions, embodiments, and performatives of aging and old age. The articles in *Staging Age*, however, go beyond just demonstrating the myriad ways in which age can be enacted and the enactments of age can affect viewers. In addition, the combined articles in this volume lend additional credence to the concept of *age as a performative*.

The chapters offer analyses and theories intended to stimulate further research and undergird pedagogy, as we hope to broaden interest in studying age across disciplinary boundaries. This collection is, in part, inspired by Margaret Morganroth Gullette's call in *Aged by Culture*: "About age as a performance, we need to start the arguments" (159). The volume also follows in the footsteps of Kathleen Woodward's discussions of the masquerade of youth and old age, and Anne Basting's connections among aging, identity, culture, and performance.

Staging Age rests on the premise that age is both a performance and performative. While this study will employ the common meanings of the term "performance," a brief review of performativity in relation to age is appropriate. We begin with the foundational *Gender Trouble*, in which critic Judith Butler posits a performative as a constant iteration that transforms an action into a reality, "a doing that constitutes a being, an activity that creates what it describes" (Hedges). We contend that age as well as gender can be viewed as performative, in that each of us performs the actions associated with a chronological age minute by minute, and that the repetition of these performances creates a so-called reality of age both for the subject and for those who interact with the subject. Critic Mary Russo has suggested that "a theoretical reconsideration of aging as cultural repetition or performativity" would be valuable, but scholarship has yet to pursue this avenue thoroughly (21).

In positing age as a performative, age studies scholars encounter criticism similar to what Butler met: As with gender, age is at least in part biological; a person does not get to choose a different age or gender from the wardrobe each morning (Butler, *Bodies* x). And that critic would be right, of course. As Butler argues, though, the *meanings* associated with the biological aspects of gender (or age) *are* constructed: "[T]he matter of bodies will be indissociable from the regulatory norms that govern their materialization and the signification of those material effects" (*Bodies* 2). One cannot discuss the materiality of the body without engaging the issues of power associated with it. As with gender, age may be socially constructed and performative, but that performativity is in tension with the undeniable ongoing change of the body as it physically ages. With each performative iteration, a person's age changes ever so slightly, and the performance must accommodate the shift. Because the change happens so slowly, the repetition that is the hallmark of performativity seems more salient than the shift in the individual performance; however, the constantly changing body cannot be dismissed, no matter how imperceptible physical change may be from moment to moment.

Those performative alterations are enacted in a variety of media. As we assembled this volume of essays, we focused on arts that center on the performer's body: theatre, film, and dance. These media lend themselves readily to critiquing the multifaceted relationship between art and the construction of age in Western culture. In *Aged by Culture*, Gullette asserts that live theatre is the most promising site for examining the "'meatiness' of bodies" (163). Moreover, Gullette posits that viewing the performance of age on the stage holds out the possibility that individuals will then regard "*themselves* as bodies with watchable presence" (177). We extend the discussion to include other media that are concerned with the appearance of age, so that scholars may not only analyze textual messages about age in scripts and choreography, but also attend to the performers' attitudes toward their own aging processes and the opportunities and limitations of their fields. The darkened theatres of stage and screen become sites of potential transformation, challenging actors, dancers, and audience members to reassess social norms and assumptions about age.

Among those social norms is the belief that the only people who will take aging and old age seriously are the aged. As Anne Davis Basting mentions in her foreword to this book, for years, attention to aging in the arts has met resistance from scholars and artists, mirroring the general anxiety about aging in Western culture. For example, leaders of the Senior Theatre focus group of the Association for Theatre in Higher Education have even tried omitting the word "senior" from their conference session titles so that people reading the program would be more likely to attend. During the past generation, much scholarship has questioned and perhaps transcended binaries of race, class, gender, ability, and other categories of identity; too often, age has been overlooked, omitted, or "Othered" with a vengeance, a marginalization that age studies scholars suggest is a manifestation of fears about aging. Rashād questions these anxieties: "Why are you nervous about growing older? What are you scared of? What kind of way is that to live? How can you live being afraid of the inevitable? Please, darling, are you the same as you were at age two?" Of course, none of us is, but the impression that only the aged would be interested or qualified age critics lingers in far too many circles.

Scholars such as Gullette have attempted to remedy this situation by repositioning the field of inquiry as age studies rather than aging studies, welcoming the exploration of all aspects of the age spectrum. Ageism can rear its ugly head against the *too young* as well as the *too old*. Expanding the field to all ages, critics hope, will increase scholars' comfort with age issues, so that they overcome their often-unconscious fears of being stigmatized by the association with aging. When the field of inquiry is called aging studies, the focus is on those who have traditionally been marginalized; age studies denotes age as a topic relevant across the lifespan, but contains the potential for old age to remain a peripheral "Other." In addition to grappling with that fundamental understanding of what the field is or should be, scholars have struggled to find common ground in this research area, situated as it is in a way that crosses every disciplinary line.

A text that focuses on the performance and performativity of age might not resolve these knotty issues. Such a text can, however, engage more and more diverse scholars while providing that elusive commonality of approach and perhaps a shared language to undergird wide research interests. For *Staging Age*, we sought articles not only about the performance of aging or the aged, but also of performances across the lifespan, and across other categories of diverse identities. That being said, we note that the chapters contributed to *Staging Age* tend to focus on the performance of middle and older ages; only one chapter (Klein) concentrates on the performance of childhood, and few articles address diversity of race or class. The inclusiveness we seek in this field evidently will take time to develop. Nonetheless, we are pleased that this volume offers an introduction to the criticism of age studies, one that considers how age is performed on stage and off. As this discipline continues to develop, we look forward to participating in a field that contains more broadly inclusive scholarship.

We are painfully aware of how long the scholarship has taken to come even this far; a small scholarly group has been making the case for the inclusion of aging studies and age studies issues throughout the academy for multiple decades. However, we also are encouraged that diverse critics now are showing interest in the field. The time is ripe for expansion and for increased critical engagement with the category of age, allowing age to take its rightful place with other intersectional classifications, such as gender, race, class, and ability, which have garnered more scholarly attention for the past generation.

Sheer numbers at the Othered end of the age spectrum may signal a shift in priorities. As the 78-million-strong Baby Boom generation navigates middle age and heads toward traditional retirement age, the subject of aging has attracted wider media attention. Not surprisingly, this burgeoning general interest in aging is reflected in the entertainment media, as the performing arts participate in cultural interpretation in the United States and beyond. Although the Academy Award for Actress in a Leading Role traditionally has gone to women under age forty, a shift has occurred in recent years. Nominees for the 2006 award included Meryl Streep (b. 1949), Helen Mirren (b. 1945), and Judi Dench (b. 1934); Mirren won. Julie Christie (b. 1941) was nominated for the 2007 top honor, and Streep was nominated again for 2008 and 2009 awards. Instead of playing out the traditional aging narrative of decline, these older actors are poised atop Hollywood's peak. In addition to the big screen's welcoming these shades of gray, the worlds of theatre, dance, and similar media also are turning attention to the presence of older people, presenting a broader range of ages.

The higher profile of aging in the arts has generated increasing interest among critics within the arts and academia. Even Hollywood idol Robert Redford voiced a sense of alienation from the aging body, an experience that millions of Americans share: "There is a difference between the way I look and the way I feel inside" (Gillmor). Woodward has described various elements of age that support Redford's observation: "In addition to being a state of mind, aging is a biological phenomenon and a social construction. To subjective or personal age [how old we feel we are], we must add social age [how age affects the ways other people treat us], which is mediated by chronological age (how many years old we are) and biological age (the state of health of the body)" (149). Performances that foreground age touch on all these elements, as the audience considers the apparent chronological age of the performer and the performer's ability—physical and emotional—to represent various social constructions. Performers routinely make adjustments that add and subtract markers of age, creating art that reflects and shapes contemporary culture.

The chapters collected in *Staging Age* point toward issues of performing age that are common from one medium to another, as well as age issues that seem specific to each medium. The film section addresses constructions of middle and older ages in movies ranging from an early silent film to a recent taboo-breaking work. Likewise, the theatre section treats not only Shakespeare and Molière, but also Beckett and works designed for young audiences. Chapters on dance explore choreography for intergenerational troupes, received notions about who is "allowed" to dance, and the types of dance that welcome a full range of performers' ages. Several chapters explore the relationships between aging performers and their roles, whether that may involve an iconic Hollywood star, a Shakespearean actress, or a venerated dancer. Aiming at inclusivity, *Staging Age* features scholars and artists from a variety of disciplines—from sociology to French, as well as from the expected humanities- and arts-oriented disciplines. The authors hail from multiple locations: from New York to Nova Scotia, Kansas to Dublin.

Their writing presents fresh understandings of theatre scripts, dance choreography, and film plots, as well as of the bodies performing those texts. In addition to focusing on young performers' smooth skin and lithe muscles, the authors present thoughtful considerations of more seasoned performances, as well as ways in which performers are, as Margaret Cruikshank puts it, "learning to be old." About the movement into advanced age, says Rashād, "this is when you're getting good. This is when your understanding is ripening and this is when you get saucy and juicy and subtle and you can play. You can play!" In the theatre, from Shakespeare's women to Beckett's voice lessons, authors include lines, stage directions, and costuming suggestions to specify a character's age.

Dancers' stage presence grows richer over the decades, while their physical agility peaks early in their careers. In action movies, do aging cops get the bad guys or desk duty? Audience members respond to performances of age based on their own experiences of age. Combining performance studies and aging studies, the chapters in this collection examine both the performativity inherent in age and the ways in which age is portrayed in multiple media, in numerous disciplines.

About the challenges of working across disciplinary boundaries in age studies, Margaret Gullette wrote: "What we can hope is that if we err or omit and someone objects, the field grows" (*Aged* 115). In that spirit, then, we hope that many readers find this book to be lacking, and we look forward to the continuing conversation.

Notes

1. Rashād is perhaps best known for playing Claire Huxtable on *The Cosby Show*. She was fifty-six years old when she spoke with National Public Radio's Michele Norris about Rashād's role in *Gem of the Ocean*.
2. See Deats and Lenker's introduction and Waxman (78–79) for brief overviews of the theoretical bases of using literature in this way.

Works Cited

Butler, Judith. *Bodies that Matter*. New York: Routledge, 1993.
———. *Gender Trouble: Feminism and the Subversion of Identity*. New York: Routledge, 1990.
Cruikshank, Margaret. *Learning to Be Old: Gender, Culture, and Aging*. Lanham, MD: Rowman and Littlefield, 2003.
Deats, Sara Munson, and Lagretta Tallent Lenker, eds. *Aging and Identity: A Humanities Perspective*. Westport: Praeger, 1999.
Gillmor, Alison. "Act Your Age: Why Old Men Shouldn't Be Action Heroes." Feb. 16, 2006. *Canadian Broadcasting Corporation Cbc.ca*. Oct. 19, 2006. <http://www.cbc.ca/arts/film/age.html>.
Gullette, Margaret Morganroth. *Aged By Culture*. Chicago: U of Chicago P, 2004.
Hedges, Warren. "Terms and Definitions." *Swirl: Your Guide to Post-Millennial Paradigms*. 3 Dec. 2003. <http://www.sou.edu/English/IDTC/Terms/terms. htm>.
Rashād, Phylicia. "Creative Spaces: Phylicia Rashad's Nature Escape; Actress Finds Inspiration at the New York Botanical Garden." Interview with Michele Norris. *All Things Considered*. Natl. Public Radio. KNOW, St. Paul, MN. Aug. 17, 2002. <http://www.npr.org/features/feature.php?wfId=3855 543&sourceCode=RSS>.

Russo, Mary. "Aging and the Scandal of Anachronism." *Figuring Age: Women, Bodies, Generations.* Ed. Kathleen Woodward. Bloomington: Indiana UP, 1999. 20–33.

Waxman, Barbara Frey. *From the Hearth to the Open Road: A Feminist Study of Aging in Contemporary Literature.* Westport, CT: Greenwood Press, 1990.

Woodward, Kathleen. *Aging and Its Discontents: Freud and Other Fictions.* Indianapolis: Indiana UP, 1991.

SECTION I

FILM

CHAPTER 1

"THAT YOUNGER, FRESHER WOMAN": *OLD WIVES FOR NEW* (1918) AND HOLLYWOOD'S CULT OF YOUTH

Heather Addison

Aging in Early Twentieth-Century America

Age studies scholar Margaret Gullette argues that aging is a culturally constructed rather than a strictly biological process. "The basic idea we need to absorb," says Gullette, "is that whatever happens in the body, human beings are aged by culture first of all" (3). Our current understanding of growing older as a process of decline and potentially debilitating loss may be traced to a specific constellation of historical forces that emerged in the late nineteenth and early twentieth centuries, forces that, as I will argue in this chapter, had an impact upon the representation of aging in *Old Wives for New* (1918), a popular silent film directed by Cecil B. DeMille.

Prior to the late nineteenth century, a model of aging that had originated with the Puritans was in ascendance. It acknowledged the potential infirmities and loss as well as the redemptive spiritual potential of old age, offering a contradictory but essentially hopeful vision of the human life cycle (Cole 39–40). Furthermore, as historian Howard Chudacoff has noted, the preindustrial American economy of artisanship and agriculture was one in which age did not play a vital role in stratification; different generations routinely lived and worked together and relied upon one another to survive (10), producing a strong sense of interdependence and mutual respect. By the late 1800s, however, the rural economy that had been the bulwark of the pre–Civil War era gave way to a factory-based system in which accumulated experience mattered less than strength, endurance, and speed. According to Chudacoff, "Shifts in the manufacturing process began to squeeze workers into more sharply defined age and skill categories" (18), which tended to isolate different age groups and even to pit them against one another in the competition for employment. At the same time, Victorian morality, with its emphasis on self-control and productivity, evolved a dualistic model of aging that lauded "good" old age (health, vigor, self-reliance) and devalued "bad" old age (decay, dependence). According to historian Thomas R. Cole, "Victorian moralists dichotomized and rationalized experience in order to control it. Ideological and psychological pressures to master old age generated a dualism that retains much of its cultural power today" (231).

The positive pole of this dualistic model of aging remained dominant throughout the nineteenth century, but with increasing industrialization and the rise of a scientific worldview, a more pessimistic interpretation of aging as "disease" gained prominence after the fin de siècle. Old age was medicalized, and the sciences of "geriatrics" and "gerontology" were established to deal with its ravages upon the body. As Cole explains, "The formative literature of gerontology and geriatrics helped complete the long-term cultural shift from conceiving [of] aging primarily as a mystery or an existential problem to viewing it primarily as a scientific and technical problem" (195). Aging became something pathological that could be avoided—or at least delayed—if the proper preventive treatment(s) could be identified and undertaken.

The increasing efficiency of manufacturing processes in the 1910s and 1920s accelerated the impact of the Industrial Age upon American culture, particularly in regard to attitudes toward aging. Citizens habituated to hard work, thrift, and a relative scarcity of goods had to be indoctrinated as consumers who could absorb the new manufacturing capacity of factories. Industry leaders turned to advertisers, who abandoned the low-key, product-centered approach that had characterized most Victorian-era ads in favor of high-pressure, psychological methods that preyed upon consumers' fears and insecurities, bred dissatisfaction and envy, and fostered a desire for a stylish, carefree way of life. The cornerstone of this emerging consumer culture was an exaltation of youthfulness, which provided a foundation for both production and consumption of goods.

Young adults, advertisers argued, were less set in their ways and therefore more receptive to the constant clarion call of the consumer age: Buy, buy, buy. Youthfulness itself was promoted as an advantageous state that could ensure continued health, beauty, and employment; those who became frail, ill, or decrepit were at risk of being discarded by a modern, fast-paced, industrial society. In the early twentieth century, this quest for youthfulness provided a continually expanding market for diet products, exercise machines, and cosmetics as Americans attempted to stop or reverse the inexorable process of aging.[1] This market was skewed toward females, who typically faced graver social and economic consequences as they aged than their male counterparts did. Men's power and capital tended to increase as they accumulated age and experience, thus according them a measure of compensation for their lost youth. Women's appeal was more dependent upon their possession of youth and beauty, which became crucial markers of their "exchange" value.

Thus, Hollywood's emergence in the 1910s coincided with a gradual yet fundamental alteration in Americans' experience of growing older. As Hollywood became established, it quickly gained fame not only as a center of film production, but also as a cultural institution that valued conspicuous consumption, sexual display, physical culture, and youth, especially in its female performers. Throughout the late 1910s and 1920s, the popular press, including motion picture fan magazines, consistently emphasized Hollywood's youthfulness. Motion picture stars served as "heroes of aging," public figures who attempted to remain forever young in their physical appearance and work habits (Featherstone, "Post-Bodies" 227). Hollywood, with its spectacular moving images of elegant young bodies, romantic interludes, and extravagant living standards, obligingly provided the consumptive capacity to absorb industry's excess of goods by promoting the new standards of behavior, appearance, and lifestyle to which the public was to aspire.

Cecil B. DeMille and the "New Woman"

There was perhaps no figure more closely associated with Hollywood's celebration of youthful consumerism than director Cecil B. DeMille, whose films have been credited with—and sometimes derided for— bringing Hollywood into the "modern age" by dispensing with Victorian morality and embracing extravagant consumption. In 1914, DeMille directed his first film, *The Squaw Man,* for the Jesse Lasky Feature Play Company (later Paramount Pictures), which he had founded with Jesse L. Lasky and Samuel Goldfish (later Goldwyn). He quickly developed a reputation as a skilled director whose profitable films featured melodramatic plotlines and elaborate costumes, often in historical settings. In 1918, however, he made a contemporary film that helped to establish him as Hollywood's purveyor of modern values: *Old Wives for New,* an adaptation of a popular novel of the same name. The story chronicles the travails of Sophy and Charles Murdock, a middle-aged couple who have been married for twenty years. Charles has retained his dignity and youthful looks, while Sophy, in DeMille's words, has become "wonderfully disgusting": fat, slovenly, and wrinkled. Flashbacks reveal that she was once slender and beautiful.

Each of the main characters is out of sync with modernity: Charles, because he is tied to a woman bordering on decrepitude, and Sophy, because she has unwisely allowed her youthful, slender appearance to slip away from her. Sophy's body, which the film presents as decayed and out of control, provides Charles the motivation—and justification—to pursue and eventually marry a younger, trimmer woman. The narrative does not abandon the misguided Sophy, however; after she rejuvenates herself by trying to slim down and undergoing beauty treatments, she marries her husband's male secretary, suggesting that society will not forsake those women who commit themselves to disciplining their bodies. What I wish to suggest in this chapter is that the gendered performances of aging in *Old Wives for New* can be understood as a manifestation not simply of DeMille's splashy showmanship and prurient interest in objectifying women, but as evidence of broader social pressures operating in Hollywood and the culture at large in the early twentieth century—pressures that put a new premium on youthfulness.

Indeed, the novel upon which the film is based was published a full decade before the film was produced. Author David Graham Phillips was arguably a literary version of Cecil B. DeMille; he began as a journalist, but by his mid-thirties was able to wrest a living from the publication of titillating "social issue" novels like *The Great God Success* (1901), *The Master Rogue* (1903), *The Fortune-Hunter* (1906), and *Old Wives for New* (1908).[2] *Old Wives for New*, which provided the foundation for DeMille's 1918 film, is rich with drama distilled from the collision between "old" and "new": between those who cling to outdated ideas about personal hygiene, attractiveness, filial duty, and unchanging traditions and those who understand that youth, beauty, happiness, and continual change and excitement are the paramount goals of life. Phillips's book is striking for its implied horror of aging and fat, a theme to which it returns again and again, primarily through the vilification of Sophy Murdock. Sophy does not bathe frequently, wears shapeless clothing about her large girth, and feels that she has done her part in life simply by marrying and having children:

> Plainly, she regarded her life as past its climax; and the state of physical and mental deterioration, indicated in slovenly corpulence, in carelessness of toilet, in stale, monotonous expression of eyes, proclaimed that she had

been of this mind for some time, several years at least. . . . To glance from her to her husband was to have the impulse to commiserate [with] them both—and to wonder. For, it was as obvious as her having ceased to live and having begun a long placid death of the dry rot that the man to whom she was married stood just at the beginning of the age of achievement. (Phillips 27)

Here, the narrator conveys his disgust for those who allow themselves to trod upon a path of decline, becoming little more than "dry rot." The story offers a female as the representative of this disturbing fall from grace, reiterating women's tenuous position in the ideological universe that the film embraces. If Sophy were a man who had grown slovenly and corpulent, she may still have had other forms of cultural capital, such as involvement in business, to keep her connected with the modern world. But Sophy, a housewife and mother, has no such means to validate and engage herself. Her husband is the wealthy and powerful "Oil King," while she has become obsolete.

Sophy understands that somehow the modern world is passing her by, but she is not quite sure how to remedy the situation:

She thought little about abstract matters, yet she could not help realizing that everything was unsettled and unsettling in this modern world. She dimly saw how these new and therefore wicked impulses to change were affecting all ages and impulses and stations and both sexes, were disregarding the matrimonial and the family barriers—in fact, all the barriers which religion and tradition had established. Husbands and wives no longer had the habit of contentedly and decently growing old together, as unmoved by change as oysters in deep-lying beds by swing of tide or whirl of tempest. Instead, one or the other, or both, became tainted by this craze for change; and there were scandals, domestic upheavals, divorces. (87–88)

The novel suggests that Sophy is an obtuse person with limited capacity for sophisticated thought, someone who is able neither to understand nor to cope with the shifting demands of the modern world. Yet her position is tautological: She is ignorant because, in her passive position as a wife and mother, she is insulated from the very forces that the narrator mocks her for failing to understand and embrace. Detached from the powerful modernity that surges outside of her domestic sphere, she becomes more and more apathetic (and pathetic).

When Sophy fears that her husband, disgusted by her unkempt appearance and overwhelming girth, has begun to look elsewhere for affection, she consults her doctor, desperate for help. "Didn't I tell you that fat was a disease?" he chides her. "Didn't I warn you that if you let that disease run a few years longer, you'd be a shapeless mass before you were forty?...You're a young woman. You've been letting yourself go to rack and ruin" (74–75). Her doctor recommends a strict diet and exercise, but Sophy is unable to follow either.

Ultimately, her salvation is her husband's male secretary, Melville Blagden, who sees in her situation a chance for his own prosperity: If Sophy divorces, she will assume control over half of the fortune that her husband's business acumen has generated, so Blagden maneuvers to marry her. He admires fleshy women, but Sophy still needs to slim down before she can approach his ideal, so he flatters her into taking more exercise and eventually visiting one of the new "aesthetic surgeons" who performs youthful "renovations." Since Sophy is still relatively young and has a "superb constitution," Dr. Secor does not endorse "drastic measures," but instead prescribes a system of "massage, breathing, diet, and walking" (294) to reduce her weight and restore a measure of her attractiveness. Once she has taken a physical culture course and purchased a new, more attractive wardrobe, Blagden accepts her as a suitable mate. She has demonstrated her devotion to the imperatives of consumer culture: She is willing to spend time and money in the pursuit of youth and beauty, the two key ingredients in a woman's success. In other words, her possession of a fortune is a necessary but not sufficient condition to make her wife material. Blagden is interested in her, but is not *convinced* that she is a suitable mate until her appearance undergoes a transformation.

DeMille's film, scripted by Jeanie MacPherson, echoes and magnifies the novel's endorsement of youthful modernity. Historians have gushed over the film version's significance to DeMille's career, to Hollywood, and to American culture. In *Cecil B. DeMille's Hollywood*, Robert Birchard claims that *Old Wives for New* "created a sensation and led directly to the social comedies with which DeMille would be identified into the early 1920s. With this film Cecil B. DeMille closed the door on the 'age of innocence' and ushered in the Jazz Age" (124).[3] More than any of his previous films, *Old Wives for New* heralded DeMille's embrace of modernity—a modernity that was sharper and more unrelenting than that of Phillips's novel, written just ten years earlier. "Phillips was sympathetic about [Sophy's] failings, attributed in part to rural family origins, but DeMille proved merciless in deconstructing the sentimental image of the American wife and mother in favor of the 'new woman,'" observes Sumiko Higashi in *Cecil B. DeMille and American Culture: The Silent Era* (146).

This "new woman" was one who purchased all the latest products, including fashionable clothing; followed a daily schedule of personal hygiene; and maintained a slender, youthful body, even after childbirth.

DeMille's film did not create the "new woman," but it did, perhaps even more than Phillips's novel, help her gain a firmer purchase in American culture, reinforcing ideas that had already begun to seem natural and obvious. "*Old Wives for New* has its inexorable logic," declared a review in the *Los Angeles Times*. "The story is built of facts that no sane man or woman will deny. The physical side of love may not be ignored—the body must be kept as a temple for the soul. This is the theme of *Old Wives for New*, and rightly considered, it is a big theme, one worthy of a story, a poem or a picture" (Anderson).

In 1919, the year after the film was released, newspaper advice columnist Dorothea Dix called attention to the continued relevance of the subject—and its close association with DeMille's film—by titling one of her columns in early 1919 "Old Wives for New." She cites a case in which an older gentleman who wishes to marry a young girl is chagrined that his wife will not divorce him: "I think it very selfish of her [to refuse], as she is old and rheumatic, and no longer attracts or interests me." Dix rails against this "bad business" of swapping wives, but her spirited defense of the value of aging wives suggests that, in the face of a new focus on youth and personal satisfaction, exemplified by such artifacts as Graham's novel and DeMille's film, older women—especially those not actively engaged in maintaining or recuperating their youthfulness—had lost a measure of their cultural capital.

"For Pity's Sake, Spruce Up!"

The version of *Old Wives for New* shot by DeMille and written by Jeanie MacPherson begins with an interesting stand-alone quotation that does not appear in the novel and is not attributed to any of the film's characters:

> It is my belief, Sophy, that we Wives are apt to take our Husbands too much for granted.
>
> We've an inclination to settle down to neglectful *dowdiness*—just because we've "landed our Fish"!
>
> It is not enough for Wives to be merely virtuous any more, scorning all frills. We must remember to trim our "Votes for Women" with a little lace and ribbon—if we would keep our Man a "Lover," as well as a "Husband"!

The intertitle suggests that the implied omniscient narrator of the film is herself an experienced wife who can counsel Sophy—and other females watching the film. This narrator advises women that virtue is no longer

enough for a wife to be valued; in an age of greater female liberty, sym-
bolized by the campaign for suffrage, women must take care to cultivate
an appealing, youthful femininity. Thus this initial quotation insinuates
that the film can be read as a helpful, cautionary tale for wives: It may
insult or frighten women, but all for a good cause. "Yes, you worried married women," concluded one review of the film, "better see *Old Wives for
New!* Of course, you may not have a thing in common with . . . Sophy, but
if you have, for pity's sake spruce up and do it quickly" (Tinée). If women
exhibit "dowdiness," a condition that suggests not only frumpiness but
also an antiquated appearance, they risk losing their spouses.

Like the novel, the film stages a series of comparisons between characters' behaviors and the dictates of modernity. Those in harmony with
modern values—youth, dynamism, consumerism—are rewarded. Those
who are not in concert with such values are punished with a degree of
social exclusion, economic exclusion, or both, unless and until they find a
way to transform themselves. Largely due to the cinematic advantages of
mise-en-scène (pictorial composition) and editing, the comparisons that
the film makes between those characters who are in sync with modernity
and those who are not are generally more striking than those in the novel.
The film employs parallelism and crosscutting extremely effectively as it
assesses characters' engagement with modernity.

The first character introduced, Charles Murdock (Elliot Dexter), is
described in an intertitle as an "Oil King" whose name "spells *Genius*
to the Financial World and *Pocket-Book* to his Family." This intertitle
is followed by a shot of oil derricks and then an image of Murdock sitting at a desk in a large office, near two telephones and a ticker tape
machine, surrounded by the symbols of successful capitalism. He wears a
suit with a bow tie; a round iris mask (a common stylistic feature of silent
films) frames his youthful face. Despite his apparent wealth, he appears
unhappy. Watching a man and a woman eat lunch outside his window,
he exclaims, "They don't own the house they live in—and they haven't
any automobile, but they're happier than I am—because they have *Love!*"
Thus, Charles has a sore lack in his life; yet the film, by presenting him as
youthful, attractive, and financially successful, leaves us hopeful that this
deficiency can be overcome.

Immediately after Charles Murdock, we are introduced to "The Five
Pairs of Hands that Were to Weave the Threads of His Destiny." Each
pair of hands represents one of the five secondary characters who affect
Charles's life in various ways over the course of the film. Each of them
has a specific role in the hierarchy of modernity. The first of the five
is "Sophy Murdock—his Wife." After an intertitle announcing her, the
film fades in on a close-up of two large hands searching through an

Figure 1.1 Middle-aged, slovenly Sophy Murdock (Sylvia Ashton) spends her days lounging and eating chocolates.

enormous box of chocolates. A dissolve reveals Sophy Murdock (Sylvia Ashton): fiftyish, thick about the middle, straggly haired, and dressed only in a robe as she reads the comics. Her passivity, size, and lack of personal hygiene mark her as radically out of step with the modern age (see figure 1.1). The second pair of hands—dainty and youthful—belongs to Viola (Marcia Manon), a "Painted Lady" who inveigles Charles Murdock into a brief, illicit relationship. She is on the opposite end of the spectrum from Sophy: She uses so much makeup and finery that her youthful beauty no longer appears natural. She is a consumer, but not a discriminating one. She leers and winks directly at the camera, suggesting her lower class, "vulgar" status. The third "Pair of Hands" is Juliet Raeburn (Florence Vidor), a fashionable New York dressmaker and the woman with whom Charles Murdock eventually falls in love when he meets her on a hunting trip. She presents the proper mixture of modern derring-do and old-fashioned modesty. Juliet's elegantly clad hands cut delicate fabric, implying that she is a working woman intimately acquainted with contemporary fashions. Her face is made up, but much more discreetly than Viola's; she smiles, but sweetly and not directly at the camera, as Viola did. Despite Juliet's long working hours and her leadership role as the owner of a business, she maintains a demure youthfulness. Her suitability as a potential mate for Charles Murdock, a hardworking capitalist who has also preserved his youthful attractiveness, is apparent.

The fourth and fifth "Pairs of Hands" are those of the narrative's secondary male characters, providing insight into the film's gendered treatment of the imperatives of modernity. The hands of Melville Blagden (Gustav von Seyffertitz), Charles Murdock's middle-aged secretary, type busily and efficiently. He is a poor man with an aristocratic background who must use his brains to get ahead in the modern world. The final pair of hands belongs to Tom Berkeley (Theodore Roberts), Charles Murdock's business partner, who is introduced as a "shrewd Sensualist who wants only what he pays for—and gets it." His hands are in front of a knob, fumbling with a key ring as he searches for the means to unlock the door to his mistress's apartment. As he enters, we see her urge a handsome young man wearing a tuxedo into hiding. Thus, we learn that the elderly Berkeley's money is not enough to ensure his mistress's fidelity, for she seeks a younger man.

This clever series of character introductions deftly establishes the value of youth, beauty, brains, and wealth. Females are more likely to possess and exploit youth and beauty, while males skew toward brains and wealth. One or more of these qualities can be helpful and bring a degree of satisfaction, but all four are necessary to secure oneself a haven of love and happiness in the modern world. Viola and her friend Jessie, both kept women, use their youth and beauty to get ahead. Sophy benefits from the fortune she receives as a consequence of her divorce, but the film presents her wealth as a product of her husband's labors, not her own. Melville Blagden employs his brains to change his penniless situation into one of largesse by marrying Sophy. Tom Berkeley, Charles Murdock's partner, has an ample fortune that he uses to attract a series of young women. The only two characters who achieve success in both the public (business) arena and their personal lives are Charles Murdock and Juliet Raeburn, each of whom has youth, attractiveness, brains, and (self-generated) wealth. Both benefit from their physical appeal, although the standards of youthful beauty that the film upholds for its female characters are arguably less forgiving than those it applies to men.

This is certainly true for Sophy, whose castigation for allowing herself to appear frumpishly middle-aged begins in earnest after all of the characters have been introduced in the "Hands" scenes. In the very first of DeMille's lavish bathroom sequences, which became a signature feature of his silent films, *Old Wives for New* cross cuts between

Charles Murdock in the couple's elegantly appointed bathroom and Sophy Murdock, who is still asleep in their bedroom. This fascinating sequence reveals private space and showcases luxury that few could afford at the time: a bathroom with two impressive pedestal sinks and a claw-footed bathtub. The first shot is an iris in that introduces the space. A well-dressed servant assists Charles with his striped bathrobe; the two are initially turned away from the camera. The film cuts to a medium long shot of Sophy in bed. Then, Charles approaches one of the sinks and stands stock-still, a revolted look on his face as he regards his wife's hair in the drain (see figure 1.2).

He picks it up rather gingerly and drops it out of a nearby window, then removes a toothbrush and hair-filled comb from the edge of his sink and deposits them at Sophy's sink, which is crammed with bottles, cups, and other odds and ends.

Meanwhile, Sophy begins to awaken as Charles, back at his own sink, wipes it clean. Sophy gets out of bed, puts on slippers, and enters the bathroom. She is on the right side of the frame, looking blowsy and aged in a robe and disheveled dark hair sprinkled with patches of gray. He stands on the left side of the screen: tall, slender, clean, his bared biceps flexing. She holds her head as if she is ill and turns on the tap at the

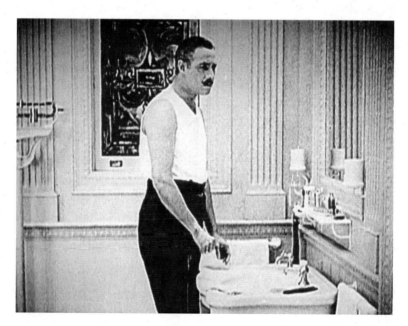

Figure 1.2 Trim, fastidious Charles Murdock (Elliot Dexter) is disgusted when he sees his wife's hair in the sink.

tub; we get close-ups of her hands, the water flowing down the drain, and then her weary face. She shuts the water off, and then notices the window that Charles opened. Giving him a repressive look, she stalks across the room and pulls it down. He regards her as if she has just closed the last chapter of their life together, and she returns to bed, choosing not to avail herself of the bathroom's amenities.

This sequence, more obviously than any other series of shots in the film, dramatizes Sophy's disengagement with the modern world. She is blessed with a beautiful bathroom with which to attend to her personal needs, but she can keep neither herself nor her surroundings in proper order. Her slatternly state is brought into stark relief—and perhaps seems more foolish and even "offensive"—in the midst of an elegant bathroom that audiences of the period would have associated with the ultimate in sanitation and splendor. Her sink is littered with jars and bottles that might help her to recover her beauty, but she ignores them. Meanwhile, her husband resolutely allies himself with the modern age; he disdains chaos and filth in his surroundings and in his person. He keeps his area of the bathroom as neat as his frowzy wife's habits will allow, while his body is carefully attired, youthful, clean, and trim. The mismatch between the two is painfully obvious: Charles must shed Sophy if he is to remain part of the modern world.

The narrative reminds us that both sexes can be penalized for their failure to engage with modernity, however. For instance, Tom Berkeley, Charles Murdock's business partner, is cuckolded by his mistress because he can offer her money but not youth. Yet the film—and the novel—suggest that aging women suffer more than aging men. Berkeley may be deceived by his young mistress, but he cruelly discards her for an even younger woman when she begins to bore him. Even after marriage and motherhood, women of the period were urged to retain their attractiveness, lest they lose the affection of their families. "Not a Day Older!" trumpets a 1923 ad for Palmolive soap in *Motion Picture Magazine*. "Fortunate is the wife and mother whose youthful appearance evokes this compliment on the day of her china wedding [twentieth anniversary]." The ad features an adored, youthful mother surrounded by her husband and two adolescent children. Mothers who remained youthful enjoyed the embraces of their families, but those same family members, such ads implied, could just as easily turn away if Mother showed signs of advancing age. This is the disdain that Sophy, the mother of two young adults, encounters in DeMille's *Old Wives for New*—until, at the behest of her husband's secretary, who is attracted to her fortune, she recuperates her youth via the ministrations of a beauty doctor (whose staff rolls Sophy on the floor, puts her in a steam box, and then straps her into a punishingly tight corset).

In the Victorian era, motherliness was associated with devotion, sacrifice, and a mature, matronly body. In the Jazz Age, popular culture urged mothers to be as slim and youthful as their daughters, to shed the "old-fashioned" ideas of the nineteenth century. This is why actress Sylvia Ashton was an interesting choice for the part of Sophy Murdock. Most female motion picture stars were young and slender, but the industry did provide limited opportunities for older, more physically substantial women as "character" actresses. Dubbed the "Mother of Hollywood" because of her maternal roles and her emotional support of many young stars, Ashton was described by a fan magazine of the period as "tremendously fat—almost incredibly so.... And she can cook. Oh, how she can cook!! It's no wonder that Hollywood has adopted Sylvia Ashton as its unofficial mother. She has every one of those God-given propensities that mothers have. And in her heart is the love that passeth all understanding" (Handy 28). Mature mothers were laudable for their devotion to old-fashioned morality and selflessness, yet removed from the stream of modern life because of their age and their full-blown, fleshy figures. Ashton was beloved because of her extensively publicized maternal generosity (among other things, she liked to feed people and even opened a restaurant). While the film excoriates the character of Sophy on all levels—she is thoughtless, greedy, self-centered, and old and fat—DeMille's decision to cast Sylvia Ashton as Sophy implies that she can and will be redeemed if she is willing to devote herself to a body improvement regime. By extension, the film may provide an encouragement (or a warning) to "Victorian" mothers like Sophy: If they discipline their bodies with exercise programs and beauty products, they too can recuperate their youthful attractiveness.

Early in the film, Sophy denounces Juliet Raeburn, her husband's new love, as a "younger, fresher woman." By the film's conclusion, however, she has absorbed the precepts of modernity, finally recognizing not only that *anyone* can be younger and fresher (with the right products and effort), but also that *everyone* has a responsibility to cultivate youthfulness. When a system of physical culture and careful hygiene gradually allows her to recover a degree of her attractiveness and good humor, Sophy finally agrees to divorce Charles, who immediately marries Juliet. The transformed Sophy is also able to secure a mate: Melville Blagden, who is attracted to her rehabilitated body—and her lavish divorce settlement. Thus the title of the narrative, *Old Wives for New*, is revealed to be quite precise. The events of the plot actually produce two new wives: Sophy, who marries Melville Blagden, and Juliet Raeburn, the young dress-maker who marries Charles Murdock.

If one considers age, however, the couple shuffling in the film dif-fers rather markedly from the couple shuffling in the novel. In Phillips's prose version of the tale, the four principal characters are within a decade of one another in age: Charles is fortyish, Sophy is in her late thirties, Melville Blagden is in his thirties, and Juliet Raeburn is at least thirty (having owned a business for ten years). In the film, no ages are men-tioned, but the ages of the actors are quite suggestive of DeMille's (and by extension, Paramount's and even Hollywood's) attitudes toward male and female aging. Elliot Dexter, who plays Charles Murdock, is forty-eight years old. Sylvia Ashton is thirty-eight—ten years his junior—but the streaks of gray in her hair and her matronly attire make her seem older. She appears closer to her chronological age by the end of the film, when she has dyed her hair, applied cosmetics, and updated her wardrobe. Charles marries Juliet Raeburn, played by Florence Vidor, who was then twenty-three years old. Sophy marries Melville Blagden, played by Gustav von Seyffertitz, aged fifty-six. Thus an askew uni-verse is brought into alignment by pairing off a forty-eight-year-old man with a twenty-three-year-old woman and a thirty-eight-year-old woman with a fifty-six-year-old man. The film codes it as pairing youth with youth (Charles with Juliet) and age with age (Sophy with Melville), reinforcing the notion that, in Hollywood, a woman had to be in her twenties to be considered young, while a man could be youthful well into his forties.

In endorsing this paradigm, DeMille was arguably responding to wider historical trends, such as industrialization, consumerism, and the rise of age stratification, particularly as they affected women. Yet the cel-ebration of youth—and the concomitant dismissal of age—are prominent and excessive in DeMille's film, as they were in much of early Hollywood discourse. Respect for old age was losing ground in American culture, but the trend was exaggerated in Hollywood.

Established in sunny California, far from traditional Eastern centers of civilization, dependent upon an intangible visual product that high-lighted personal appearance and brought the possibility of substantial largesse, Hollywood quickly began to favor and reinforce the values of youthful consumerism: self-interest, sexual appeal, satisfaction gleaned through the purchase of appropriate products, and so on. Motion pic-ture stars conspicuously consumed their wealth; exhibited their bodies at swimming pools and beaches; and worked to keep themselves slim, young, attractive, and vigorous, so that the "cruel eye" of the camera would not reveal wrinkles or adipose tissue. Hollywood's predilection for youth, especially youthful females, was well established by the late 1910s—and is still apparent nearly a century later.

Notes

1. For a detailed discussion of the relationship between the youthful body and its role in consumer culture, see "The Body in Consumer Culture" by Mike Featherstone in *The Body: Social Process and Cultural Theory*.
2. The melodrama in Phillips's novels pierced the veil of reality in 1911, when he was summarily shot and killed by a man who believed that Phillips had cast aspersions on his family in *The Fashionable Adventures of Joshua Craig*, a book published two years earlier.
3. DeMille has argued that he had no investment in suggesting to husbands that they should get rid of dowdy, dilapidated wives, or, indeed, in making the picture at all: "The fact is," he says, "that I made *Old Wives for New* only after repeated urging from the New York office" (211). According to DeMille, Lasky purchased the rights to the novel, and then hounded him to produce a film based upon it: "Remember," Lasky said in a telegram to DeMille, "'that we are holding *Old Wives for New* until you decide whether or not you want to produce it. I am strongly of the opinion that you should get away from the spectacle stuff for one or two pictures and try to do modern stories of great human interest.' So I did. The reader may, if he chooses, consider that my original sin. He may write down...the date on which I bade a last good-by to integrity and art" (DeMille 212).

Works Cited

Anderson, Antony. "Old Wives for New." *Los Angeles Times*, June 17, 1918, sec. 2:6.

"At the Theaters This Week—*Old Wives for New*." *Washington Post*, June 24, 1918: 9.

Birchard, Robert S. *Cecil B. DeMille's Hollywood*. Lexington: UP of Kentucky, 2004.

Chudacoff, Howard P. *How Old Are You? Age Consciousness in American Culture*. Princeton, NJ: Princeton UP, 1989.

Cole, Thomas R. *The Journey of Life: A Cultural History of Aging in America*. New York: Cambridge UP, 1992.

DeMille, Cecil B. *The Autobiography of Cecil B. DeMille*. Ed. Donald Hayne. Englewood Cliffs, NJ: Prentice-Hall, 1959.

Dix, Dorothea. "The People and Their Troubles: Old Wives for New." *Los Angeles Times*, Mar. 26, 1919, sec. 2:2.

Featherstone, Mike. "The Body in Consumer Culture." *The Body: Social Process and Cultural Theory*. Ed. Mike Featherstone, Mike Hepworth, and Bryan S. Turner. London: Sage, 1991. 170–96.

———. "Post-Bodies, Aging, and Virtual Reality." *Images of Aging: Cultural Representations of Later Life*. Ed. Mike Featherstone and Andrew Wernick. London/New York: Routledge, 1995. 227–44.

Gullette, Margaret Morganroth. *Declining to Decline: Cultural Combat and the Politics of the Midlife*. Charlottesville/London: UP of Virginia, 1997.

Handy, Truman. "Mother O'Hollywood." *Motion Picture Magazine*, Aug. 1922: 28+.

Higashi, Sumiko. *Cecil B. DeMille and American Culture: The Silent Era*. Berkeley: U of California P, 1994.

"Not a Day Older!" Palmolive Soap advertisement. *Motion Picture Magazine*, Mar. 1923: inside cover.

Old Wives for New. Dir. Cecil B. DeMille. With Sylvia Ashton, Elliot Dexter, and Florence Vidor. Artcraft Pictures, 1918.

Phillips, David Graham. *Old Wives for New*. New York/London: D. Appleton, 1908.

Tinée, Mae. "Forget Your Woes; Take off Some Fat—Get Some Clothes." *Chicago Daily Tribune*, July 9, 1918: 14.

CHAPTER 2

THE UNCONSCIOUS OF AGE: PERFORMANCES IN PSYCHOANALYSIS, FILM, AND POPULAR CULTURE

E. Ann Kaplan

In the growing field of age studies, scholars have analyzed how cultures think about age across a range of perspectives—economic, sociological, political, and ideological—as well as studied representations of age in a variety of media. There is, however, less research on what I call the "unconscious of age," using the term in three distinct but related senses. First, building on work by humanities scholars and essays by clinicians, I look briefly at how psychoanalysts have thought about age—the "unconscious" of age in the sense of biases in traditional psychoanalytic theory. Second, I explore more recent clinical case studies of the elderly, looking at the "unconscious of age" in a sense that humanists have rarely studied— namely, the unconscious conflicts that reemerge with aging. Finally, I use this background to illuminate the central character's dilemma in Roger Michell's film *The Mother*,[1] which is about May, a middle-aged woman involved in a sexual relationship with a much younger man. Anne Reid's performance as May challenges ongoing (if dated) stereotypes of aging and staging. Furthermore, an examination of May's differences from psychoanalytic case studies reveals traces of ageist stereotypes in some clinical work.

These three approaches to the unconscious of age depart from methods that, as noted, predominate in age studies. Over the years, sociological, ideological, economic, anthropological, and multicultural perspectives have delivered vital information about older women, along

with directives for needed changes in policies and practices for dealing
with women's increasing numbers worldwide. However, we also need to
better understand the inner, psychic lives of older people—information
that is much harder to access. What happens to sexual desire as we age?
How do unconscious desires—love, lust, and infatuation—change with
age? Why do some cultures assume the aged are sexless or have lost desire,
or if not, that their desire is grotesque, while others value older women
as bearing wisdom and experience? I turn to psychoanalysis and film to
find accounts of the inner lives of older people so absent in the often vast
bibliographies about aging in fields such as gerontology and those noted
above.[2]

Julia Kristeva remarked that literature is "like hysteria, which Freud
saw as a 'distorted work of art'...a *staging* of affects both on the inter-
subjective level (characters) and on the intra-linguistic level (style)" (179)[3];
her comments are applicable to film as well. It is this *staging* and *performance* of affects in regard to sex and middle-aged western women that
I explore in this article, via psychoanalytic theory, psychoanalytic case
studies, and fiction film.[4]

The Unconscious of Age in Psychoanalytic Theory

The irony of Freud's doubting that older people could benefit from psychoanalysis, while he himself as an elderly man was doing some of his most
creative work, has not gone unnoticed. Harold Blum (2001) notes that
while analysts themselves continued to work into very advanced years,
"the problems of the geriatric analyst or elderly impaired patient were
hardly considered" (109). It seems that analysts' unconsciousness about
age enables them to provide accurate assessments of patients while hiding from themselves their own age. If they are still innovative therapists
at midlife or later, helping ever-new patients, why should they deny the
same flexibility and creativity to their older clients? Kathleen Woodward
(1991) further notes that at the age of seventy-seven, in his lecture "On
Femininity" (published in 1931), Freud contrasts men and women in
regard to their possibilities for change in analysis. While to Freud a man
at thirty still appears youthful, women, he says, are already old, rigid, and
incapable of change. The woman's libido has, for Freud, "taken up final
positions and seems incapable of changing them for others. There are no
paths open to further development; it is as though the whole process had
already run its course and remains thenceforward unsusceptible to influence" (qtd. in Woodward, *Aging* 192). This shockingly negative assess-
ment of the aging psyche, especially in its reference to women whom
today we would consider young, shows how far consciousness has come
today, even if, as I argue here, we still have further to go.

Some attention was given in early psychoanalytic literature to Freud's comments about working with elderly patients. Karl Abraham wrote a short paper in which he briefly described a few cases, mainly of obsessional neuroses in older people whom he cured. However, the ages he calls "old" are again to readers today shockingly young—between thirty-five and fifty.[5] In addition, Abraham still accepts Freud's concept of "involution," by which he means that the human psyche starts to go backwards as people age. Age staging and stereotyping must unconsciously shape such perspectives.

Numerous critiques of Freud's views include rebuttals of his assumption that little can be achieved through working with elderly people.[6] In a Festschrift honoring Pearl King (whom I discuss below), Blum quotes Freud, writing at age forty-eight, explaining that patients' ages are important in determining their fitness for psychoanalysis: "Near or above the age of fifty," Freud says, "the elasticity of the mental processes...is as a rule lacking—old people are no longer curable" (qtd. in Blum 108). Blum notes that not only did analysts assume the personality to be "consolidated" and inflexible in old age, but they also thought narcissism and narcissistic investment would increase with age, along with a lack of motivation to change and diminished opportunity for producing changes in the external world (108–9).

It seems ironic that the unconscious of the elderly was ignored by psychoanalysis not only because older people were not considered possible subjects for analysis, but also because Freud's focus on childhood and on conflicts from infancy in the young adult seemed to rule out older people. As the studies show, however, it is precisely youthful conflicts that emerge to trouble older people as well. A further irony is Freud's claiming that the unconscious is timeless, and then considering the unconscious of the elderly as bound by time. From my point of view, the unconscious does not grow old; it does not get "rigid"; it remains to trouble one as much as ever, as the dreams of older people (evident in the case studies discussed below) show.

From these small beginnings, psychotherapists in the 1950s and increasingly in the 1970s and onward found support to go much more deeply into the debate about undertaking psychoanalysis with older clients. As we will see, Erik Erikson's work in the 1950s on generativity and his 1970s research on the life cycle provided important support for rethinking age across the life span and for bringing elderly clients into psychoanalysis.

As case studies show, personality alters in later life, and as Blum and others have noted, the way life is lived and experienced changes (109). The unconscious is formed through interactions with parents, siblings, and caregivers from the moment the child is born. Oedipal conflicts, intense sibling rivalry, urges to kill and devour the mother or replace the father as mother's lover are all feelings and traumatic experiences that cannot be consciously accepted or cognitively processed. They remain deep in the individual's mind and are not normally subject to change over the life course.[7] But a person's way of being in social interactions, his or her "personality" may change as a result of life experiences (such as the death of a loved one, the incapacities of an aging body, a divorce, or a remarriage). Such changes may provoke repetition of neuroses apparently at rest, showing the benefit of treatment in later life. Freud's ideas are called into question by analysts such as Pearl King, Hanna Segal, Harold Blum, and others who took the trouble to work with older patients, and some of whom I consider in what follows.[8]

The Unconscious of Age in Clinical Practice with the Elderly

After Freud's death, although British psychoanalyst Pearl King was not the first person to address psychoanalysis with the elderly, in the 1970s and 1980s she was a major pioneer in rethinking Freud's concept of the older patient and in engaging in clinical work with the elderly.[9] Together with Hanna Segal, King took the lead in developing psychotherapy that better suited the older patient. Their case studies show the importance of bringing older people into psychotherapy, a procedure that counters the now common practice of putting them on medication.[10] Studies reveal Freud's mistake in thinking that "elasticity" of mental processes was lacking in older people, or that old people were no longer curable. Hanna Segal's 1957 paper (reprinted in the Festschrift to honor King) details her work with a seventy-three-year-old man who, separated from his family for years, underwent a psychic crisis on visiting his son and brother in London. This case study shows how the crisis that shook this man's defenses against fantasies of persecution and punishment, constructed during a difficult childhood in Nazi-occupied Europe and which now returned him to adolescence, was successfully worked through in the transference with Hanna Segal.

Pearl King also contributed by introducing into psychoanalysis Erik Erikson's concept of the life cycle: Here the subject is seen within a life considered as an ongoing process. In this view, life is dynamic, rather than having the rigidly fixed stages so dear to classical psychoanalysis. In her pioneering 1980 essay, "The Life Cycle as Indicated by the Nature of the Transference in the Psychoanalysis of the Middle-Aged and Elderly," King notes that she is the first to give a paper at an International Psychoanalytical Congress dealing with the psychoanalysis of middle-aged and elderly patients (153). Uncertain whether "psychoanalysts will agree that such patients are suitable candidates for psychoanalysis," she treads carefully where Freud is concerned. She finds a comment by Freud (missed by Segal and Blum) in his paper on "Types of Onset of Neurosis," wherein he notes "the *possibility* that *developmental biological processes* may produce an alteration in the equilibrium of the psychic processes, thus producing neurotic breakdowns at *key phases of the life cycle* at puberty and menopause" (153; Freud 236, King's emphasis). King finds support in the psychoanalytic tradition from Karl Abraham's paper noted earlier, singling out Abraham's statement that "the age at which the neurosis breaks out is of greater importance for the success of psychoanalysis than the age at which treatment is begun" (153). Erik Erikson's notion of phase-specific and psychosocial tasks enables King to take note of different developmental phases in her patients, each with its own anxieties and pressures brought forward from earlier periods in the life cycle. Yet her theory is not in the end teleological, for she states that "middle-aged and elderly patients may be functioning within a number of different time-scales," which may include "a chronological time-scale, a psychological one, and a biological one, alongside the time-scale of unconscious processes, which are, paradoxically, timeless" (154).[11] This observation is crucial for the analyst's effective handling of the transference: "An understanding of the time-scale within which an elderly patient is currently functioning," King says, "gives the analyst an important key to the understanding of transference phenomena in such patients. The analyst can be experienced in the transference as any significant figure from the elderly patient's past, sometimes covering five generations" (154).

Before going to her case studies, King usefully lists a number of common pressures of aging (most of which are familiar to scholars today), such as fears regarding retirement, awareness of aging and bodily changes, possible illness and dependence on others, and the inevitability of one's own death.[12] The two most relevant to this project, however, are first, anxieties in marital relationships once children have left home, and fear of diminution or loss of sexual desire or possibility.[13] Such pressures of aging (amazingly widespread) are increased in individuals with specific neuroses.

I will mention briefly one case that King's paper discusses, which shows what can be achieved with older women. The woman's crisis was brought on by the early retirement policies in Britain at the time. Faced with retirement at age sixty-three from a job as manager of a children's home, the woman lost her sense of self worth, self-esteem, and her identity, so parasitical on her role had her ego become due to narcissistic investment in her job. The analysis reveals the woman's difficulty in passing from childhood to adulthood, due to being situated as the "baby" in a family without warmth or closeness. Envy of her siblings for having a better time was now transferred to her younger colleagues who could continue in their careers. She was able to work through "her paranoid and depressive anxieties" that had made transition to adulthood difficult and, King notes, kept her a "spinster" [sic]. She was now able to accept losses, including sex, and "ego growth and phase appropriate sublimation could take place" (160). This ability to live with and work through the inevitable losses of aging—coming to terms with them but also learning to take appropriate advantage of one's new life stage—is partly what interests Roger Michell in *The Mother*.

Two other case studies, from many that could be cited, are worth mentioning, even though they do not directly deal with sexuality and older women.[14] In his "Repetition and Modification in the Ageing Process," Blum explores "the continuity of the personality and of unconscious conflict throughout the life cycle" (109). Usefully, he emphasizes that "there is no standard chronological or psychological definition of the terms 'old' or 'elderly,'" since "these terms have many social, cultural, medical, and economic dimensions," to say nothing of enormous variety in regard to aging amongst individuals (110). After noting the many contemporary contributions to treatment of older patients, Blum focuses on Freud's case of the Wolf Man, which ironically (because Freud did not attend to these aspects) provides a unique longitudinal study of a human being's "unfolding" from childhood to old age (110, citing Anna Freud). Many of the pressures King listed are evident in the Wolf Man's autobiographical commentary (again, very unusual), such as depression arising from retirement, loss of sexual potency, increase in aggression, and anxiety about impending death. The Wolf Man's mother, someone whose hypochondria disappeared at midlife and who was much happier in old age than in youth, offers a counterexample of aging. Blum concludes that lessened self-expectation on the part of the older person can benefit the individual: Harsh internal demands to live up to personal ideals and values fortunately lessen with age. "Changes in self-representation," he says, "are found with changes in the ideal self and ego ideal during the lifecycle and the ageing process" (113). In a second case study, Blum discusses interesting aspects of the transference of a male client, and concludes that "the shaping influence of the ageing process on the way the present and past are experienced...allows for present meanings to be retrospectively transferred to the past, as well as to the neurotic behavior of later life" (117). We will see how May in Michell's film finally is able to confront her past mothering inadequacies and her inability to leave her husband: In forgiving herself, she is able to move forward to new experiences.

Blum's final case, a midlife woman, demonstrates how with "the onset of ageing [sic] and transition into older years," old symptoms may revive. The phrasing of the woman's situation by Blum as a conflict between what Erikson called "generativity versus stagnation" will be revisited in discussing May's situation in *The Mother*. In the course of describing the case, Blum once more critiques Freud's assumption in "On Femininity" that older women manifest "anal regression" becoming "quarrelsome, vexatious and overbearing, petty and stingy...traits which they did not possess earlier during their period of womanliness" (qtd. in Blum 119). While he does not see in Freud's comments the blatant nineteenth-century stereotypes of old women, Blum does suggest that the limited role of women in earlier historical periods might account for negative traits in contemporary elderly females (119). Blum shows how this woman's losses and disappointments were conceived by her through the lens of aging, when "[n]ew conflicts and personality problems stood out in relief, and old problems were re-experienced in terms of her being an older woman who had lost loved ones, her youthful attractiveness, and her earlier determination, vigor, and vitality" (120). These losses are similar to those suffered by May in Michell's film, as will be clear in what follows.

In the years since King, Segal, and Blum did their pioneering clinical work with the elderly, privileged Western older people have drastically altered their practices of growing older, to say nothing of new attitudes toward older people as scholars and writers have drawn public attention to aging issues. Clinicians today do not have the same reactions to older clients as did earlier therapists, partly because discourses are changing, but also because older people are healthier and more energetic, and able to retain a vigor not available to the population Freud and even later clinicians served. In other words, there may have been some objective reality to the designation of rigidity in the elderly.

Despite changes in practices and in public discourse regarding aging, however, strong, often negative emotions about the elderly and their social presence remain. Even the pioneering clinical work performed with older people and cited above sometimes retains unconscious biases about age, as in the concept of "transcending old age," which retains the notion that old age *requires* "transcending" in the first place; or the concept of "the onset of age," as if it were an abrupt change. If the elderly are shut away, safely out of sight, those aging (as we all daily are) can forget their progress into middle-, late-, and then deep old age. If the elderly freely mingle with us in person and on the screen and if their performances challenge how we unconsciously think they should behave, then we cannot so easily forget. Anxiety will result; strong feelings such as disgust may emerge. On the other hand, some might argue that not having the elderly highly visible (if one could control that) would lessen the likelihood of disgust. I think that familiarity through seeing the elderly in life and on the screen is likely over time to enable younger people to overcome negative feelings.

As practices and performances of advanced age change, so new public and private emotions are provoked—feelings that I argue express complex unconscious fears and fantasies about the elderly as Other. In Eurocentric cultures, the elderly (and especially the extremely old) are "Othered" to defend against our recognizing ourselves in them. Analysis of performances that move beyond stereotypes may reveal what disturbs us about aging, while also allowing viewers glimpses of unconscious conflicts that emerge with age. As noted earlier in referring to Kristeva, fiction allows us a space between reality and fantasy where inner lives can be safely displayed: Winnicott's concept of play as neither a matter of inner psychic reality nor a matter of external reality, but what he calls a "third space" approaches what I have in mind for the "in between" of fiction (qtd. in Rudnytsky xii). As Peter Rudnytsky puts it, "The intermediate quality of transitional objects between fantasy and reality foreshadows that of works of art, which likewise partake simultaneously of reality and illusion" (xii).

Like Claire Kahane, I would add to the transitional space model the framing of this space by symbolic and ideological forces that affect how inner lives are imaged; that very frame is what makes art fascinating and important. The journey the viewer is invited to take into these lives, as framed by politics and cultural context, creates the friction or tension between viewer and text. I appreciate the concept of transference between reader/viewer and text, and find it especially relevant to textual performances of older women; we may learn more from fiction than from normal interpersonal relationships. People in the lived world have social identities that rest on complex cultural norms and they may prefer to keep daily practices and values hidden. Fictional protagonists, since they do not exist in the lived world, do not have to be responsible to any lived community for what they reveal. Even in the post-1960s, postmodern era, when the media's display of bodies and feelings seems to be limitless, in our social and professional lives we do not expose our innermost fears, fantasies, or feelings, or those of our loved ones. But we can "enjoy" watching screen lives where we may be led behind the appearance to inner lives, as constituted by the frame of the authors. This is not to deny that these "shadow" or "ghost" lives have real impact in the lived world—a fact easy to show by examples of films such as Mel Gibson's *The Passion of Christ* or, closer to my topic here, D.H. Lawrence's

Lady Chatterley's Lover.[15] If in Lawrence's case the borders between class in Britain especially troubled the adultery in the text, in the case of Michell's *The Mother,* it is not so much the class (although that figures somewhat) that troubles viewers as it is the ages of the lovers and their contexts. Good fiction, like psychoanalysis, if in a very different form, can take us to places inside people where we cannot normally go, and provoke our prior conceptions and values with images that challenge stereotypes. That is part of the fascination and function of good fiction, as I hope to show below.[16]

The Unconscious of Age in Roger Michell's
The Mother (2002)

Michell's film provides an example of intimate access to a midlife woman's fears and desires, access normally not available publicly. Because the film reveals May's inner psyche, it allows for an exploration of the unconscious of age in the third sense of the term, focusing on unconscious public feelings about older people, which are ripe with dated stereotypes, and exploring the differences between May and the clinical cases discussed earlier. Images of midlife women involved with younger men have been shown on the screen before, perhaps most obviously in Hollywood's *All That Heaven Allows* (1957).[17] But *The Mother* goes much further in showing an older woman in explicit sexual performances. Even Fassbinder (although not working in Hollywood) did not show older woman–younger man sex, despite the fact that his film broke taboos in place at the time in the interracial nature of the relationship (see also *Far from Heaven* in this regard).[18] *The Mother,* set in the UK (where Michell lives), deals not only with how "Grandma won't go home," but with a midlife British mother crossing boundaries that are usually inviolable in mother–daughter relationships. Performances in *The Mother* further breach cultural norms about aging women and sex through the graphic nature of the sex scenes.

Affects to do with retirement and middle age dominate the opening sequences, which show an older couple, Toots and May, preparing to go on a visit to their children and grandchildren in London. Advanced age is staged as entailing passivity, depression, and indeed, even though May and her husband, Toots, are a couple, loneliness. Hanif Kureishi (who wrote the script) presents an experience common in Britain, where at least until recently, retirement was mandatory in a person's early sixties, and people found themselves in comfortable homes but far from cultural activities and their children. Therefore, this is a cultural image—part of the unconscious framing—rather than necessarily a stereotype about older people.

Toots and May arrive at their son's house as everyone is busy leaving for work and school. Darren, a friend constructing a conservatory in the house, is a peripheral figure in the arrival sequence, but when the older couple wanders into his space, the camera sweeps past May as Darren moves to greet Toots. Is an older woman, dressed plainly in bland colors, simply not worth regarding? Has she disappeared into the background while the larger, more social Toots is fodder for male bonding? Certainly, that is what happens. The men are soon happily discussing carpentry and cricket, while May walks into the garden, alone.

Suddenly, there is quiet; we hear the birds and faint sound of a plane or traffic. The scene initiates a focus on May's consciousness, if not her unconscious, yet suggesting someone at a life stage of reflection, pause, uncertainty. The camera behaves differently now. As May walks on the green lawn, looking up at the trees, the camera quietly pans across the lawn with the house in long shot so that we can see the men using wood to demonstrate cricket plays. The effect is somewhat uncanny, or fore-boding, reminiscent of tracking shots in films of Renoir or Antonioni. The effect is striking in part because most of the shots have been still, with movement within the frame. The moving camera indicates a change in May, anticipating future change. We are in a space with May, alone. It seems first that age is staged normatively, in that a younger man does not consider an older woman to be worth a second look. But second, the shots of May alone signal something awakening in her, perhaps already unconsciously through meeting Darren, indicating age being staged differently.

Characters in the film are aware of age, even if indirectly referenc-ing passing time as much as human age. For example, passing time is alluded to by Helen, the daughter-in-law, who yells at Darren to finish the conservatory since "it's taking longer than Michelangelo took on the Sistine Chapel." Darren retorts that it will last longer. A bit later, Toots comments that the conservatory will be a nice place for the young couple in their old age, but he adds that they will not know what to do with themselves, presumably reflecting on his own feelings about his life. We see here how older age is staged as a period of passivity, emptiness, lack of motivation or activity, rather than as a new beginning as we might now want to conceive it.

Shortly after this scene, Toots suddenly dies of a heart attack. This event provides the turning point in the film in its impact on May in regard to aging. Age is perhaps most tellingly staged in the scene immediately following Toots' sudden death, when May's son, Bobby, drives her home. We understand the degree to which May has closed off feeling at this point in her life, since she has little emotional response to her husband's death: Bobby's age-staging confronts May's refusal to buy into the stage where the family now attempts to put her. The camera fixes on Toots's slippers as they enter May's house, as it had when May and Toots left the house, and May finally shows emotion. She then makes the first of several statements that show that she is at some turning point in regard to staging age. When Bobby tells her to sit down, she retorts, "If I sit down, I'll never get up again." "Sitting down" implies not living any more, and May understands she has to fight that sort of slow death. "Age" is "staged" by Bobby and May, but with opposite stances toward the staging. Bobby wants her to accept her stage, and like the other "old girls," eventually go into a home. May absolutely refuses this staging, knowing that this leads to death and she has to save herself somehow if she wants to live. Her reaction to his suggestions seems to stem from her instinct for survival—something very unclear to her but something she absolutely has to do. It is interesting that Toots's death initiates the family's infantilizing of May, and a desire to keep her safely "controlled" in a home for the elderly. As long as she had a husband, the family did not consider her "old." The gendering of growing old reemerges once May takes a lover, of course.

One reason more women do not resist like May is that it takes guts, if not a stubborn selfishness many cannot muster: It may also involve imposing oneself, as May proceeds to do, on the young family, an especially awkward move given how distant May has been as a grandmother and (as we will learn) as a parent. But she is desperate and insists. On their arrival back at the London house, there is a shot of her sitting on the bed in the spare room of her son's house, back to camera, foreshadowing sex scenes on this same bed later. The cool, fresh white in the shot echoes the soft colors in earlier sexless bed scenes with her husband, Toots, as if to remind us of what was lacking in that marriage.

In his responses to May, on her return to her son's house, Darren, parading a classic muscular manhood, shows from the start a sensitivity lacking in her children. As May leaves the house to go for a walk, he comments, "We'll be like that one day, no one wanting us." In a sense, Darren and May emerge as the ones left out, not wanted. Darren is a drifter being paid by Bobby for doing carpentry, and he does not fit in anywhere. At this point, we do not know about Darren's relationship with May's daughter, Paula, but as the film moves on, May goes to live with Paula, allowing Michell to explore first May's relationship with her daughter, and then May's affair with Darren.

Staging of Age and Sex

May's moving in with Paula initiates May's sexual awakening. One night, drawn to the sounds of lovemaking—attesting to her awakening sexuality—May sees that the lover is Darren. She overhears Paula's ungainly pleading with him to stay, to give up his wife and to love her. May looks out the window and mutters: "Leave her alone, you blasted brute"—words that later ring oddly in the viewer's ears because May herself seduces Darren, but which attest to May's initial genuine concern for her daughter's welfare.

May intends to talk to Darren about Paula, as Paula had asked, but instead a relationship between May and Darren gets underway. Somehow, these two find it easy to be together. Suddenly, May confesses, "I can't go home. I don't know what I'm doing. I'm frightened." Darren takes this in stride, but responds that he thought one would get less frightened as one got older, being better able to deal with things. It is another moment when age is staged, but now in a positive way as supposedly (in Darren's mind) making life easier. Darren is able to move beyond the "other-ing" of older people in which he had earlier engaged in ignoring May when she arrived at the house. It is also a recognition of their age difference without its seeming to be important: The two discover shared non-age-based interests in art and life.

May's growing sexual desire for Darren is shortly communicated to viewers as May watches Darren at his workbench, his pants revealing flesh. Given prevailing cultural codes, we would not expect a sixty-plus, widowed woman to feel such powerful desire, especially for a man nearly half her age, and if so, certainly not to act on it, yet Michell and script-writer Kureishi manage to make this seem absolutely normal. That is, in presenting this performance of age and sexuality, the team challenges prevailing concepts of what is appropriate for whom at what chronolog-ical age without making it grotesque. This does not mean that viewers accept or like what they see; cultural codes they bring to the film may prevent them from valuing what Kureishi and Michell are doing. Clearly, here May slips into another age zone, refusing to bind her desire just as she has refused to stay home. She broaches the topic of Paula with Darren again but ends up talking more about herself and her own desires, "to do interesting things—things I love." As Darren goes back to work, the camera focuses on May's face. The viewer sees that it has color and life that was absent before; her skin looks less wrinkled—most likely as a result of the revitalizing effect of her growing sexual desire. Her eyes stare at Darren with longing, and she mutters under her breath, "Let us be alive before we die."

On the spur of the moment, Darren invites May to lunch at a pub. This scene beautifully prepares for what follows in showing their ease together. Darren takes her to Hogarth's grave nearby and May reads a poem on the grave that includes the line, "Through the mind connect with the heart"—in a way describing what Darren and May are doing.

We learn that May likes to draw (important later), and as they move away she says, "I like being with you so much." Shortly afterward, as she slips on a muddy path, she reaches up and kisses Darren, accounting for her behavior because of drinking at lunch.

This moment marks a decisive change in May's body language and performance. We cut to her looking in the mirror and arranging now colorful clothes—a blue outfit and bright orange scarf. The camera dwells on her face in close-up, looking younger and flushed. Paula asks if she has a date, and she replies, "That would be my lucky day." Paula takes May to her writing class, having in mind setting May up with an older man in the group, Bruce, whom I discuss below.

The intimacy between May and Darren develops as they find themselves alone in the house while the children are at school, the adults working. May gives Darren a book of Durer prints (a significant choice since Durer's works include pictures of older women sexually attracting younger men) and he is moved. She sketches him at work and talks about her life—the norms of being a wife and mother in her era, the difference for Helen and Bobby in the present. She is suddenly empowered, alive, smoking a cigarette as if to highlight her new feeling of freedom. May talks of an affair she had during her married life but how she was ultimately unable to upset her family and leave—very much the situation Darren is now in. May's confession shows that she has sex on her mind. Normative age staging is here directly challenged in the actions of both the young man and the older woman. Their interest in one another, the growing sexual tension, the intimate discussion between near strangers: All of this moves the viewer beyond images common in popular culture.

Shortly after, May asks Darren if he will go to the spare room with her. With music on the track composed especially for these sex scenes, the camera slides along the wall outside the spare room, echoing the shots of this bedroom when May first arrived, and the earlier one in May's house. It is afternoon, so there are sounds of children playing, a plane going by, normal life outside, yet in this room, something dramatic is happening. The camera catches May with her back to it, while she and Darren undress. May's older body is not hidden but only seen from the back. We see that May is a large woman, but Michell refrains from shooting her naked body in full light, softening the scene rather through careful lighting and the gray/white colors in the room, the soft curtains blowing in the breeze. She asks if Darren sees what she thinks she is, namely "a shapeless old lump." He shakes his head. She is nervous and breathless, and asks if she can do something to him. We cut to a deliberately blurred image of them in bed. Perhaps Michell wanted to bring viewers gently into this supposedly "taboo-bashing" (as reviewers put it) part of the story.[19] May says she thought "no one would ever touch her again except the undertaker," as Darren brings her to orgasm. The director (perhaps a bit heavy-handedly) underscores the rebirth aspects of the scene by showing May afterward bathing her face in water while the piano music plays as a way to lift us out of the scene, into May's inner world. With a sense of humor, Michell moves the camera through the water to the next scene where May is washing Paula's floor and singing a rock song, David Bowie's "Space Oddity," about feeling free of the world.

What is curious is how the film downplays the betrayal of May's daughter, in part by making Paula a rather unattractive character, while showing May and Darren, at least in the world they create, as (at first) sensitive and responsive to each other's inner loneliness and yearning. Darren comes to dinner at Paula's house and a mirror shot wonderfully choreographs the emotional awkwardness and difficulty of the guilty pair vis-à-vis Paula. May faces the camera and the door, while the mirror shows her back and Paula and Darren embracing. The camera later pans from Paula talking about plans to get her life in shape to Darren and May, who, separated by a table, are wanting but unable to look at one another. Later, May looks in the mirror in the foreground of the shot (her face distorted as in an earlier mirror shot; the music signals a return to May's inner consciousness), while Darren and Paula talk in the background. May turns to the camera, in a close-up shot, her face now clear but determined—determined, it seems, to keep Darren despite betraying her daughter.

The viewer has a dilemma here: We (or at least this viewer) partly want May, the older woman, to get what she wants, and partly feel that what she is doing is wrong. That is, it seems that a mother ought not to get involved with her daughter's lover, and May and Darren have something quite wonderful in ways that Darren and Paula do not. Paula's relationship with Darren is of course also illicit, and includes Paula's damaging possessiveness and anger, while May and Darren, in the beginning at least, fold together in a rare way. In a scene reminding us of the earlier one in which May watched Darren leave after making love to Paula, May again watches Darren get in his car. Her face atop her dark clothes and the darkness of the night make her foreboding.

The next sequence attempts to grasp May's inner turmoil. She is shown first on the Millennium Wheel, reflecting and reflected, looking down at the busy street, then enmeshed in glass and traffic and people, her figure distorted by the overlapping shots in which we barely see her troubled face as she bends over and cries, lost among a mélange of images. The sequence recalls an earlier one in which we saw Toots and May walking in a lively, bustling and noisy modern London, colorful and bright but with cars and buses rushing by in front frame coming between the characters and us to create this sense of rush and noise. Lots of huge ads and glass shop windows add to this sense. That time, the scene anticipated Toots's heart attack, since he was caught in this rush of cars. Now May is caught in a moral dilemma directly linked to Toots's death.

Shortly, May returns to her son's house in a new and different mood, hoping for sex with Darren. In their commentary on the DVD version of *The Mother,* Michell and producer Kevin Loader suggest that May is now addicted to sex with Darren. This gave me pause. I wondered if this comment indicated stereotyping older women's sexual awakening, as if the only way such women could be sexual was if their actions were a result of uncontrollable lust, or as if there is something pathological about old people having sex, whereas lust and infatuation are fine in young people. Michell belies the progressive aspects of his project in calling May "addicted" just because she now eagerly seeks out and enjoys sex. Turning her character a bit later on into the obsessive woman suggests Michell's own ambivalences about showing an older woman engaged in sex.

Certainly, the film now presents May as full of passion. The following sex scene makes clear her pleasure and shows Darren more engaged. The camera moves from their bodies to photographs on the wall and Darren's face reflected there. These are graphic sex scenes without dwelling too much on the bodies as such. One may wonder again if this deliberate avoidance of close-ups of the older woman's body in the sex is based on the director's sense of audience expectations, worries about conventions of a certain "aesthetics" assumed for sex scenes on the screen: Are these scenes shot to protect Michell's film from criticism and turning off viewers? Even to suggest that we might be "turned off" by an older woman's body engaged in sex already suggests underlying bias about what such a scene might look like. The camera focuses just on May's head on the pillow and Darren's body giving her pleasure. Meanwhile, unusual is how the graphic sounds of May's pleasure and multiple orgasms dominate the scene—perhaps a strategy to avoid too many explicit body shots while communicating a very sexual sequence. May massages Darren's back—something new for her. She watches Darren dress with pleasure but becomes motherly when he takes mouthfuls of pills, asking why he does it.[20]

We get a glimpse of what is in the relationship for Darren when he says: "I love these afternoons, the peace." He talks about his autistic son, and then about how lost he is in his life. These are reflections that Darren would not share with the younger woman because of their joint expectations about masculinity and strength, and Paula's neediness. But such confidences seem appropriate to reveal to the older woman, suggesting special intimacy for men across the age stage. Responding to Darren's intimacy, May describes her past home life with a controlling husband who would not let her have friends or go away. Her stubborn determination to break the codes of middle-class respectability, to become indeed the rebel Darren called her, seems understandable. "We didn't have this feminism then," she adds, seeming perhaps for the first time to appreciate what feminists are about. In this scene, interestingly, age does not seem "staged," although it is there discreetly in the conversation as noted. May gets pleasure from teasing Darren about his supposed rival, Bruce. "You old tart," he says. She looks lovingly at Darren, complicating the notion that this is all just sex addiction.

Michell and Kureishi offer contradictory images of May and Darren as their relationship continues, and this is perhaps the one fault in an otherwise powerful portrayal of an older woman's sexuality. The final sequences of *The Mother* consist of the unraveling of the triangle in a rather unsatisfactory manner that entails Darren's becoming truly ugly for the first time and presenting May indeed as an addict pleading for sex instead of as a woman who is about to lose an emotional and physical closeness that has fulfilled her for the first time.

Another perspective on older people and sex emerges in a scene that not only rings true but also is really disturbing. While many reviewers (of which more later) talk about the violation of codes involved in the sex between Darren and May, the real comment about aging sexuality and women may be found in the scene with Bruce. A seemingly pleasant, intelligent older man in Paula's writing workshop, Bruce (with Paula's encouragement) asks May on a date. The date ends in a truly unsettling sequence not mentioned by one reviewer.[21] While a man of any age may coerce a woman into sex, such duress has especial poignancy for people who may not usually be sexually active. The act becomes desperate. May passively goes along, but once the intercourse begins, she clearly does not want it and regrets having allowed it to happen. The emptiness of the sex, lacking any real relationship, makes it ugly. Through the lens of age, viewers understand the difficulty of older people's sex lives—finding appropriate partners, understanding the other person's needs, men abandoning sensitivity in their desperation for sexual release. While younger men also behave insensitively, there is a distinctive emotional inflection in the case of Bruce, who is well-meaning and generally kind.

The next sequence continues the sense of crisis and violence that characterizes the film's ending and seems melodramatic—at odds with the prior performances. First, Paula burns all her work in order to punish her mother for not supporting her creativity; Bobby then suggests his mother go for counseling. He cannot imagine any other solution for bringing his mother under control; May has strayed too far from his (and his wife's) expectations of how older people should behave. Darren comes in, already drunk; he and Bobby fight, and Bobby fires him for not completing the conservatory. Darren takes cocaine, and then roughly asks May for sex. She tries to satisfy him but wants tenderness and he pushes her away. At this point, May begins to plead with Darren to be kind. Darren becomes anything but, turning ugly, asking for money, and finally wrecking the conservatory he has been building. We cut to a low angle shot of May's face as she takes a knife from the nearby kitchen, presumably thinking of suicide. Paula confronts her mother, hits her, and this finally releases the tension between them.

It seems Michell/Kureishi now want to indicate that Darren was all along using May for sexual release—taking advantage of her loneliness and need—as would fit the stereotype of such a relationship. This goes against the emotions conveyed earlier in the film, to this viewer's disappointment. However, the filmmakers recoup something in the film's ending: May decides to leave Bobby's house on her own accord. Once again dressed in her prior nondescript gray pants and coat, she looks dejected, bruised, depressed, and passive as before. The camera surveys the room with all the different people looking at May, echoing the first scene in the house, but with the difference that now *she* is the central focus while before she was on the margins, sitting on the couch. Her defiance of what her culture considers age-appropriate actions has brought her to visibility, if not happiness. It is as if to be noticed, older women have to defy social norms. Her deviant behavior, unrewarded as it was, perhaps seems at this point not to have been worth it.

The train journey back repeats the outward journey with Toots. Back in her house, May looks at Toots's slippers in the room in which she and he sat waiting for the taxi at the start of the film. Once again we get the half-frame image, which forces us to concentrate on what Michell wants us to see. There is a cut to a mirror shot of May in bed, identical to the one in the film's opening, except now we see the bruise on her face from Paula's blow—to remind us of her betrayal of her daughter. The next shot through the door shows May packing. We see light clothes and a passport. Then May is out on the street, dressed in bright blue, wind blowing her hair and a smile on her face. She is not staying home, not sitting down, and not going to her children, but off on a new adventure on her own.

Michell and Kureishi here provide a progressive ending for the aborted love affair between May and Darren, in that May's sexual experience and the brief emotional bond she had with Darren have evidently given her a new lease on life. May's vigorous stepping out of her house on her own belies the stereotype of the older woman who has lost a husband: the expectation that she would become dependent on her children or move into a home for the elderly. If we can fault Michell/Kureishi for the way they ended the affair, at least in this final scene, they show the positive effects on May's confidence to move out into the world on her own.

Age and Clinical Observations Regarding *The Mother*: Unconscious Conflicts in Older Women

In a sense, May's challenge to the other characters in the film is her opting out of the chronological time scale, and situating herself firmly in the present—especially after her husband dies suddenly of a heart attack. Recall Pearl King's distinguishing several time scales within which older people live, including the psychological, the biological, and chronological, as well as the time scale of unconscious processes. Michell and Kureishi evoke the unconscious time scale in the many scenes in which May wanders alone around the house and garden or the streets and parks of London. They isolate these scenes not only by abrupt silencing of the roar and rush of a busy, lively London, but also by inserting the specific piece of piano music noted earlier, composed especially for these shots, that evokes a sense of being somewhere else, reflective, not in the present (and thus perhaps in the unconscious).

The director attempts to penetrate May's affect in this way, to let us into what she is feeling, despite film being notorious for the difficulty of accessing inner feeling. In this film, as we have seen, Michell does manage through his skillful cinematic techniques to reveal May's intimate emotions. Michell often has May step out of time, out of the action, into a reflective space that suggests her feeling uncertain and lost—again something difficult for people in lived relations to communicate about themselves. At other times she lives resolutely in the present, eager for new experiences, such as sex with Darren. Both the revealing of sexuality and of inner crises rarely emerge even between close friends in life. Michell also uses the technique of mirror shots, and reflection in glass surfaces to convey the idea of questioning identity. Some of the mirror shots stage the tension between characters that cannot be spoken—reflections allow us to see characters doubled or in the background at important emotional moments. Meanwhile, the many shots of May in the mirror suggest reflecting on her life stage and on her actions and emotions (see figure 2.1). Some people, as they get older and retire from work, find themselves plummeted into the past, Proustian fashion, by unheralded associations to something in the present. Such memories may evoke past conflicts they

Figure 2.1 May explores her body.

were not aware remained in the unconscious, pushed aside by consuming daily activities.

Clinical case studies cited earlier suggested that as the personality alters in later life, so, too, the way life is lived and experienced changes. The aging process may change the way the present and past are experienced, though this will differ from person to person. Anxieties frequently arise in marital relationships once children have left home, as clinicians have noted; fears about a decrease in sexual desire, a reduced sexual desirability, and a loss of the possibility of sexual experiences are common. May and Toots are experiencing both loss of desire and ability to arouse one another at the start of the film. May's conversations with Darren confirm her sense of growing emptiness and oppression in her marriage. In addition, the various changes associated with growing older (physical, psychological, and social), along with traumatic events such as the sudden death of a husband, may provoke repetition of neuroses or arouse memories of earlier events in life with associated negative affects. May is stunned by Paula's accusations of her being a cold mother, and May's only, lame defense is that she was a naturally weak person overwhelmed by the demands of marriage and motherhood. She is a woman whose sexual desire as a younger woman was stronger than her need to mother, as we learned in her conversation with Darren. Now in later life she finally is able to achieve sexual fulfillment, and to begin to repair her relationship with her children.

In this film, the writing workshop offers viewers an opportunity not only to see Paula being effective and in a leadership role, but also for May to reveal a deeper sense of self as a mother. She writes a poem as part of the group project, and is then asked to read it aloud. In it, May expands on her earlier statement about being overwhelmed by family life. She reveals her guilt about not being able to care for her children. "I'd hate them by the end of the day," she reads. It was a struggle to get them to bed and then she could not bear her children's cries; she sometimes resorted to just closing the door and leaving them alone, making sure to return before her husband did. "I wanted to kill myself out of guilt. I still haven't recovered from those cries. What is it about those cries?"

It is clear that May has had difficulty, as have some of the older people in the psychological case studies, in being generative. Blum, you recall, phrased the situation of one of his case studies as a "conflict between what Erikson called 'generativity versus stagnation.'" By this I assume Erikson means the ability to further the lives of others through being engaged in life as against a tendency to stay within what one is used to, not giving to others younger than oneself or helping them move forward. Until Toots's death, May remained "stagnant" as she aged, suggesting that, like a woman Pearl King treated, she never passed from childhood to adulthood in a satisfactory manner. Unable to properly mother her children, she was also a distant, uninvolved grandmother. However, one notes the teleology of these formulations of the aging process, especially for women. Why should women focus on being generative after a certain age, instead of pursuing desires or interests that they did not have a chance to pursue during the age stage when being wives and mothers took up most of their time? Stagnancy is not a productive state, granted, but why is the choice only between being stagnant and being generative? Why focus on generativity at the expense of self-fulfillment? It is hard to be positively generative until one has fulfilled interests and desires. At several points in the movie, May notes that she wants to do things that interest her, things she likes. She loves drawing and never had a chance to do it. Darren encourages her in this pursuit as her husband never did. Older women should be validated for taking on new interests outside of their families or fulfilling unmet desires, sexual or otherwise. Such interests do not have to replace generativity, but may well accompany it.

It is not entirely evident what the film concludes about May's emotional development as an aging woman. The rupture to her life course brought about by the sudden death of Toots results in unplanned and extended time with her adult children. This unexpected time with her children in London, in turn, produces a psychic crisis for May: She no longer fully understands who she is. Michell makes this clear in several scenes where May walks aimlessly around the city, sometimes literally getting lost. In one scene, she finds she is physically lost, underscoring her psychic lostness. The deafening noise of traffic in close shots, and the crowds of people add to May's growing distress. When finally she arrives at Paula's house, she says, "I completely lost my sense of direction"—her unconscious recognizing her mental state and life moment having lost direction as well.

Memories of her past unhappiness as a mother and wife return to haunt her. Paula's outburst offers a chance for May to begin to confront and work through the pain she caused her daughter, and, as in the poem May writes in Paula's writing class, to acknowledge her inadequate mothering. Her impulsive seduction of Darren enables her finally to achieve full sexual satisfaction, even though she again betrays her daughter's trust. It seems that May could not enter or grow into her new life stage as an older, now widowed woman without returning to her past and, as it were, filling in what was missing. I understand her leaving her house and mundane empty life as a new beginning, a sign that she is now ready to enter her life stage with energy and hope. We do not know what her relationship to her children and grandchildren will be, but her departure appears not as a rejection of them but as an assertion of her determination to be herself as she enters her new life stage, beyond the conventional framing of the older woman's identity constructed only with the familiar roles of mother, grandmother, wife.

Epilogue: Unconscious Age-Staging in Reviews of *The Mother*

The film review is an interesting genre, especially since websites such as Amazon and Netflix encourage us all to be informal as well as more formal reviewers. The practice usefully offers more information about public response than was previously available. My random survey of reviews (mainly via the Internet) delivered a wide range of evaluations of the film. Of special interest in this context are reactions to May's character and her awakening sexuality.[22]

Taken together, this assembled set of comments conveys an overall response to the tenor of the film as loosely belonging to an independent cinema that deliberately resists the sentimental comforts audiences expect from Hollywood. The charges that the film is "cool" or "cold," "acerbic" or "hyperintellectual" [sic] interest me, since these are not terms that I would have attached to the film.[23] It seemed to me that Michell and Kureishi were deliberately creating a certain distance from the characters precisely in order to allow us to bear witness to the troubles in the family and to accompany May on her journey toward self-fulfillment. The terms "taboo-crusher," "shocking drama," "a splendidly uncomfortable watch"—the reference is mainly to May's character and actions—reflect unease with the narrative and especially with May.

David Edelstein (writing for Slate.com) asks, "Is she handsome or monstrously ugly? Do we like her or find her grotesque?" He continues, "She's watching her lover with her daughter, Paula, and the possessive fury in her eyes is, well, unmotherly: I want, I want, I want." Clearly, May challenges reviewers' concepts of norms for mothering and grand-mothering, since reference to her age and/or social role is explicit in all the reviews. Dennis Lim, writing for the *Village Voice,* titles his review "60 Going on 69," while Edelstein's column is called "The Sexual Awakening of Mom." Mark Kermode's "Passion on a Pension" cracks a joke at May's expense, and he sees the film as "a story of a grandmother who has a fling with a young builder (that) breaks the last cinematic taboo."

Discomfort increases as soon as reviewers begin to discuss their reaction to the "sexagenarian" sexuality. Will Self (included in Nev Pierce's review) puts it bluntly: "What is taboo-busting in the movie is the portrayal of the sex. Kureishi's signature is more in the graphicism of sexual depiction." On the same BBC panel about the film, Bonnie Greer busts out: "This woman is motivated by lust." Nev Pierce condemns the lovers for their "selfish, narcissistic natures," extending what these characters do to a "damning portrayal of western humanity, which runs the risk of being as hollow and callous as the people it portrays." Meanwhile, David Lim sees May as "co-opting her kids' me-me-me ethos." May's "sweet-old-lady disposition is deceptive," he says, and her "viperfish potential flickers to the surface in a remarkable scene at Paula's writing group"—a statement that, along with others here (as is clear above), I consider a profound misreading of what happens in *The Mother.*

How can we account for this misreading? Could it be that these male reviewers (why are so many reviewers male?) unconsciously encountered a displaced incest taboo in the young man's involvement with *the mother?* Do comments reflect a thwarted desire for mother's breast? The scenes are perhaps "uncanny" in provoking deeply repressed unconscious wishes from childhood that society prohibits. But surely, the overriding impulse at work is that of ageism, *tout court.* Although the discomfort noted in the reviews does not always explicitly mention May's age, the negative impressions surely arise from the unconscious ageism of the writers. Misreadings arise despite Michell and Kureishi having, to my mind, managed to make the relationship between Darren and May seem (at least for the most part) simply the coming together of two lonely, lost people.

A few reviewers overcome preconceived notions of what is proper for whom at what age and come closer to my reading of the film. Andrew

O'Hagen (another member of the BBC panel discussion) says, "I don't think she was motivated by lust at all: she is motivated by disappointment and an urge to fly in her life. She has been hemmed in by everybody." A rare female reviewer, Stephanie Zacharek, writing on Salon.com, concurs, noting that aside from being about an older woman emotionally involved with a much younger man, the film is also "about not quite fitting in, at any age—and about how, sometimes as we get older, we may feel we fit in less rather than more... It's as if [May] is simultaneously trying to assert her existence (perhaps for the first time) and fold herself up to be as small and unobtrusive as possible." Kermode understands how few films exist about retirement-age women "having flings with strapping young men" (his only reference, however, is inappropriate; i.e., the cult classic *Harold and Maude*: Harold as strapping? And there is not a single sex scene in that film), and he concludes that *The Mother* is "far more radical than its cosy Brit-pic milieu may imply." Reviewers seem to revert to the old concepts psychoanalysts first articulated, as discussed at the start of this chapter, namely the inevitability of psychological rigidity in old age.

Michell and Kureishi have to be admired for making this film. Producer Kevin Loader notes on the DVD how difficult it was to get funding, presumably because the blend of age and sex was seen as too challenging and therefore not marketable. The "unconscious of age" can be seen in biases against funding such a story. Until we fully confront unconscious attitudes toward older people and our expectations of how they should behave, it will be hard for audiences to appreciate films like *The Mother*. Do attitudes have to change first? Or might new images begin to change attitudes? Age studies scholars must continue to challenge prevailing habits of staging age in order to raise public consciousness about biases against the elderly in life and on the screen. Once consciousness begins to change, we will find more interest in and opportunity for performances that confront and move beyond stereotypes.

Notes

1. Michell's long distinguished career as a theatrical director—working first with John Osborne, Samuel Beckett, and other distinguished British writers and performers—prepared him for his successful film directing career making absorbing and intelligent films about serious social issues such as those studied in *The Mother*. In an epilogue, I also reflect on the unconscious of age in regard to unconscious cultural response to images in Michell's film.
2. For this project, I limit myself to studying representations of Eurocentric women. Comparative research is much needed and perhaps will most profitably take place in a collaborative context.

3. In the first chapter of *Black Sun*, Kristeva presents in detail her theory about the space that literature occupies: "Literary creation," she says, "is that adventure of the body and signs that bears witness to the affect—to sadness as impressing of separation and beginning of the symbol's sway; to joy as imprint of the triumph that settles me in the universe of artifice and symbol, which I try to harmonize in the best possible way with my experience in reality" (22). In writing, subjects overcome the lost objects: "I evoke, I signify through the artifice of signs and for myself what has been parted from me" (23). Here Kristeva follows both Hanna Segal (in her 1957 "Notes on Symbol Formation"), whom Kristeva cites explicitly, and Donald Winnicott (see his 1971/1984 *Playing and Reality*), whom she does not quote. Melanie Klein's theories about symbolization are also involved as per Hanna Segal's contribution.

4. Recent scholars in age studies have been careful to distinguish among life phases of older people, as does Harold Blum in work I discuss below. Briefly, distinctions have to be made among midlife issues, later life concerns, and the situation of advanced old age. Then again, specific ages cannot be attached to these distinctions: For one person, midlife worries start at fifty years, for another at seventy-five; later-life concerns may start at sixty-five or at ninety-five. There is great individual variation, which is why fixed stages should be avoided. As more and more people live to one hundred years and more, so has concern for their care, deservedly, become a central issue. In this chapter, I address sexual issues relating to midlife women from a psychological and inner-life perspective.

5. In his "The Applicability of Psycho-Analytic Treatment to Patients at an Advanced Age," Karl Abraham refers to Freud's brief comments in his 1898 "Sexuality in the Aetiology of the Neuroses," in which Freud says that psychoanalysis loses its effectiveness if the patient is too advanced in years (3:284). However, Abraham goes on to warn that one should not approach "the investigation or treatment of nervous conditions with *a priori* [sic] theories" (312). In a statement quoted by later clinicians, Abraham notes that "the age of the neurosis is more important than the age of the patient" (316).

6. See list in Calvin Settlage's 1996 "Transcending Old Age: Creativity, Development and Psychoanalysis in the Life of a Centenarian" (549).

7. Some theorists have recently argued that the process of psychoanalysis, the "talking cure," can actually alter synapses in the brain and perhaps change some deep unconscious conflicts. However, few people can afford the large number of sessions required for such change, if indeed, it really can take place.

8. Martin Grotjahn agrees that the "unconscious does not know aging and death," and thus growing old can be traumatic. However, he also confirms that therapy with the elderly, despite Freud's pessimism, can be successful and helpful. See Grotjahn's 1955 work.

9. In 1940, for example, Martin Grotjahn wrote on "Psychoanalytic Investigation of a Seventy-One-Year-Old Man with Senile Dementia," in *Psychoanalytic Quarterly*; again in 1955, Grotjahn addressed issues of the older patient in his "Analytic Psychotherapy with the Elderly" in *Psychoanalytic Review*. Several articles have, of course, appeared in the years following the work of King and Segal (see Carol Martin, Savi McKenzie-Smith, Adam Limentani, and Calvin Settlage), but the case studies by King and Segal are most useful in regard to the protagonist in *The Mother*. In work in progress, I deal in-depth with clinical research on the elderly and consider changing theories about the success of working with older patients.

10. There have been many horrifying media stories about overmedicating the elderly in senior homes. I have personal experience with an elderly aunt in several such homes, and believe that a sensitive, trained analyst could have helped her depression more than the many pills she was given. In a moving paper about his work with a woman of advanced age, Calvin Settlage demonstrates how organic symptoms such as palpitations, dizziness, and temporary memory loss may result from psychological distress in old age. His work with a female centenarian is fascinating and will figure in my future research on psychoanalysis and the elderly.

11. Kathleen Woodward also usefully refers to different categories through which age needs to be thought in her essay "Performing Age, Performing Gender" (183). In a footnote, she cites distinctions that need to be made among "chronological age," "biological or functional age," "social age," "psychological age," and "statistical age."

12. In 1980, Abraham, Kocher, and Goda also noted similar life changes and losses in their brief review of the literature on "Psychoanalysis and Aging."

13. It is clear that specific issues would be likely to be foremost at different phases of the aging process, although once again, one would find great variety.

14. For a sense of the extent of research in this area, see bibliographies in articles cited here, especially that by Calvin F. Settlage discussed earlier. Such pressures are increased in individuals with specific neuroses.

15. Because D.H. Lawrence wrote about adultery between an upper-class woman and a working-class hand on her husband's English estate with explicit and graphic description of their sexual intercourse, *Lady Chatterley's Lover* was banned in England. A drawn-out court case ensued, during the course of which prior censoring of sexuality was highlighted along with an oppressive class system that had long outlived its origins. English culture began to change in the wake of Lawrence's interventions.

16. I stress "good" here because a shallow or cliché-ridden narration of inner lives does not teach anyone anything or make a difference. With all its faults (I do not claim that *The Mother* is a perfect film), I experienced *The Mother* as taking me to places inside an older woman to which I had not been exposed in this particular manner before.

17. See also the Fassbinder remake, *Ali Fear Eats the Soul* (1986), and *The Graduate* (1967), with its follow-up project, *Rumor Has It* (2005).

18. Love affairs between older women and younger men are becoming more numerous in contemporary film, but usually sex scenes are not central. See, for example, Diane Keaton in Hollywood's *Something's Gotta Give* (2000).

19. One might argue that Michell and Kureishi lose their nerve at this point, but I rather think they did not want to do too much in one film. As it is, as will be clear in the epilogue where I discuss reviews of the film, audiences were shocked already just by there being any sexual intercourse at all. There will be time for more graphic shots of older bodies engaged in exciting sex.

20. This reference to Darren's drug use prepares us for his violent and unpredictable behavior in the last images of their relationship.

21. The only reference to Bruce in the random reviewer survey discussed below is in a user comment by someone from Ecuador who finds Bruce "a sympathetic cameo of a lonely, clumsy, not entirely likeable and very humble man who doesn't have much of a clue about entertaining a woman."

22. The following brief quotations provide insight to prevailing views of the film:
    - "An acerbic, astute comic drama about fidelity, family and sexagenarian sex..." (Nev Pierce, *BBC Film Review*).
    - "*The Mother* is a perfect union of writer and director: Kureishi and Michell are both hyperintellectual, and the frames are packed with novelistic detail" (David Edelstein, Slate, May 28, 2004).
    - *The Mother* "is cool, almost clinical, yet emotionally ferocious, and not without sympathy for its characters' fresh hells...It's unsentimental, unbearably so, yet it doesn't shut the door on the possibility of change" (David Edelstein, Slate, May 28, 2004).
    - "*The Mother* is a moving, thought-provoking, occasionally darkly funny and shocking drama with an excellent central performance by Reid" (Matthew Turner, *London, The View*).
    - "*The Mother* is a taboo-crusher that bracingly resists sensationalism and sentimentality" (Dennis Lim, "60 Going on 69," *Village Voice*, May 25, 2004).
    - "*The Mother* is a splendidly uncomfortable watch, pitting a dysfunctional family against itself..." (Mark Kermode, *Observer*, Nov. 16, 2003).
    - "At its worst, this looks like some sort of BBC Four version of Shirley Valentine. *The Mother* is a contrived and self-important drama, scripted by Hanif Kureishi and directed by Roger Michell....The movie surrounding (Reid) is strangely cold and unsubtle" (Peter Bradshaw, *Guardian*, Nov. 14, 2003).

23. These quotations by Nev Pierce and David Edelstein are cited in the previous note.

Works Cited

Abraham, Karl. "The Applicability of Psycho-Analytic Treatment to Patients at an Advanced Age." Trans. Douglas Bryan and Alix Strachey. *Selected Papers of Karl Abraham*. London: Hogarth, 1949. 312–17.

Abraham, Georges, Philippe Kocher, and Georges Goda. "Psychoanalysis and Ageing." *International Review of Psycho-Analysis* 7 (1980): 147–55.

Ali: Fear Eats the Soul [Angst essen Seele auf]. Dir. Rainer Werner Fassbinder. Perf. Brigitte Mira, El Hedi ben Salem, and Barbara Valentin. New Yorker Films, 1975.

All That Heaven Allows. Dir. Douglas Sirk. Perf. Jane Wyman, Rock Hudson, and Agnes Moorehead. Universal Pictures, 1955.

Blum, Harold. "Repetition and Modification in the Ageing Process." *Within Time and Beyond Time: A Festschrift for Pearl King*. Ed. Riccardo Steiner and Jennifer Johns. London: H. Karnac Books, 2001. 108–21.

Bradshaw, Peter. Rev. of *The Mother*, dir. Roger Michell. *Guardian* Nov. 14, 2003. *Internet Movie Database*. <www.imdb.com>.

Bruce. User comment about *The Mother*, dir. Roger Michell. *Internet Movie Database*. 2008. Jan. 16, 2007 <http://www.imdb.com>.

Edelstein, David. "The Sexual Awakening of Mom." Rev. of *The Mother*, dir. Roger Michell. May 28, 2004. Slate.com. Jan. 16, 2007 <http://www.slate.com/id/2101436/>.

Erikson, Erik. *Childhood and Society*. New York: Norton, 1950.

———. *Identity and the Life Cycle*. New York: Norton, 1980.

———. *Life History and the Historical Moment*. New York: Norton, 1975.

Far from Heaven. Dir. Todd Haynes. Perf. Julianne Moore, Dennis Quaid, Dennis Haysbert, and Patricia Clarkson. Focus Features, 2002.

Freud, Sigmund. "On Femininity." *Standard Edition* 22: 112–35.

———. "Sexuality in the Aetiology of the Neuroses." *Standard Edition* 3: 261–85.

———. "Types of Onset of Neurosis." *Standard Edition* 12: 229–38.

The Graduate. Dir. Mike Nichols. Perf. Anne Bancroft, Dustin Hoffman, and Katharine Ross. Embassy Pictures, 1967.

Grotjahn, Martin. "Analytic Psychotherapy with the Elderly." *Psychoanalytic Review* 42 (1955): 419–27.

———. "Psychoanalytic Investigation of a Seventy-One-Year-Old Man with Senile Dementia." *Psychoanalytic Quarterly* 9 (1940): 80–97.

Harold and Maude. Dir. Hal Ashby. Perf. Ruth Gordon, Bud Cort, and Vivian Pickles. Paramount Pictures, 1971.

Kahane, Claire. "Gender and Voice in Transitional Phenomena." *Transitional Objects and Potential Spaces: Literary Uses of D.W. Winnicott*. Ed. Peter Rudnytsky. New York: Columbia UP, 1993. 278–91.

Kermode, Mark. "Passion on a Pension." Rev. of *The Mother*, dir. Roger Michell. *Observer*. Nov. 16, 2003. *Internet Movie Database* <www.imdb.com>.

King, Pearl. "The Life Cycle as Indicated by the Nature of the Transference in the Psychoanalysis of the Middle-Aged and Elderly." *International Journal of Psycho-Analysis* 61 (1980): 153–60.

Kristeva, Julia. *Black Sun: Depression and Melancholia*. Trans. Leon S. Rudiez. New York: Columbia UP, 1987.

Lady Chatterley's Lover. Dir. Just Jacckin. Perf. Sylvia Kristel, Shane Briant, and Nicholas Clay. Cannon Film Distributors, 1982.

Lim, Dennis. "60 Going on 69." Rev. of *The Mother*, dir. Roger Michell. *Village Voice*. May 25, 2004. *Internet Movie Database*. <www.imdb.com>.

Limentani, Adam. "Creativity and the Third Age." *International Journal of Psychoanalysis* 76 (1995): 825–33.

Martin, Carol. "The Elder and the Other." *Free Associations: Psychoanalysis, Groups, Politics, Culture* 3C (1992): 341–54.

McKenzie-Smith, Savi. "A Psychoanalytical Observational Study of the Elderly." *Free Associations* 3C (1992): 355–90.

The Mother. Dir. Roger Michell. Perf. Anne Reid, Peter Vaughan, Anna-Wilson Jones, and Daniel Craig. Prod: BBC Films, Free Range Films, Renaissance Films; Distribution: Momentum Pictures, U.K. Sony Pictures Classics, U.S., 2003.

Muslin, Hyman A. *The Psychotherapy of the Elderly Self*. New York: Brunner-Mazel, 1992.

The Passion of the Christ. Dir. Mel Gibson. Perf. James Caviezel, Maia Morgenstern, Christo Jivkov, and Francesco De Vito. Newmarket Films, 2004.

Pierce, Nev. Rev. of *The Mother*, dir. Roger Michell. *BBC Film Review*. Nov. 12, 2003. *Internet Movie Database*. <www.imdb.com>.

Rudnytsky, Peter L., ed. *Transitional Objects and Potential Spaces: Literary Uses of D.W. Winnicott*. New York: Columbia UP, 1993.

Rumor Has It . . . . Dir. Rob Reiner. Perf. Jennifer Aniston, Kevin Costner, Shirley MacLaine, and Mark Ruffalo. Warner Bros. Pictures, 2005.

Schwab, Gabriele. "Reading Otherness, and Cultural Contact." *The Mirror and the Killer-Queen*. Bloomington: Indiana UP, 1996. 1–84.

Schwarz, Murray M. "Where Is Literature?" *Transitional Objects and Potential Spaces: Literary Uses of D.W. Winnicott*. Ed. Peter Rudnytsky. New York: Columbia UP, 1993. 50–62.

Segal, Hanna. "Fear of Death—Notes on the Analysis of an Old Man." *Within Time and Beyond Time: A Festschrift for Pearl King*. Ed. Riccardo Steiner and Jennifer Johns. London: H. Karnac Books, 2001. 214–22.

Settlage, Calvin F. "Transcending Old Age: Creativity, Development and Psychoanalysis in the Life of a Centenarian." *International Journal of Psycho-Analysis* 77 (1996): 549–64.

Something's Gotta Give. Dir. Nancy Meyers. Perf. Jack Nicholson, Diane Keaton, Keanu Reeves, and Frances McDormand. Sony Pictures Entertainment, 2003.

The Standard Edition of the Complete Psychological Works of Sigmund Freud. Trans. and ed. James Strachey. 24 vols. London: Hogarth and Inst. of Psychoanalysis, 1953–74.

Steiner, Riccardo, and Jennifer Johns, eds. *Within Time and Beyond Time: A Festschrift for Pearl King*. London: H. Karnac Books, 2001.

Turner, Matthew. Rev. of *The Mother*, dir. Roger Michell. Oct. 24, 2003. *View London*. Jan. 15, 2007 <http://www.viewlondon.co.uk/films/the-mother-film-review-5417.html>.

Winnicott, D.W. "The Location of Cultural Experience." *Transitional Objects and Potential Spaces: Literary Uses of D.W. Winnicott*. Ed. Peter Rudnytsky. New York: Columbia UP, 1993. 3–12.

———. *Playing and Reality*. New York: Basic Books, 1971.

Woodward, Kathleen. *Aging and Its Discontents: Freud and Other Fictions*. Bloomington: Indiana UP, 1991.

———. "Performing Age, Performing Gender." *NWSA Journal* 18.1 (2006): 162–89.

Zackarek. Stephanie. Rev. of *The Mother*, dir. Roger Michell. Salon.com. Jan. 16, 2007 <http://dir.salon.com/story/ent/movies/review/2004/05/28/the_mother/index.html?CP=IMD&DN=110>.

CHAPTER 3

OLD COPS: OCCUPATIONAL AGING IN A FILM GENRE

Neal King

Ageism in Hollywood

Convinced that their jobs make them special and keep them connected to others, movie cops hate to retire. As stars of action cinema, they enjoy the rush of combat and the righteous work of culling the criminal herd. What happens, then, when old age begins to slow them and threaten to end their careers? Clint Eastwood, in his late seventies as of this writing, still stars in gunfighter movies, nearly forty years after his first appearance as Dirty Harry (1971). How does cop action change as stars reach retirement age?

The appearance of old people on screen, including old cops, can call to mind the findings of social gerontology and thus matters of realism and reflection of social trends.[1] Conversely, old characters may raise the very different question of how filmmakers imagine old age as they staff an industry known for its focus on youth. This chapter pursues the second line of thought. I ask neither how accurate the portrayals of retirement age are, nor to what extent they illustrate social research, but instead how they result from the most immediate causal forces upon them—those of the industry that produces films for profit. By portraying old age as they do, particularly in old cop movies, filmmakers with ties to studios and concerns for their careers evoke the status of old people in Hollywood. I urge that we view media imagery in this more focused light, rather than as reflection of the nature of aging nationwide.

The cop movie genre began in 1967. Between then and 2008, only eighteen of the 309 Hollywood films released to international cinemas have featured cop heroes near retirement. By focusing on those nineteen old men (one film stars two of them, and there are no old women), this study reveals old masculinity to be the strenuous resistance to retirement unless ending a career offers the manhood-affirming compensation of glamorous romance. Old cops who retire either enjoy sex or suffer despair and death. The rest stay on the job, firing their weapons and enjoying the self-importance that masculine work brings. I suggest that moviegoers can view the options available to old cops as a product of how age matters within Hollywood.[2] Filmmakers often depict old people as marginal to paid work, and by doing so imply a shared view of the status of retirement in their industry. Hollywood studios have been dominated by young men and invested in both the machismo of the highest-status jobs in filmmaking (producer, director, action-movie star) and the popularity of their stars with the youth who buy most tickets. Those filmmakers appear to have been telling stories built as much around the needs of aging genre and the studios that employ them as around the larger dynamics of aging in the United States.

Much of the inequality by age, gender, and race in the United States rests upon the long-term practice of occupational segregation, maintained mostly by informal means, but also by extending divisions of labor sometimes enforced by law. Western forms of ageism—exclusion of old people based on belief in their incompetence—include a view of old people's diminishing capacities to contribute in the workplace. Thus are larger labor markets riven by age.[3]

The organization of Hollywood favors especially sexist and ageist decisions in writing and casting. This stems in part from the autonomy of executives to produce films and cast as they please: Successes are difficult to predict, and worried decision-makers need not account for the logic of their choices. Producers are thus free and highly motivated to follow both the leads of the advertisers who segment markets by age and gender, and the trends toward youth-oriented blockbuster success (Baker and Faulkner, Bielby and Bielby, Epstein). The highest status internal to the industry rests on cinema blockbusters that predict the long-term profits of studio properties,[4] rather than the larger viewership of television shows. In many circumstances, a desire for that status can motivate producers to favor the possibility of high prestige, rather than lower-profile, more reliable profits. That is, corporate owners of studios may follow such market mechanisms to the point of ignoring the stated preferences of large consumer groups (Cosgrove-Mather, Powell). Thus, even though old people watch their products and buy the goods advertised, producers tend to hire young writers and young male actors for principal roles, with the result of a "double jeopardy" for actors who are both female and old (Lincoln and Allen).

Some of these patterns have been in place for nearly a century. Looking mainly for young men and "girls" to perform on film in the 1910s and 1920s, the early Hollywood system continued to cast some aging established stars by the early 1940s, but otherwise equated vitality with youth (Addison; see also Addison's chapter in this book). During those early decades, filmmakers barely broached the topic of old age on screen (Cohen-Shalev and Marcus 87); research of the past two decades shows that depictions of old people in entertainment still include scant representation of them as purposive heroes, but frequent inclusions as the butts of jokes or as victims (Lauzen and Dozier; Powell). On film, mature white males below the age of sixty appear in control of most organizations, as justified by imputations of greater productivity and competence (Powell 187; Lauzen and Dozier 443). Indeed, older characters of all genders and races have been less likely to pursue clearly depicted goals and thus less likely to serve as the protagonists of film stories (444). Old women appear as even less active and attractive than old men, and old men are paired in romances with much younger women (Bazzini, McIntosh, Smith, Cook, and Harris; Markson and Taylor "Mirror"). Men thus appear in heroic roles more often than women do, even as they grow old.

For the most part, the careers and salable brands of Hollywood's star system require adherence to physical standards of youth and middle age. Just as early stars who wished to revive or maintain careers before the cameras "frequently had to substantiate or recuperate their youth" (Addison 11), so might stars need to perform athletic feats and romance younger partners today, especially in the sex-and-violence plots typical of genre films (e.g., action, teen comedy, horror). Addison shows that Hollywood employers have long looked to youthful stars for two main reasons. First, movie producers argued that the long hours and repetitive activity of filming require much strength (15). Second, the subplots of genre films tend to focus on erotic romance (16); in the context of the age stratification growing popular in the 1910s and 1920s, early filmmakers assumed that the youthful audiences, on whose spending they could most rely, would prefer youthful stars in romantic roles (17).[5] In short, most trends within the industry worked against old stars unless they could look or at least act like young ones.

This brief literature review thus suggests that the age-graded hierarchies and youth-oriented casting in Hollywood register on screen as the rapid *occupational aging* (the process by which employees come to seem too old to work) of women and the mixed portrayals of old men. Old women all but disappear as protagonists, and old men tend to star in films in which they enjoy romance with younger women.

Were popular culture homogenous, all reflecting one mass social psychology, then one might expect that various media and genres would paint similar pictures. But decades of research on the production of culture (Bordwell, Thompson, and Staiger; Miller) suggest that different strata of culture industries operate by different rules and thus can produce different images, even of the same phase of the life course. For instance, in science fiction, people can experience a fantasy escape from mortality; retired people are reborn to sunny childhoods (Katz). Tourism pamphlets treat retired vacationers as in need of nurturing care, community, and routine (Chaney). Study of ads created by a national government to urge safe sex found unabashed depictions of old women's sexuality, and evidence of positive viewer responses as well (Tulloch). Research on Internet and magazine ads reveals a pattern in which those texts suggest that old men with money to spend enjoy expensive sporting and leisure pursuits, and medically augmented sex lives with attractive spouses. Retired men appear coupled with women who are roughly age peers, enjoying their retirement as if in victory over the constraints of work (Calasanti and King, "Firming"; Calasanti and King, "Beware"). But such pairings and pleasure, including these images of old women as active and sexual partners, do not appear in all other images of retired life. Various types of media, and the subgenres of texts within them, are produced in different contexts, with different aims, by different parties and do not all offer the same depictions. We need to understand the images in a Hollywood genre not as signposts of postmodern change or widespread social shifts, but as expressions of filmmakers with industrial concerns of their own.

All of this bears study in part because the literature on reception of Hollywood storytelling suggests that "negative" depictions of old characters may affect the self concepts of old viewers (e.g., Lauzen and Dozier 444; Markson and Taylor, "Real versus Reel" 170); depictions of old people as "hindrances to society" are associated with negative self-concepts among their viewers (193). The fictive association of old age with unhappiness, failure, and evil is pervasive (Powell 187). This association suggests some important consequences of the patterns in popular culture that result from Hollywood's ways of doing its business. Against the background of ageist patterns in casting and writing, the most immediate causal factors influencing the depiction of retirement-age cops are the careers of the genre's retirement-age stars, and the ways in which those careers serve producers' goals. I next focus on production of the genre in order to show how the handling of cop action stars results in the depiction of cop action retirement.

The Cop Action Genre

In order to answer questions about trends in old cop heroism, this study includes every North American cop action film released between 1967 and 2008, comparing those eighteen films in which old actors (those nearing retirement age, beginning at fifty-nine)[6] appear as heroes to the 291 movies that star younger players. This allows for the observations of widespread patterns in the depiction of aging at work. Films considered part of cop action first appeared in the mid-1960s. Releases nearly stopped at the close of the 1970s, but resumed and attained the height of their frequency at the end of the 1980s. The frequency has declined somewhat since 1990, but remains steady today (see figure 3.1).

Perhaps because cop action films originate in a specific milieu developed in late-twentieth century Hollywood, and thus bear traces of that context, they tell a tightly defined set of stories—the copies and knock-offs typical of generic production (Altman). Cop action heroes tend to be working-class white men doing law enforcement and security jobs, and they tend to make similar complaints—that the world is slipping away from them (King, *Heroes*). Skilled at little other than killing ("It's the only thing I was ever good at," says the hero of *Lethal Weapon*), cop heroes feel that demands for civility (e.g., rule-bound enforcement of the law as opposed to self-defensive slaughter in the midst of furious combat) cost men like them the privileged places in male-dominated occupations and communities.

Most cop action heroes are thus deeply invested in holding jobs that call for physical aggression to solve social problems and that endear those men to the communities that need saviors. In a few ways, life as a cop hero appears as a dirty, low-paid version of being an action star: A hero plies a trade known for physical exertion and extravagant expressions of machismo, works with few female peers, dismisses other walks of life

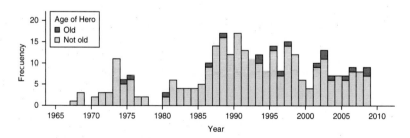

Figure 3.1 Frequency of international release of Hollywood cop action films, by year and by age of hero. ("Old" = fifty-nine years old or older)

as less dignified,[7] and resists retirement as a humiliating failure unless another form of glamour replaces the work-related action. The sense that the skilled, violent work of policing is special, and especially manly, pervades the genre.

The absence of women among old heroes fits the larger pattern of casting by age and gender in Hollywood, and fits trends in cop action movies even more closely. Though other genres (e.g., romantic comedies, musicals, dramas) feature women in principal roles, only two dozen of all cop action movies star women, and those heroes are disproportionately young—four times as likely as male actors to portray rookies (King "Generic Womanhood"). Only two middle-aged women star in cop action films.[8] The inclusion of women as heroes is relatively recent, as early experiments with gender inclusion in cop movies were few and far between, and met with little box-office success until 1990s *The Silence of the Lambs,* with its rookie hero. As a result, none of the younger actresses who have starred in successful cop movies have advanced to retirement age. There are no successful female actors established in the genre who have reached an age to play retiring heroes.[9]

Old men, however, star in this film genre's conflicts: between normalcy and a lively occupation, between restraint and physical aggression, between retirement and prestige. Genre filmmakers employ several stars of an age to play such roles and of sufficient fame to sell tickets. Though, as Margaret Gullette demonstrates in her review of stage acting, there is a difference between having an old body and playing one, film actors seldom play old for more than a few scenes (in heavy makeup) unless they are old. A successful acting career in Hollywood is a precious resource, maintained in part by the appearance of physical youth, and only one actor (Bruce Willis, in an episode of the anthology *Sin City*) has been cast as a character much older than he is. They otherwise appear to take old roles when they can no longer hide their own aging. Thus the presentation of old heroes seems to depend upon the aging of bankable stars.

Clint Eastwood, of *Dirty Harry* fame, has headlined movies into his late seventies, in most cases offering "fantasies of old age in which men are presented as initially flawed and failing but eventually valued, praised, and sexually attractive to younger women" (Gates 187). As such icons as John Wayne, Frank Sinatra, Sean Connery, Charles Bronson, Robert DeNiro, Al Pacino, and Harrison Ford have neared or reached their sixties, they also starred in movies with plots inflected by age.

I suggest that the production of these films has been driven by the presence in Hollywood of aging stars who wield clout and whose names can draw distributors to make the deals from which studios profit.

Performances in the films discussed below have resonance for those who know the genre, in that the actors are familiar, their tics and gestures known. Clint Eastwood has starred in a dozen cop action films, starting back in 1968 with *Coogan's Bluff*. Al Pacino began his cop action career at thirty-two as *Serpico* (1973); Robert Duvall was forty-two when he starred in *Badge 373* (also in 1973); and Sidney Poitier was forty when *In the Heat of the Night* spurred development of the genre in 1967. Other actors, such as John Wayne and Frank Sinatra, were further into middle age at that time, leaving them fewer years to star in the genre before they would play old heroes. In all of these cases, viewers of the old-man films could have been familiar with the actors from their younger years, and might have been aging right along with the movie stars they had watched for decades. Producers can sell modestly priced genre films on the basis of such stars, even when those actors' popularity as headliners of block-busters in the United States may be fading. The story of a retiring cop can star such an actor and thus meet at least a second-tier industrial need. These industrial dynamics have altered the vision of retirement within the genre, from the darkest view of it as a precursor to death, to one more accepting of the transition so long as romance compensates.

Avoidance of Retirement

The Development of Cop Action Stars

The genre's first decades provided the fewest and grimmest views of retirement, either by associating it with death or by avoiding the topic. I illustrate those in turn, and briefly discuss other films that include old men as secondary characters—supportive sidekicks rather than starring heroes. I suggest that the change in view of retirement, from the dim view in early years toward more optimistic accounts, resulted not from some larger shift in age relations nationwide, but rather from the fact that the genre was too new in the 1970s to have many established actors associated with it. Old stars of the time (e.g., John Wayne) had worked in other genres and had no investment in urban cop personae. Without years of association between actors and police roles, and thus expectation that audiences would pay to see old cops played by actors well known within the genre, there was no demand for such films to meet.

A few cop action films of the 1970s acknowledge occupational age and impending retirement, in most cases depicting the end of one's career as a fate to avoid. For instance, the senior sidekick in *The New Centurions* (played by Oscar-winning actor George C. Scott) retires and loses his connections to colleagues and to the street he had patrolled with pride. He kills himself with a revolver after months of isolation.[10] Frank Sinatra's swansong, *The First Deadly Sin* (1980), also features the hero's retirement, after which he has nothing left but grief for his dying wife. The film closes with a shot of him in tears, ending the 1970s-era depiction of cops' retirements on a sour note. Such early films starred actors known for diverse performances rather than the cop genre in particular, and offered views of old manhood that were particularly dark and dramatic.

Other early films starring actors in their sixties denied old age as a curse not fit to mention. For instance, John Wayne starred in two mid-1970s films (see table 3.1) without so much as acknowledging that he had entered his late sixties. His characters shoot with perfect aim from long distance, take dives to dodge bullets, outgun mobsters during car chases, and enjoy flirtations with women half their age. Such films depicted men able to do manly work without having to worry about weakening bodies or dismissal from the job.[11]

The *Lethal Weapon* cycle (1987, 1990, 1992, and 1998) stars younger men and maintains the oppositional stance toward retirement. The leads joke about the senior partner's relatively advanced status. The dialogue never stipulates the elder man's age (actor Danny Glover was forty during the filming of the first installment, and fifty-one during the filming of the last), but shows him preparing to retire and then deciding otherwise during the third film. Throughout the series, this gently paternal partner responds to stress by telling himself that he is "too old for this shit." By the fourth film, the younger partner (played by Mel Gibson, forty-one at the time of filming) has also adopted the series' trademark line, joking that he also is now "too old for this shit." Occupational old age comes quickly for these adrenaline-charged cops, whose jobs require near-daily doses of combat. But such relatively young men dismiss retirement as a dignified option. They talk their insecurities away in locker-room coaching sessions and then wade back into battle. Their movie-star-driven personae fear not violent death, but the undignified normalcy that retirement could bring. Such films star actors in middle age and could easily treat retirement as an option to avoid.

However, the matter of race confounds this measure of the impact of age on cop heroism. Where the larger genre tends to focus on white working-class heroism, its black heroes are more likely to be buttoned-down or suave professionals unaccustomed to dirty work (e.g., the older, black partner in the *Lethal Weapon* films). The genre focuses on white men as those most alienated from their society, most in need of some uplift, and most likely to wade into violence on a regular basis. In a reversal of older American racial stereotypes, black men in cop action

Table 3.1 Cop action films with old heroes

Title	Date of release	Lead actor	Age during filming	Resolution
88 Minutes	2008	Al Pacino	65	Status quo (professor)
Along Came a Spider	2001	Morgan Freeman	63	Status quo
Blood Work	2002	Clint Eastwood	71	Retirement/romance
Brannigan	1975	John Wayne	68	Status quo
Falling Down	1992	Robert Duvall	61	Restoration of job
The First Deadly Sin	1980	Frank Sinatra	64	Retirement/mourning
Hollywood Homicide	2003	Harrison Ford	60	Status quo
In the Line of Fire	1992	Clint Eastwood	62	Retirement/romance
Insomnia	2002	Al Pacino	61	Death
Just Cause	1995	Sean Connery	64	Status quo (attorney)
Kiss the Girls	1997	Morgan Freeman	59	Status quo
McQ	1974	John Wayne	67	Restoration of job
Murphy's Law	1986	Charles Bronson	64	Status quo
Righteous Kill	2008	Robert DeNiro/ Al Pacino	64 / 67	Status quo/suicide
The Rock	1996	Sean Connery	65	Escape from prison
The Sentinel	2006	Michael Douglas	61	Retirement/romance
Shoot to Kill	1988	Sidney Poitier	60	Status quo
Sin City	2005	Bruce Willis	49★	Suicide

★ Willis plays a character described as being about two decades older than the actor.

films tend to be more refined in demeanor and professionalism than their white counterparts; the black men are played by such stars as Denzel Washington and Laurence Fishburne.[12] This pattern dates to the 1960s, when producers realized that they could enjoy massive success with Sidney Poitier's stirring depictions of professional-class competence. His string of hits included a seminal cop action film (*In the Heat of the Night*, 1967), which gave rise to two sequels and helped to define the genre and focus its racial politics on assimilation rather than black-power rebellion. Hollywood producers were impressed enough with their ability to draw black audiences without offending white ones that they generally stuck to the depiction of middle-class black cops (with the notable exception of Eddie Murphy characters in the 1980s).

Indeed, the two old black male stars of the 1980s and 1990s are upscale urbanites working professional-class FBI jobs (Sidney Poitier in 1988's *Shoot to Kill*, and Morgan Freeman in the "Noah Cross" films *Kiss the Girls* and *Along Came a Spider*, from 1997 and 2001). Poitier's hero chases a killer through the mountains of the U.S. northwest in winter, and lags behind his younger (white) partner, nearly succumbing to hypothermia. Though one could attribute the difference between the two men's physical performances to age, the Poitier character's urban-tenderfoot status confounds the matter. At the end of the story, he takes a few bullets in the chest before killing his foe in hand-to-hand combat—under freezing Canadian seawater, no less. He trades quips with his sidekick from an ambulance stretcher. Although his injury might serve as a sign of his being "too old for this shit," no one says so, and his heroic performance testifies to his masculine toughness. The genre thus confounds class and race; black men engage in less reckless violence across the genre, making it difficult to assess whether the old black heroes restrict their aggression because they are old, because they are professional class, and/or because they are black.

Consider also Morgan Freeman, who began to star in cop movies in 1995 (with *Seven*), by which point the actor had reached his late fifties. He plays mature detectives who maintain measured paces, more interested in solving puzzles than in racing cars or firing weapons. The hero of *Kiss the Girls* (filmed when the actor was going on sixty) and its sequel, *Along Came a Spider*, only fires weapons, with lethal aim, when necessary. With his love of fine music and clothes, his educated vocabulary and thoughtful demeanor, he cuts a more urbane figure than the average working-class, athletic, white cop. Like Sinatra's retiring character in *The First Deadly Sin*, Cross ambles through his story without having to test his strength. Thus can the mixture of race and class confound one's attempt to measure the effect of age on black heroes.

By the time such films appeared, the presentation of old cops had become more common. Actors long associated with the genre had reached that age and could thus be used to sell stories of older men to genre fans worldwide. A producer had simply to figure out how to depict retirement age without too quickly degrading the marketable personae. The next cop action films to confront their starring heroes with retirement came at the height of the genre's popularity, in the early 1990s.

Falling Down

Robert Duvall, supporting actor in *The Detective* (1968) and star of *Badge 373* (1973), was among the first of the cop action generation of actors (after Sidney Poitier) to reach his sixties on screen. His last cop action starring role, in *Falling Down* (1992), presents the genre's first extended discussion of retirement. I consider this film at greater length in order to show how the genre has continued to depict the end of a career as a fate to avoid.

Falling Down tells the story of Martin, a white Los Angeles Police Department officer who, on what is meant to be his last day on the job, happens upon a case that changes his wavering mind. At story's end, he kills a criminal and then defies his colleagues and wife by rescinding his decision to step down. Martin's backstory tells of a wife—a full-time homemaker afraid to lose her remaining kin—who has talked him into working a desk job and then into retiring. He is humiliated not to work cases on the street, in harm's way like "a real cop." During his last day on this vestige of a job, he assembles clues collected by other cops and realizes that he can locate and arrest another aging white man. The developing comparison between these two men provides the crux of the story.

Martin ultimately realizes that the other aging man has become a violent criminal out of his rage at having been left behind—laid off at work, divorced by his wife, and denied custody of his daughter. Like Martin, this killer wants to regain his status as breadwinning patriarch. Both wear the professional breadwinner uniform of white shirt and tie, and Martin can track his prey because he empathizes with his displacement—that sense of having been left behind by a society that has little use for old-fashioned, white-male heroism. Thus do the two serve as opposing images of aging white men in trouble who must pursue violent conflict to the point of death in order to remain heroic.[13]

Held to the standard of constant aggression, Martin seems to fall short. Other cops consider the deskbound hero a coward; a sidekick mocks his aim to retire ("Lake Havesu?" his partner asks in disbelief. "What are you going to do, watch the cactus grow?"). Martin volunteers to help with physical work but is shrugged off by a younger cop. He tries to share insights with a detective, who dismisses him as no longer useful. Only at the end of the story, when he defies his wife and the men around him and tracks his doppelgangerdown, does he put his body to work. Having already given up his badge and gun to retirement, Martin rushes into harm's way with nothing but his hands in front of him, in a scene of unarmed pursuit unprecedented in the genre. As a defenseless cop looking to face a killer, he is both brave and emasculated—the picture of ambivalence about old manhood. He grabs his fallen partner's gun and finishes the chase, blowing the killer away and then vowing to remain on this thrilling job over his wife's objection. An old man in danger of fading, he is reborn. His remarkable courage contrasts with his disarmed status, as if he could compensate with pure force of will for the degradation of occupational old age.

Robert Duvall's performance enhances the sense of an aging man struggling with his position. Modest in demeanor (with downcast eyes, soft voice, and a stooped posture), Duvall brings to the film a history of playing tough men who remain tight-lipped, mixing stoicism with gentle humor. Such is the sidekick character that he played in *Colors* (1988), in which he serves as the sage, senior partner to an impetuous rookie (at the end of the film the old partner is shot to death). In *Falling Down*, Duvall leaves most of his feelings unstated, acting with expressive eyes and mouth the ambivalence of a man who wants to be a good husband but wants even more to be a cop. He wears a starched white shirt and tie, and is bald enough to look like an old-fashioned teacher. He looks away and keeps quiet when insulted, allowing other cops to think him a coward until he proves otherwise in battle. Even in the ultimate face-off with his crazed double, Martin is mature enough to plead with the criminal to stand down rather than force a gunfight. Martin entreats the suicidal killer to go quietly, up until the moment he has to fire in self-defense. However modest he might be about his capacity for combat, once awakened by the rush of police work, Martin realizes that he cannot give up the job. His performance is that of a man entering old age with apprehension (the actor was sixty-one at the time of filming), ashamed of the effect that it has had on his stature at work (others tease him about his reticence to do street work), reserved but containing the rage of one who knows that he was a hero once and can be again.

Martin's lethal action in the finale even suggests that the physical performance was more a matter of modesty (that of a devoted husband to a fearful wife) than of age. Perhaps the hero has adopted the pose of a man in decline because he has dutifully surrendered to retirement. Hastening to the chase, he perks up again, decks a flippant colleague, rushes into harm's way, outfights his younger partner, and puts a killer down, even before announcing that he will refuse to retire. The plotting raises the possibility that signs of age are but a mask he has donned and can doff when he pleases.

The movies discussed so far depict retirement as a sad fate, of stardom in eclipse. They leave open the possibility that being old is more a pattern of behavior (retiring, ceasing to perform like one's younger self) than a number of years lived. But before I turn to visions of successful retirement, I look at another equation of old manhood with death.

Insomnia

One other film depicts an old cop in a way that does not acknowledge age directly, but nonetheless provides a performance of manhood on the wane. *Insomnia* (2002) foregrounds a sixtyish white cop's physical limits and moral corruption, but links them to the film's titular disorder rather than to age directly. Though senior in his role as a homicide detective, the hero (played by Al Pacino) shows no interest in retirement, and the issue does not arise in the dialogue. Nevertheless, his occupationally old status seems congruent with the moral and physical exhaustion that his story chronicles.

Insomnia tells, among other stories, the tale of the hero Will's guilt over a past misdeed (evidence tampering), and then the investigation of his accidental killing of a fellow cop. The plotting allows both for increasing exhaustion as insomnia wears him down, and for a growing sense of guilt as he covers up the shooting and dwells on his crooked past. *Insomnia* focuses on Will's growing weakness rather than the strength with which he brings a killer down. This old cop dies a truly fallen man, as though sleeplessness had drained him dry.

The central performance features the actor's raspy smoker's voice, hunched posture, slurred speech, and the droopy eyes and yawning mouth that are indicative of Will's sleeplessness. Several montages affirm his physical suffering as he tries to block Alaska's summer sun in the middle of night. In conversation, he increasingly appears to drift, which he later does during a car chase. He hallucinates and generally comes undone. The dialogue ties the insomnia to his guilt, when the rookie investigating Will's accidental shooting begins to realize that he may be tampering with her evidence. Suspecting him of crime, she says to him, "A good cop can't sleep because a piece of the puzzle is missing; and a bad cop can't sleep because his conscience won't let him." Will shrugs off the implication, but then, during the film's climax, changes his mind. He resolves to come clean, hunts down the killer, suffers a mortal wound, and, with his last breath, commands the rookie to tell the truth of his own misdeeds.

The hero's physical exhaustion, just like the other physical frailties of aged cops in other films, hardly prevents a robust confrontation with the killer. He chases, wrestles, and outguns his foe. And neither need his death betray weakness. Across the genre, corrupted heroes die at the conclusions of the films in which they star, after all. However, that performance of exhaustion is tied to the hero's senior status—he enjoys renown among detectives in training, has many famous cases to his credit, but also has committed at least one crime (manufacturing evidence to gain a capital conviction) for which he must pay. Though the plot avoids the issue of impending retirement in its depiction of a senior hero who loves his job, the descent into insomnia implies his long-term guilt and the exhaustion that it brings. Will's conscience will not let him sleep, and it is time for him to stop working. The tragedy is that to cease is to die. Like some of the other films that treat retirement as a stigmatized status to avoid, *Insomnia* skirts the subject in its dialogue but implies it with plotting and performance. Retirement is death.[14]

In both of the cases just reviewed, heroes act as if they are slowing down, but for reasons aside from aging per se. Martin of *Falling Down* has chosen a desk job to please a demanding wife; Will of *Insomnia* suffers guilt and disease. Martin's desk-cop persona is revealed to have been a mask for the real Martin, an action hero; *Insomnia*'s Will dies restored to the moral ideals of his youth. Both films star retirement-aged men but provide alternate reasons for any appearance on their part of failure to live up to the standards of youth. They thus go to some lengths to allow that their stars are able to meet those youthful ideals, even if they choose to *act* like old men. The mask of aging appears as just that—the performance of an aging but still potent star. Hollywood is thereby able to offer movies that feature aging stars, as long as they conform to the formula for box-office success: The *mask* of old age is equated with unhappiness, failure, and evil, but redemption is possible when the actor's "true"—that is, *unaged*—self is revealed or restored.

Compensation for Retirement

Although the films reviewed thus far deal with occupational old age as a problem and retirement as a fate to avoid, three films depict contented retirement by heroes in love. *The Sentinel* (2006) stars Michael Douglas as a Secret Service agent enjoying an affair—with the First Lady, no less, played by ex-model Kim Basinger. With her real-life status as a media star, Basinger represents both Academy Award–winning talent and the high end of Hollywood standards of physical beauty. Douglas's cop character retires from active duty to an instructor position at the end of the story, with a round of jokes about playing golf and wearing Depends. His affair has been exposed to his boss, and so the hero must leave his action-oriented job. In this film, (semi)retirement results not from the cop's physical failure but from a physical achievement of sorts—an illicit romance with a glamorous woman.

Two other films, both starring Clint Eastwood, also pair retirement with romance. *In the Line of Fire* (1992) features him as another Secret Service agent. He romances a younger colleague, played by Rene Russo, and then retires at the end of the story. Russo is another ex-model and paragon of Hollywood beauty, and twenty-four years younger than Eastwood. She played romantic sidekicks in several action movies of the 1990s, including the third and fourth *Lethal Weapon* movies. She represented the ideal middle-aged partner of a high-status white male hero: not simply attractive, but gorgeous by Hollywood standards, as though aging male action heroes need exceptional romantic foils in order to compensate for their age and the way that such age erodes their machismo on the job.

As the hero of *In the Line of Fire*, Eastwood performs advanced age with signs of exhaustion: labored breathing, sweating, and confusion while on duty, and a midafternoon nap for which the other cops mock him. The dialogue calls attention to his senior, legendary status, with references to his having guarded President Kennedy. The film even employs a photograph of a young Eastwood, which calls attention to the physical transformation that age has wrought: a gain of weight and a loss of hair. The hero takes a bullet in the line of duty, right before he helps to kill the criminal; however, his ultimate retirement comes not for reasons of injury or exhaustion but rather because he can more easily pursue his new romance with his young colleague (against Secret Service policy) if he gives up his job. He retires, an apparently happy man, walking into the sunset with his new lover.

Eastwood's other romance with a younger, beautiful woman provides the third example of this trend, the 2002 film *Blood Work*. It tells the story of a retired white FBI agent who takes to private investigation (without a license, in the rogue activity that has become a cliché of this vigilante-oriented genre) on a citizen's request. By the end of the complicated story, this hero has solved his case, romanced his new client (played by a woman who is thirty years younger than Eastwood), helped her murder a killer in vengeance, and retired once again. In this

film, the impulse that drives him is neither revenge nor dedication to
career (the motives of younger heroes in other films), but rather his guilt
at even being alive—it turns out that he received the transplanted heart
of the victim whose murder he must solve. The pairing of such guilt
with the hero's old age suggests doubt about the worth of an old man, to
which he responds by wading into a case in defiance of orders to drop
it. Here, retirement without love comes not as a time to slow down, but
as an opportunity to resume the actions of a cop, now without the constraints of the law. He takes a new case from a client who will become
his new love.

As a contrast to this pairing of infirmity with age, consider *Heart
Condition*, in which another cop (played by Bob Hoskins, who was
forty-seven at the time of filming) receives a transplanted heart and
pursues the killer of his heart's donor. This similarly plotted story plays
not on age but on vice; the hero has eaten so much bad food, drunk
so much alcohol, smoked so many cigarettes, and spewed so much rac-
ist venom that he has poisoned his system. The story appears to have
originated with a writer who really wanted to focus on a heart transplant as part of a fable of race relations (see hooks and King *Heroes* for
discussions) and thus secured work for Hoskins not despite his age but
because of it.

In *Blood Work*, however, the heart transplant is more obviously a
matter of age, and the story centers on (temporary) renewal of employment rather than racial reform. In other words, where the hero's flaw
is racism in the earlier film, it is old age and retirement in the latter
(though it bears mention that the donor of the heart in both films is
a person of color). In this film, employment is more than a means to
expiate an old man's guilt at being alive. Midway through, the hero
of *Blood Work* discusses the rewards of his job when his neighbor asks
him what it was like: "How did it feel? I mean, back in that day, back
when you were going up against all of those sickos?" The hero replies,
"That was my job. Connected.... That's what it was, when I was at
the top of my game. I felt connected to everything: the victim, the
killer, the crime scene, everything. Just felt like it was all part of me. It's
beginning to feel that way again." The hero takes obvious pride in this
renewed sense of importance and the attention that it will bring him.
He soon becomes the subject of media interest again, the stardom that
had eluded him in retirement restored. Across the genre, heroes show
that they prefer the wild action of police violence to the mundane normalcy of any other job; they are stars of their own world. And only in
the context of retirement must they consider alternatives for themselves
in more than the abstract. Retirement threatens to leave them living

that dreaded normalcy, which might feel like occupational death, as at the desk job of *Falling Down*.

Such exposition provides a frame for a viewer's interpretation of Eastwood's physical performance in *Blood Work*. Raspy of voice and hunched at the neck, prone to holding his hand to his chest, slower to move than we have seen the actor before, this character pauses to swallow pills, removes his shirt for chest exams, and generally takes it easy. He even loses a struggle with a younger man early on, allowing a suspect to pin him and escape. Demonstrations of physical weakness come rarely from cop action heroes—nearly all of them from actors near retirement age. But none of this prevents the hero from challenging, arresting, and shooting the killer at the end of the story. He even bluffs the killer with a pantomime; at the moment when he suffers his initial heart attack, he feigns greater weakness than he feels to draw the killer close and get a shot off, wounding his prey even as he succumbs to a certain sign of aging—once again, the genre reminds us that old age can be a mask easily doffed by a potent man. This hero remains a forceful presence throughout, able to do his old job despite his old age. But his frequent indications of postoperative and aged status inflect his masculine heroism nonetheless. His age weakens his hold on the thrilling life of connectedness; he retains that hold only until he can trade it for another glamour.

As with *In the Line of Fire*, the end of *Blood Work* suggests the conditions under which retirement is an acceptable concession to physical decline. The hero's client becomes his lover (thirty years of age divide the actors); they bed down in cop action style, after getting to know each other for only a short while. After the case is closed, he literally sails off into the sunset with her.[15]

All three of these examples pose unusual romance (with women decades younger, or living in the halls of power, or both) as compensations for retirement from the job of violent policing. The romantic pairings echo the lives of actual cops, and ordinary old men, far less than they do the lives of wealthy and famous male stars, who often wind up with wives many years younger. The casting decisions have less to do with the needs of plots than with the expectations of stars whose names market the genre films. Valuable commodities in their twilight years, after having built the loyalties of fans for decades, such stars bear flattery within the industrial context. However, the effect on the storytelling is to paint a picture of retirement years as ones of intergenerational romance. Only under that condition, with its alternate approach to the reassurance of masculinity, do cop action heroes embrace the transition with ease.

Conclusion

I have argued that Hollywood's filmmakers serve organizational needs—selling genre films, maintaining stars' careers—in the ways that they tell their stories of retirement—age cops. They use actors long familiar to genre fans and thus sell product in a global marketplace. With women among the genre's successful stars (e.g., Jodi Foster, Jennifer Lopez, Angelina Jolie) not yet aged enough to play old cops, and with little inclusion of women in the executive ranks of studios, the genre has yet to make room for old women. Instead, it flatters its male stars, treating mundane retirement as a fate to avoid by one of three Hollywood means: by staying on the job, by lapsing into dramatic death, or by pairing with lovers decades younger. The oldest heroes may put away their guns, but their other attributes of manhood work just fine, the genre says. The cop heroes look and act like aging stars in these respects.

One can imagine other stories of work and power, which offer different visions of age, and in which actresses such as Judi Dench and Meryl Streep, Susan Sarandon and Alfre Woodard, or former cop action stars such as Sigourney Weaver and Whoopi Goldberg confront criminals and prove their mettle. Hollywood could tell stories of the graceful acceptance, by both women and men, of the changes that aging can bring—of contribution, contemplation, or relaxation under conditions more varied than the polar opposites of violent death and glamorous romance. Such stories could provide a validation to aging viewers that Hollywood currently withholds, and a life course that young viewers rarely see.

A different industry would have to make such films, however, as it would express a different common sense based on a different social organization. It would be less beholden to the men among its marquee stars, less focused on global markets for genre films, less dominated by men in executive positions who remain unaccountable to consumer groups. Perhaps such an industry will develop as women gain more authority in Hollywood, or as old people come to form a more powerful consumer group, and as aging comes to pose less of a threat to filmmakers' careers.

In the meantime, the genre contributes to the mass media's tendency to depict old age with ambivalence. Few of its heroes are old men, and none are old women. The former do best by staying active, in terms of sex or violence; and the latter appear not to exist. From the larger genre we learn that "normal people suck" because they do not work this particular, violent job. Pity those men who must leave cop work without the compensation of lively romance, for they descend to pathetic status: disarmed, disconnected, and dismissed, or dead. They are fallen stars.

For students of age relations, this exercise offers a methodological caution: *caveat spectator*, let the viewer beware. Occupational aging in film is not merely about what happens on the real-life job depicted. It is shaped by the status of aging among those who make the films more than among those who enforce the law. We should not assume that images in cop action, or in any other genre or medium, simply reflect retirement policy, widespread experiences of retirement, or mass social psychology. Neither do they illustrate findings of social gerontology, as if they had been produced to serve as companion texts to scholarship. Instead, one may study the conditions under which storytellers work, in order to understand industry-specific variances in popular ageism. Further study will show how depictions of retirement age emerge from other production contexts. On the basis of the most casual appraisal, it seems that cinema genres such as romantic comedy make more room for women as stars, and therefore have featured dozens of characters in middle and old age (for example, played by such actresses as Meryl Streep, Diane Keaton, Susan Sarandon, and Shirley MacLaine). Hollywood's genres feature different kinds of stars, draw from different kinds of traditions, and tell different kinds of stories to suit them.

Notes

1. Decades of research have revealed patterns in the ways in which real people face retirement: taking short-term bridge jobs, trying to keep busy, and reentering the paid workforce for short periods. See Ekerdt; Ekerdt, Bossé, and Levkoff; Pampel; Quinn, Burkhauser, and Myers.

2. By "Hollywood," I refer to the commercial filmmaking firms that are geographically concentrated around the Los Angeles basin (Scott). They are hierarchically stratified, with the major studios of the Motion Picture Association of America at the top, and various independent producers and supplementary firms lower down. Feature filmmaking for the global cinema market enjoys the highest status, while production for television and for direct-to-video markets enjoys respectively less. My analysis bears on the output of the major studios, whose filmmaking occurs within a dense network of personal connections—a shared subculture.

3. Pathbreaking social gerontology, conducted since the 1970s, includes histories of employment policy shifts over the past two centuries in Europe and North America. This research shows that a changing ideology of the natural life course has portrayed old age as decline and obsolescence, such that old workers often face repudiation from younger people as being weak, sick, and unable to learn, and as nearing death. Casual dismissal of the competence of old people often turns to formal policies of retirement, "early exit," "redundancy," "age management," "job sacrifice," "job

release," and "stipend worker" programs. Important histories of the labor market include Achenbaum; Brooke and Taylor; Chudacoff; Duncan; Graebner; Laws; and Phillipson.

4. Blockbusters are multiplatform, saturation-advertising releases that rely on widespread, coordinated consumer awareness to generate "event" status and thus sell many tie-in products and generate revenues for years to come through multimedia rereleases. Young men in groups are the principal consumers. The massive profit margins created by these hits sustain the major-studio business model in Hollywood (Epstein, Gomery).

5. Addison points out that this focus on youthful audiences and stars was not necessary, but resulted instead from a national trend toward age segregation, which resulted in turn from a mode of industrialization: "[I]f motion pictures had more regularly featured a diverse range of ages in their leading players and narratives, perhaps those at or beyond middle age would have attended films in greater numbers" (17).

6. I chose fifty-nine as the cutoff age because Morgan Freeman had reached that age when he filmed the first of the two Noah Cross movies, *Kiss the Girls* (released in 1997). The other films considered in this study starred actors who were at least sixty years old during filming. Because few films specify characters' ages, I use actors' ages as proxies.

7. "Normal people suck," says a hero in *Running Scared*, while the hero of *Heat* joins a criminal in dismissing the family man's life of "barbecues and ball games."

8. These female cop heroes are played by Holly Hunter and Sigourney Weaver, both in 1995's *Copycat*.

9. Perhaps because of its lesser status in Hollywood, television has been more open to portrayals of aging women on the job, such that actors Angie Dickinson and Tyne Daly (who had played one of Dirty Harry's sidekicks in 1976) starred as cops in such television series as *Police Woman* (1974–78) and *Cagney & Lacey* (1982–88). Holly Hunter, star of the feature film *Copycat* (1985), went on to star in a television show about a cop (*Saving Grace*, 2007–). Movement back into feature films is unusual for actors in an industry so focused on elite status. On a popular British series centered around a female detective, portrayed by an actress (Helen Mirren) aged forty-five to sixty, see Gray & Jurik (2004).

10. In his review of research on stereotypes of aging, Thompson argues that later-life masculinities seem to be defined by norms of sociability and reveal more vividly men seeking connections with others, instead of the acts of individuation. Older men's experiences become more centered on the emotional work of relational concerns and reflection and less by the triumphs they had used to define themselves as younger men (634). In this respect, old men might be seen to pursue their sense of connectedness into more feminine worlds of purely social relationships rather than instrumental bonds at work. Though we have no evidence of causal connection between the expectations Thompson documents and the production of cop action films, such stereotypes might be seen to play out

in these cop movies as the search for the stardom that interaction with criminals, crime reporters, and public officials brings.

11. Some of the more recent films that star actors who had nearly turned sixty make little mention of their ages in the dialogue. *Hollywood Homicide* stars Harrison Ford at sixty, and settles for a Viagra joke and a scene in which he rides a child's bike during a chase. The matter of eventual retirement does not arise.

12. See King, *Heroes in Hard Times*, for a general discussion of the intersection of class and race in the genre.

13. The film's dialogue pokes fun at its comparison of the two men by having a witness tell the hero that the criminal "looked like you, except he was taller and he had hair."

14. In a recent cop action film (*Righteous Kill*, 2008), Pacino plays a man who elects suicide at the end of his career, motivated by his embrace of lawless violence. Paired with *Insomnia*, it suggests links between corruption, age, and death.

15. The most recent old-cop movie, as of this writing (*Righteous Kill*, 2008), pairs the hero (played by star Robert DeNiro) romantically with a woman played by an actress twenty-eight years younger—another former model, no less (Carla Gugino). The hero ends the film talking of his daughter and coaching a softball team of little girls, as his young girlfriend looks on in approval. In the 2008 release *88 Minutes*, Al Pacino has a brief affair with a character played by an actress thirty-four years younger; and the film's plot surrounds the hero with several women, decades younger, and nary an age peer in sight. Though young women and girls abound, older women have no place in the genre. Finally, note that the only old cop hero played by a younger actor—Willis's old character in *Sin City*—receives amorous attention from a female character one-fourth the hero's age.

Films

88 Minutes. Dir. Jon Avnet. Wri. Gary Scott Thompson. Prod. Randall Emmett, et al. Sony. 2008.

Along Came a Spider. Dir. Lee Tamahori. Wri. Mark Moss. Prod. David Brown and Joe Wizan. Paramount. 2001.

Badge 373. Dir. Howard W. Koch. Wri. Pete Hamill. Prod. Jim Digangi and Howard W. Koch. Paramount. 1973.

Blood Work. Dir. Clint Eastwood. Wri. Brian Helgeland. Prod. Clint Eastwood and Judie G. Hoyt. Warner Bros. 2002.

Brannigan. Dir. Douglas Hickox. Wri. Christopher Tumbo, et al. Prod. Arthur Gardner and Jules V. Levy. MGM/UA. 1975.

Colors. Dir. Dennis Hopper. Wri. Michael Schiffer. Prod. Robert H. Solo. Orion. 1988.

Coogan's Bluff. Dir. Don Siegel. Wri. Dean Riesner, Herman Miller, and Howard Rodman. Prod. Don Siegel. Universal. 1968.

Copycat. Dir. Jon Amiel. Wri. Ann Biderman and David Madsen. Prod. Arnon Milchan and Mark Tarlov. Warner Bros. 1995.

The Detective. Dir. Gordon Douglas. Wri. Abby Mann. Prod. Aaron Rosenberg. Twentieth Century Fox. 1968.

Dirty Harry. Dir. Don Siegel. Wri. P. M. Fink and Dean Riesner Harry Julian Fink. Prod. Don Siegel. Warner Bros. 1971.

The First Deadly Sin. Dir. Brian G. Hutton. Wri. Lawrence Sanders and Mann Rubin. Prod. George Pappas and Mark Shanker. Warner Bros. 1980.

Falling Down. Dir. Joel Schumacher. Wri. Ebbe Roe Smith. Prod. Arnold Kopelson, Herschel Weingrod, and Timothy Harris. Warner Bros. 1992.

Heart Condition. Dir. James D. Parriott. Wri. James D. Parriott. Prod. Steve Tisch. New Line. 1990.

Hollywood Homicide. Dir. Ron Shelton. Wri. Robert Souza. Prod. Ron Shelton and Lou Pitt. Columbia. 2003.

In the Heat of the Night. Dir. Norman Jewison. Wri. Stirling Silliphant. Prod. Walter Mirisch. United Artists. 1967.

In the Line of Fire. Dir. Wolfgang Petersen. Wri. Jeff McGuire. Prod. Jeff Apple. Columbia. 1993.

Insomnia. Dir. Christopher Nolan. Wri. Hillary Seitz. Prod. Broderick Johnson, Paul Junger Witt, and Andrew A. Kosove. Buena Vista. 2002.

Just Cause. Dir. Arne Glimcher. Wri. Jeb Stuart and Peter Stone. Prod. Arne Glimcher, Steve Perry, and Lee Rich. Warner Bros. 1995.

Kiss the Girls. Dir. Gary Fleder. Wri. David Klas. Prod. David Brown and Joe Wizan. Paramount. 1997.

Lethal Weapon. Dir. Richard Donner. Wri. Shane Black. Prod. Richard Donner and Joel Silver. Warner Bros. 1987.

Lethal Weapon 2. Dir. Richard Donner. Wri. Shane Black, Warren Murphy, and Jeffrey Boam. Prod. Richard Donner and Joel Silver. Warner Bros. 1989.

Lethal Weapon 3. Dir. Richard Donner. Wri. Jeffrey Boam and Robert Mark Kamen. Prod. Joel Silver and Richard Donner. Warner Bros. 1992.

Lethal Weapon 4. Dir. Richard Donner. Wri. Channing Gibson. Prod. Joel Silver and Richard Donner. Warner Bros. 1998.

McQ. Dir. John Sturges. Wri. Lawrence Roman. Prod. Arthur Gardner and Jules V. Levy. 1974.

Murphy's Law. Dir. J. Lee Thompson. Wri. Gail Morgan Hickman. Prod. Pancho Kohner. Cannon/Media Home Entertainment. 1986.

The New Centurions. Dir. Richard Fleischer. Wri. Stirling Silliphant. Prod. Robert Chartoff and Irwin Winkler. Columbia. 1972.

Righteous Kill. Dir. Jon Avnet. Wri. Russell Gewirtz. Prod. Avi Lerner, et al. Overture Films. 2008.

The Rock. Dir. Michael Bay. Wri. Douglas S. Cook and Mark Rosner David Weisberg. Prod. Jerry Bruckheimer and Don Simpson. Buena Vista. 1996.

The Sentinel. Dir. Clark Johnson. Wri. George Nolfi. Prod. Michael Douglas, Marcy Drogin, and Arnon Milchan. 2006.

Serpico. Dir. Sidney Lumet. Wri. Peter Maas, Waldo Salt, and Norman Waxler. Prod. Martin Bregman. Paramount. 1973.

Shoot to Kill. Dir. Roger Spottiswoode. Wri. Michael Burton and Daniel Petrie Harv Zimmel. Prod. Ron Silverman and Daniel Petrie. Buena Vista. 1988.
Sin City. Dir. Robert Rodriguez and Frank Miller. Wri. Frank Miller. Prod. Elizabeth Avellán. Buena Vista. 2005.
The Silence of the Lambs. Dir. Jonathan Demme. Wri. Thomas Harris and Ted Tally. Prod. Kenneth Utt, Edward Saxon, and Ron Bozman. Orion. 1991.

Works Cited

Achenbaum, W. Andrew. *Old Age in the New Land: The American Experience since 1790.* Baltimore: Johns Hopkins UP, 1978.

Addison, Heather. "'Must the Players Keep Young?': Early Hollywood's Cult of Youth." *Cinema Journal* 45.4 (2006): 3–25.

Altman, Rick. *Film/Genre.* London: BFI Publishing, 1999.

Baker, Wayne E., and Robert R. Faulkner. "Role as Resource in the Hollywood Film Industry." *American Journal of Sociology* 97.2 (1991): 279–309.

Bazzini, Doris G., William D. McIntosh, Stephen M. Smith, Sabrina Cook, and Caleigh Harris. "The Aging Woman in Popular Film: Underrepresented, Unattractive, Unfriendly, and Unintelligent." *Sex Roles* 36.7–8 (1997): 531–43.

Bielby, Denise D., and William T. Bielby. "Audience Segmentation and Age Stratification among Television Writers." *Journal of Broadcasting & Electronic Media* 45.3 (2001): 391–412.

Bordwell, David, Kristin Thompson, and Janet Staiger. *The Classical Hollywood Cinema: Film Style and Mode of Production to 1960.* New York: Columbia UP, 1985.

Brooke, Libby, and Philip Taylor. "Older Workers and Employment: Managing Age Relations." *Ageing & Society* 25.03 (2005): 415–29.

Calasanti, Toni, and Neal King. "'Beware of the Estrogen Assault': Ideals of Old Manhood in Anti-Aging Advertisements." *Journal of Aging Studies* 21.4 (2007): 357–68.

Calasanti, Toni, and Neal King. "Firming the Floppy Penis: Age, Class, and Gender Relations in the Lives of Old Men." *Men and Masculinities* 8.1 (2005): 3–23.

Chaney, David. "Creating Memories: Some Images of Aging in Mass Tourism." *Images of Aging: Cultural Representations of Later Life.* Ed. Mike Featherstone and Andrew Wernick. New York: Routledge, 1995. 209–24.

Chudacoff, Howard P. *How Old Are You?: Age Consciousness in American Culture.* Princeton, NJ: Princeton UP, 1989.

Cohen-Shalev, Amir, and Esther-Lee Marcus. "Golden Years and Silver Screens: Cinematic Representations of Old Age." *Journal of Aging, Humanities, and the Arts* 1.1 (2007): 85–96.

Cosgrove-Mather, Bootie. "Fighting Ageism in Hollywood." 2002. CBS News. Aug. 1, 2009 <http://www.cbsnews.com/stories/2002/08/01/entertainment/main517206.shtml>.

Duncan, Colin. "Assessing Anti-Ageism Routes to Older Worker Re-Engagement." *Work, Employment & Society* 17.1 (2003): 101–20.

Ekerdt, David J. "The Busy Ethic: Moral Continuity between Work and Retirement." *Gerontologist* 26.3 (1986): 239–44.

Ekerdt, David J., Raymond Bossé, and Susan Levkoff. "An Empirical Test for Phases of Retirement: Findings from the Normative Aging Study." *Journal of Gerontology* 40.1 (1985): 95–101.

Epstein, Edward Jay. *The Big Picture: The New Logic of Money and Power in Hollywood.* New York: Random House, 2005.

Gates, Philippa. *Detecting Men: Masculinity and the Hollywood Detective Film.* Albany: State University of New York Press, 2006.

Gomery, Douglas. "The Hollywood Blockbuster: Industrial Analysis and Practice." *Movie Blockbusters.* Ed. Julian Stringer. New York: Routledge, 2003. 72–83.

Graebner, William. *A History of Retirement: The Meaning and Function of an American Institution, 1885–1978.* New Haven, CT: Yale UP, 1980.

Gray, Cavender, and C. Jurik Nancy. "Policing Race and Gender: An Analysis of 'Prime Suspect 2'." *Women's Studies Quarterly* 32.3/4 (2004): 211–230.

Gullette, Margaret Morganroth. *Aged by Culture.* Chicago: U of Chicago P, 2004.

Katz, Stephen. "Imaging the Life-Span: From Premodern Miracles to Postmodern Fantasies." *Images of Aging: Cultural Representations of Later Life.* Ed. Mike Featherstone and Andrew Wernick. New York: Routledge, 1995. 61–75.

King, Neal. "Generic Womanhood: Gendered Depictions in Cop Action Cinema." *Gender & Society* 22.2 (2008): 238–60.

———. *Heroes in Hard Times: Cop Action Movies in the U.S.* Philadelphia: Temple UP, 1999.

Lauzen, Martha M., and David M. Dozier. "Maintaining the Double Standard: Portrayals of Age and Gender in Popular Films." *Sex Roles* 52.7 (2005): 437–46.

Laws, Glenda. "Understanding Ageism: Lessons from Feminism and Postmodernism." *Gerontologist* 35.1 (1995): 112–18.

Lincoln, Anne E., and Michael Patrick Allen. "Double Jeopardy in Hollywood: Age and Gender in the Careers of Film Actors, 1926–1999." *Sociological Forum* 19.4 (2004): 611–31.

Markson, Elizabeth W., and Carol A. Taylor. "The Mirror Has Two Faces." *Ageing & Society* 20.02 (2000): 137–60.

———. "Real versus Reel World: Older Women and the Academy Awards." *Women & Therapy* 14.1–2 (1993): 157–72.

Miller, Toby, ed. *The Contemporary Hollywood Reader.* New York: Routledge, 2009.

Pampel, Fred C. *Aging, Social Inequality, and Public Policy.* Thousand Oaks, CA: Pine Forge Press, 1998.

Phillipson, Chris. *Capitalism and the Construction of Old Age.* Critical Texts in Social Work and the Welfare State. London: Macmillan, 1982.

Powell, Lawrence A. "Mass Media as Legitimizers of Control." *Aging and Public Policy: Social Control or Social Justice.* Ed. John B. Williamson, Judith A. Shindul, and Linda Evans. Springfield, IL: Charles C. Thomas, 1985. 180–205.

Quinn, Joseph F., Richard V. Burkhauser, and Daniel A. Myers. *Passing the Torch: The Influence of Economic Incentives on Work and Retirement.* Kalamazoo, MI: W.E. Upjohn Institute for Employment Research, 1990.

Scott, Allen John. *On Hollywood: The Place, the Industry.* Princeton, NJ: Princeton UP, 2005.

Thompson, Edward, H. "Images of Old Men's Masculinity: Still a Man?" *Sex Roles* 55.9 (2006): 633–48.

Tulloch, John. "From Grim Reaper to Cheery Condom: Images of Aging and Death in Australian Aids Education Campaigns." *Images of Aging: Cultural Representations of Later Life.* Ed. Mike Featherstone and Andrew Wernick. New York: Routledge, 1995. 263–79.

SECTION II

THEATRE

CHAPTER 4

PERFORMING FEMALE AGE IN
SHAKESPEARE'S PLAYS

Janet Hill and Valerie Barnes Lipscomb

In Shakespeare's *Antony and Cleopatra,* in moments of glorious self-irony, Cleopatra dismisses her youthful "salad days, / When [she] was green in judgment, cold in blood" (1.5.73–74). Instead, she acknowledges an older but still enticing body that is "with Phoebus' amorous pinches black / And wrinkled deep in time" (1.5.28–29). In the twenty-first century, a seeming celebration of female "post-salad days" has become a fashion: Thousands of websites tell women, "Sixty is the new forty." However, for women in theatre, Shakespeare's plays offer limited stage opportunities once they are beyond their salad days,[1] a situation that many older performers lament. After providing an overview of what older female performers encounter in Shakespeare's plays, this chapter presents and discusses excerpts from Janet Hill's interviews with women who have been acting in those plays for many years. Their words provide a valuable perspective not only on the profession, but also on attitudes toward age/ aging and performance. The interviews' revelations are twofold, exploring both what the roles themselves say about older women and what the performers observe about aging in their profession. The performers remain fascinated by Shakespeare's roles, even though most of the aged female characters are minor compared with the Shakespearean female characters that these actors portrayed when they were younger. The actors face the irony that as seasoned performers, they bring the capability for greater performance depth to their roles, while the Shakespearean roles available for older women become more limiting; as the women's skills develop, the depth of the available roles diminishes. Analyzing and performing Shakespeare's older women has prompted these actors to confront their own aging experiences, both confirming and transforming their preconceptions about aging.

The considerations of Shakespearean theatre expressed in the interviews may be seen as presenting a mirror of contemporary and Elizabethan societies. Harriet Walter was just over fifty during a 2004 interview in which she expressed regrets about age and female characters in Shakespeare: "If Shakespeare's got a weakness, it's there somewhere around the lack of description or lack of examples of lover/ mother. There just aren't that many. There are girls." As Shakespeare often is considered the pinnacle of English-language theatrical achievement, Walter pinpointed the importance of Shakespeare's influence in the canon, regarding attitudes toward older women: "It's a scary legacy because it makes you feel in a way that it's influenced all the playwrights right along. And you sort of feel that now in modern drama that it's if you're just a wife and mother you're not dramatic." Sir Ian McKellen echoes Walter's concern when he refers to "the dearth of possibilities in television and theatre for older actresses," noting that this "complaint [is] familiar...among actresses." The seventy-year-old McKellen suggests that the lack of roles for aged women is "in part due to the dominance of male roles in the classical canon." He continues, "It's not fair that, particularly in the classics, although there are some great parts for older women, there aren't nearly as many as there are for men, say, in Shakespeare. Judi Dench has now really run out of parts to play in Shakespeare" (quoted. in Smith).

Walter shared McKellen's bleak view when she positioned Shakespeare's work as a determining factor in the older female's place in the theatrical arena: "I love Shakespeare but [at my age] there are few parts left except harridans and bitter old women. The classical tradition has affected modern writers like fairy tales [have]. To be old and female is to be of no interest." Some actors, then, perceive a troubling cutoff age for roles that offer them deep professional satisfaction. Walter also wryly observed that perhaps a factor in this lack of interest is that people in general do not find middle-aged (or older) females intellectually, emotionally, or physically interesting.

This observation is supported by long-standing feminist theory that a patriarchal society tends to devalue and ignore women, particularly when they are no longer of childbearing age. One could question, however, how much a multicentury history of uninteresting depictions in theatre and other media create, rather than just reflect, a cultural understanding of middle-aged and old women as boring. Walter mused that middle-aged women's lives lack the conflict demanded by drama and are perhaps better suited to the ruminative style of the novel; age theorist Margaret Gullette counters this way of thinking with a call for more novels that reflect the progress and development that many women experience at midlife and beyond.

The lack of central, substantial roles for older women in part reflects Renaissance society. Casting conventions in the era's theatres governed the number of female parts available. We have long known that Shakespeare's players, as well as actors in other professional companies, were all male, and that on the professional stage, women (of any age) were completely absent. On and offstage, men's words were heard, written, and read more than women's (with the notable exception of England's Queen Elizabeth)—and by more people; men moved more freely than women between public and private worlds.

It is worth noting, though, that while excluded from the stage, working women of all ages were in fact involved in theatrical activities. Scholar Natasha Korda explores the interactions between Renaissance theatre and women, describing how many women worked in and around the London playhouses in various supporting jobs, plying trades and skills behind the scenes: "The webs of commerce in which the theatres were intertwined were hardly all-male preserves." Women served as the equivalent of box office clerks and ushers, hawkers who sold refreshments, peddlers, and pawnbrokers (212).

Nevertheless, since Shakespeare wrote for exclusively male players, men played women on his stage; the quasi-female bodies are widely held to have belonged to boy apprentices who played in those roles only until their voices broke (MacMillan, "Sharer" 233).[2] John Wilders argues that these youngsters were likely to have been highly trained and able to play girls and women such as Cleopatra convincingly:

> Shakespeare would not have written such accounts of [Cleopatra's] effect on others, however, unless he had known that a boy could himself convey something of her magic to the audience, and in the prolonged final scene he had to display Cleopatra's greatness more or less on his own. If we are skeptical about an adolescent boy's ability to do justice to the role it is probably because we underestimate the intelligence of children of that age. Moreover the boy actors were the products of a tradition which went back well beyond the playing of John Lyly's sophisticated court comedies to the performances put on by choristers during the course of the two previous centuries. (11)

Like most critics, Wilder speculates that boys played every female role.

A rare voice, that of Anne Higgins, questions the assumption that boys played *all* women. Higgins is not persuaded that a boy actor would have the emotional or experiential capacity to play Cleopatra. Higgins contends

> Cleopatra herself makes it plain she is well aware of her age and looks, and it is a significant theatrical gesture, one that calls attention not just to the fullness and surprising realism of this characterization, but to the fact that the role can be well played, both dramatically and physically, by a skillful mature male actor.

Perhaps, then, a significant obstacle to Shakespeare's creating more substantive older female characters would have been the availability of actors who could portray older women. Even the technical aspects of such performances—performing a mature female voice, for example—present physical challenges for the most talented males of any age.

Whether or not mature men played some roles, such as that of Cleopatra, the most prominent female roles in Shakespeare's plays are mainly those of *young* women, about whom literary critics and theatre practitioners have speculated at length. The young female figures have been anatomized as victims, rebels, central, marginalized, vocal, silenced, and so on. Their voices, gestures, and bodies have been disarticulated and dissected, rearticulated and reconstructed. Many studies scrutinize Shakespeare's (and other Renaissance playwrights') cross-dressing practices, engaging in debate about the convention's social, religious, and political implications, as well as its potential, then and now, for homoeroticism. For example, critic Lisa Jardine argues

> that these [cross-dressed] figures are sexually enticing *qua* transvestied boys, and that the plays encourage the audience to view them as such. The audience is invited to remark [upon] the "pretty folly," the blush, the downcast shameful glance of the boy player whose "woman's part" requires that he portray female qualities, but in *male* dress. (29; see also Belsey 129–221; Gay; Howard 102; Newman 40–41; and Rutter)

Shakespeare's *mature* female characters, however, seem to attract little of the critical fire sparked by the young women and—apart from Cleopatra—galvanize almost none of the controversy.

One could make the case that Shakespeare sometimes shortchanges his aging females. Take Queen Margaret in *Richard III*, whose plight and character could evoke pity and critical attention. After all, she is a foreigner, an outsider, suffering bereavement and madness: a dislocated, marginalized figure. Still, the incantatory rhythms of Margaret's curses may sound with flattening artifice when measured against the madness of Shakespeare's old men, such as Lear and Gloucester in *King Lear* or Titus in *Titus Andronicus*.

Nevertheless, the actor is obligated—and desires—to animate and vitalize each character to the best of her ability. In a 2000 interview with Janet Hill, Anna Cartaret said that she discovered a rounded character when she performed Margaret, one in whom she could divine a depth of humanity and dramatic validity. Cartaret remembered how she developed her attitude to the role: "[Margaret]'s an outsider. I based her on women on the tube who talked non-stop. She'd be capable of killing, wandering about dispossessed. I found her masculinity." Another Margaret, Susan Engel, who also was interviewed in 2000, overthrew any superficial notions of this old woman's curses. She insisted, "What's important is the music of Margaret. Sometimes [actors] don't hear the tune right. But music is the thought. The text won't let them miss it." Readers of the plays may miss hearing this "music of age"; experienced female actors reveal these character features. Instead of seeing Margaret as a flat character, Cartaret and Engel found in their work a way to feel *for* and *with* their Margarets and to expose these insights. These depths were not imposed; they were latent in the text. The discussions with Engel and Cartaret directly connect the expertise that comes with experience and age, and their ability to understand fully and thus develop this aged Shakespearean female character.

Experiences such as Cartaret's and Engel's challenge many of the critical assumptions about Shakespeare's construction of older women. It is time to reenvision these characters, to take them seriously, and to explore their complexities; the voices of the interviews in this chapter begin that work. Since no close studies of Shakespeare's older women exist, we cannot "recuperate" these characters. We must begin with fresh critical and theatrical readings, analyzing the older female characters in ways thoroughly distinct from those in which Shakespeare's younger women are read.

Who are the few, often-maligned older women, the figures who represent Shakespeare's staging of women's age? Apart from Margaret, the characters are not old; they are older. Their actual years are mostly left uncertain, simply dramatically positioned as an older generation, subject to the years we choose to impose on them. For instance, Juliet's Nurse may be about twenty-eight years old. Nurse's dead child, Susan, would have been fourteen years old, and Nurse herself, like Juliet, might have been a fourteen-year-old bride.[3] Even so, as Juliet's caretaker, Nurse is "old" in the world of the play. Similarly, Emilia, Desdemona's woman-servant, has no age attached to her, but she is a sort of surrogate mother to her inexperienced mistress. Other characters are more clearly established as old: Mistress Quickly via her long liaison with Falstaff, Volumnia in her familial position as grandmother, and Cleopatra by means of her comments and jokes about her advanced age.

The plays give us another two broad groups of these women: aristocratic or upper class, and workers. In the former group, we find Cleopatra, Volumnia, Gertrude, Queen Margaret, Elinor (*King John*), possibly Lady Macbeth, and certainly Beatrice, who, though not old in our usual understanding of age, is older than the conventional unmarried heroine. In the latter group are Shakespeare's women-servants, companions, or members of a female underclass: Emilia (*Othello*), Paulina (of special performative interest since, like her mistress, Hermione, she ages over the course of *The Winter's Tale*), the tavern keepers and bawdy house hostesses such as Mistress Overdone and Mistress Quickly, and Juliet's Nurse. Unlike "newborn" Perdita or Miranda, or inexperienced Olivia or Rosalind, each older character is drawn as a woman with a past; while existing in the stage "now," each enunciates an historical view that includes time before the play began. Cleopatra, for instance, lives vividly in the present, yet, as she herself makes clear, she has also lived a long and vital "before."

The interviews in this chapter track a "re-visioning," a critical journey with English actors who have played Shakespeare's older women. Each one speaks frankly about her unique way of approaching her role, describing first encounters with the character in the script, then discussing how she realizes the figure in performance. In the following section, two Cleopatras, a Volumnia, an Elinor, and some "working women" offer insights into staging female older age. Occasionally, Janet Hill's interview method includes drawing on the performers' direct responses to her questions, but largely she presents issues they themselves have raised and quotes the women verbatim. Their ideas and what they choose to say about playing female age vary widely: They speak of how they mesh stage representations with "their personal chemistry"; they describe their life experiences as older women and what in themselves or their characters they feel the need to expand on or to rein in; they consider where the older female fits within the overall vision of the play and its staged society. All ponder what they think is particularly important that the audience should "get" about age and how to go about achieving this audience response using voice, gesture, and stage positioning. They talk, too, about how they enact the physicality, sexuality, power, and powerlessness they see residing in age. Most of these performers find the roles of Shakespeare's older women to be complex representations, although a few think Shakespeare's constructions were cramped by exigencies of writing for a male company. The majority believe in the fullness of Shakespeare's constructions of aged women. The responses are as diverse as the women themselves.

Sandra Voe
Age, Loyalty, and Pride in Working Women:
Juliet's Nurse and Mistress Quickly

Hill interviewed Sandra Voe after seeing her play Mistress Quickly in Parts 1 and 2 of *Henry IV* at Stratford's Swan Theatre.[4] Voe began the interview by comparing how she is usually cast to playing Shakespeare's working women.

> Usually I play quite subdued parts—sort of grannies and aunts and school-teachers and psychiatrists and social workers. But [playing Shakespeare's women] is finding a chance where you can sort of flower.

Although Shakespeare's older female characters are often considered inconsequential, like Carteret and Engel, Voe spoke of the power she found in those roles. First, she spoke about the first time she played Juliet's Nurse.

> The nurse in *Romeo and Juliet* I've played twice, both times totally differently. The first time I played it, I was about forty-five, maybe a bit younger even, and we had a very youthful Romeo and Juliet, you know, just out of drama school, and the director wanted to set it in a kind of Spanish town [...] . So the nurse was got up very sexily in a beautifully cut black outfit, quite low-cut, and a mantilla, and I stood up there and I thought I looked divine. I thought if this is Nurse, give me Shakespeare's low life. It was wonderful. [...] In the first scene with Juliet and Juliet's mother, she takes over; she doesn't mind taking over at all, so she is very at home, very sure of herself. Very secure in her position as the nurse. And plays a surrogate mother practically.

Voe compared the roles of Nurse and Mistress Quickly. Even having played the role of Mistress Quickly, Voe clearly reflects the general understanding of Quickly as a minor character. As the interview progresses, however, Voe relates the strengths that she finds in the character, and discusses the basis for her coming to that understanding.

> Juliet's Nurse has a kind of fuller [stage] picture than Mistress Quickly, who just seems to come in and strikes while the iron's hot. She comes in and says, "Today I'm coming in to say, 'No, Sir John. I did not find the money, there are no pickpockets in my house.'" When he accuses her of taking his money, she absolutely goes for him, hammer and tongs. The first time we see her, she's having fun with him in the Boar's Head together. And she says let's do the play within the play, when they swap parts, the king and Prince Hal. And she's just having a complete laugh and she's laughing till she cries, and she's falling about and it's all good fun.

You see nothing about the way that Falstaff has been leeching off her, sponging off her for months and years on end, quite likely, and he's really seriously in debt. In Part 2 she speaks about him eating her out of house and home. He's taken all her substance to put into his great fat belly. She gets the Lord Chief Justice in to deal with him because she can't handle it any more. She gets Fang and Snare to arrest him because he owes so much money. And, then it comes out, she has quite a long spiel where she accuses him of promising to marry her, which he has done over the years. In this production, we think that he has been promising and promising and promising.

Voe's starting point for her ideas about the older female characters is always the text:

Going through the text is the only way I can arrive at something solid enough to get a springboard off. Mistress Quickly really genuinely cares about Falstaff. And cares for him. And having known him for so long and had this checkered relationship all the way through, and then in Henry V (her elegy on Falstaff), of course, she's the one who makes the beautiful—so simple—yet one of the most beautifully written pieces of prose I can think of.

What's terrific about it, I would say? She always seems to be going on about something and telling a long convoluted tale. Last time, she had a long tirade and kept whining on about.... I thought, "Oh god, I hate playing parts like that. All at one level." How can one make some light and shade? I tried to take it from a woman who's been wronged first of all, and then there's a cross on top of that. She had been promised something in love, but it's never been followed through, but that also made her whine quite a bit.

So there are three different strong things to play there for Mistress Quickly: knowing she's got the Prince of Wales in her house, so I have my dignity; "O, Jesu!" she's always saying. "O, my lord the prince!" and she's always extolling him. I can play that dignity. She's a cockney lady and she's trying ever so hard and tripping over the words a bit, you know [heavy cockney accent from Voe here].

Voe's portrayal finds depth in the intersection of class and age. Quickly's strength stems from both her foundational ability to survive the struggles of working-class women during the play's time period and her endurance in overcoming those obstacles for many years. Voe bases her interpretation of Mistress Quickly on observations of behavior among modern older women.

Some days you have a huge breakthrough. That was a big help to me because then I could see the fun in life and I do like a bit of fun. That she could be making as much noise as the drunks and everything. And the next time you see her in the pub, she's coming in and they have a huge set-to. They call each other names and she brings up the fact that she's bought him a dozen new shirts. And he says they're made of rough old stuff I've had to give it away to farmers' wives to make muslin cloths. She'd know about cloth. She'd go to the best tailors.

That was another thing to play, her great strength of character. She could take on this great hog's head of a man who can out-talk her and outwit her. A thousand to one. Nevertheless she would take him on. And say, "How dare you say I've got pickpockets in my inn. Nobody's ever lost anything here." She calls him vile and knave and all the bad words she can think of. Not quite in the Doll Tearsheet scene where she has a whole vocabulary of really raucous sayings. Absolutely brilliant. So I have to really stand my ground with him. That was a tough bit to do—to make it angry enough.

In his introduction to *1 Henry IV,* David Scott Kastan argues that the women in the play come off poorly, holding only peripheral, ultimately powerless places:

> Women thus offer consequential, imaginative alternatives to the public world of politics and rebellion—the anarchic, carnival world of the tavern and the passionate, domestic world of the household—but that public world always dominates. If the women ensure the recognition of social domains excluded from aristocratic history, they are finally most notable in this play for their small number and few words, and for their inability to act or speak in any public arena. Their marginalization, however, comes at a heavy price. (76)

In *Shakespeare in Performance,* Scott MacMillan's comment on playing in *Henry IV* is one with which Voe would certainly take issue: "*1 Henry IV* is not an attractive play for actresses. The female roles are slight and, in most of the big moments, invisible" (30). Voe, as a player of female roles, agrees it takes work to establish Mistress Quickly's presence in the play. However, even though Quickly lacks public power, Voe sees her place in the play as neither "slight" nor "invisible," finding strengths in Quickly's stage presence, even in her garrulousness.

Voe talked about Juliet's Nurse as a character who often suffers from being performed as a parody of underclass old women, a buffoon, a "type." Voe, though, takes this potential for caricature as a very human characteristic; indeed, she relishes both Quickly and Nurse as representations of disinhibition and lustiness that often emerge in age.

> I remember the second time I did the Nurse, which was here. Then I played her kind of lustful and lusty; that was before I was trying to contain her lust a bit. Here I let it all hang out....

[H]ere's Mercutio and he's good looking. We just played it up to the hilt. One day at rehearsal, I wore a really sexy T-shirt, thrust it all out and came on. It was right at the end of rehearsals. The boy who played Mercutio was a very tall Anglo-Indian, absolutely gorgeous. He and I had a wonderful rapport and we just got on so well, so we played it as she was really coming on to him and getting him to respond. And it ended up with him lying on top of me on the rostrum thing we had at the center of the Swan stage. It was an absolute riot when the place fell apart at the noises we were making. I played it completely differently: Before it was "How dare you?" Whereas the first Nurse I played was a simple country lady, this one was a bit past it, with a bit of a glow about her, using loads of double entendres.

Shakespeare's role, which can be played as a stereotypical older female, also allowed Voe the range to convey sexual energy, to defy norms about mature female behavior. Although the gusto provoked laughter, Voe's own sexual appeal was not in doubt, as she subverted traditional limits on older women.

June Watson
Age and Class: Volumnia,
Juliet's Nurse, Mistress Quickly

Janet Hill first met June Watson when she played Nurse in *Romeo and Juliet* in 2004 at the Stratford Main Stage.[5] At the beginning of the interview, they talked generally about the difference in the number of roles for young and old women in Shakespeare's repertoire.

[Laughs] He didn't write enough [roles for women to play]. But simply because there were no women in his company. You know they were all boys—young boys, I would say, most of them. I suppose there were quite a few doddery old men, but not really men who you would think would want to play older women. I think he probably only wrote for women when he had to. And when he wrote those wonderful parts like Rosalind and Viola, you know they were no sooner on the stage when they became men or boys....

Hill mentioned that some say Shakespeare's older women—apart from Cleopatra—are stereotypes, not fully rounded characters. Watson disagreed and talked about playing Volumnia.

[W]hat do I think about Volumnia? Well, she's almost a man, isn't she, in her strength? I mean she's a great matriarchal figure, of course, and she rules the roost. Her son is under her thumb. But I wouldn't have said she wasn't a rounded figure. I mean she's as rounded as a woman of that class in that period could be.

Even in the twenty-first century, we posit people as becoming less gendered as they age; women, particularly aged women, who allow their age to show and who demonstrate a strength of character often are defeminized, just as older men who demonstrate more sensitivity and caring are described in emasculating terms. The observation that Volumnia is "almost a man" calls attention to the inextricable link between age and gender in Shakespeare's work. Perhaps Volumnia's manlike strength adds credence to the theory that a man (rather than a boy) played her.

Watson described her time with the English Shakespeare Company (ESC), founded by Michael Bogdanov and Michael Pennington. In this company, as well as playing Volumnia,[6] she took several roles in the Henriad.[7] MacMillan, in *Shakespeare in Performance,* praises the "iconoclasm and intelligence" of the company's Henriad. Eventually the interview returned to the ESC's productions of the Henriad and a performance of Mistress Quickly, whom Watson played as a woman still much in love with Falstaff while painfully aware that she is "past it" as the object of his affection.

I played Mistress Quickly again with the ESC. In fact, that was the first part I played with them. And I played her in both *Henry IV*'s and into *Henry V* because we did the whole of the Wars of the Roses. [...] Mistress Quickly is fantastic fun, but I played her that she was absolutely besotted by Falstaff. She was deeply, deeply in love with him. Always had been. Of course he's not deeply in love with her. Of course he might have been, he might have, when he was younger, have had a bit of a thing like he and Doll Tearsheet have a bit of a relationship, and maybe years before he had that kind of relationship with Mistress Quickly. But I just played her that she gets so hurt by him in the second play. She doesn't appear much in the first play—she's just sort of the hostess of the tavern—but [in] *2 Henry IV* she gets really hurt by him, and I played her that when he does go off with Doll, although she's organized it all, set it all up, when they do go off, I played it that she's absolutely broken-hearted. There's no lines to say that, but then, of course, in *Henry V* she has the speech about Falstaff's death, and sometimes it's played for laughs. I didn't play it for laughs.

She has a long history with Falstaff. I think there's a lot in that relationship. He's bored with her. She's just become the one who organizes things for him. She's past material really.

Watson's reading of Quickly emphasizes the character's loss of her cultural capital: youth and beauty. Although she had appealed to Falstaff in her youth, the double standard of aging allows Falstaff to continue pursuing romantic connections many years later, while Quickly is relegated to arranging affairs It is intriguing that Watson points out "there's no lines to say that"; she interprets the character in a way that rounds out Shakespeare's text, while reflecting contemporary attitudes about aging women.

Sorcha Cusack
Visceral Age in Queen and Servant:
Elinor and Juliet's Nurse

In 2000, Janet Hill interviewed Sorcha Cusack, having seen her in *Romeo and Juliet* the night before.[8] While the production's attempts to relocate the play as blood feuding in Sicily were controversial, Cusack's performance as Juliet's Nurse was convincing, at times moving. Cusack arrived straight from first rehearsal of *King John*, which was to be staged later in the season at the Swan, and in which she would be playing Elinor. Fresh from her rehearsal, Cusack talked first about her upcoming role of Elinor, King John's widowed mother. She regarded Elinor as an unconventional, energetic model of female age and power.

> Elinor's a forceful presence. She was forty-five when John was born. She was a bit of a goer—lots of illegitimate children. She went over the Pyrenees to get Constance [John's wife]. She was the grandmother of Europe.
>
> You get a feeling at the beginning of the play that John seems in control, but then she is. She adored Richard the Lionheart. But she's in a difficult older women's position. She has no rights, but she's a political brain.
>
> While Constance shrieks, Elinor knows which buttons to push. Women were the underbelly of political power, like the village of Westminster today.

Then the conversation turned to the ongoing production of *Romeo and Juliet*. She reflected on Juliet's Nurse, who, although older and more experienced than Juliet, is outgrown in emotional understanding by her young charge. Paralleling the critics of many twentieth- and twenty-first-century texts that focus on younger characters, Cusack asked, "Where are the mothers in Shakespeare?" Such a query recognizes that the guidance of experience, which older women can offer, functions as a stabilizing influence in younger characters' lives. Stability is not the best grounds for story; thus, the profusion of physically or emotionally absent mothers in Shakespeare's tales allows for more drama.

Cusack also saw complex links between gender, class, and intelligence in Shakespeare.

> Class wasn't an impediment to being bright. Shakespeare never put intelligence all in one kind of figure. Yet the nurse has all the motherly qualities but not much else besides. She's an earthy, basic, primal, underdeveloped person. There's a crossover [in who's the adult] and Juliet outgrows her. That happens in the court scene when Tybalt is dead. The nurse can't grasp Juliet's understanding. All she knows is that Juliet must have a man and says Juliet must marry Paris. She can't "get" the kind of love that Juliet feels. She's all motherly and earthy, but doesn't get the largeness that Juliet experiences.
>
> In a few productions I've seen the nurse has been a "turn" and she does have an urgency to find Romeo for Juliet. But she's not just a bawd— she's earthy but not vulgar. This [vulgar] is what the director called her, but I rejected it. It occurs to me now [in talking] that Juliet is open to this love because she's been nurtured by this nurse. The older I get, [the more] I see the [painful] rituals that young people go through at twenty and twenty-two as natural, biological.

Cusack draws on her aging experience to realize the fullness of the nurse's character, and brings this experience to bear on understanding Juliet. Like the other experienced female Shakespearean players, Sorcha Cusack has a personal and professional history that allows her to perceive the characters' internal motivations more fully than she did when she was in her salad days playing characters such as Charmian.

Sinéad Cusack
Now Ready for the Role: Cleopatra

Sinéad Cusack[9] played Cleopatra in a lavish, technically sophisticated production on Stratford's Shakespeare Memorial Theatre (SMT) stage.[10] Janet Hill had seen the performance twice before they talked. The mystique attached to performing Cleopatra was at first "off-putting" for the actor. The day before, at a discussion with students, Sinéad Cusack had said she had not felt ready to play Cleopatra earlier. Now she explained why.

> I thought she was unplayable. And I've seen many, many, many Cleopatras, and some great, some good, some indifferent. But I've always thought what I was left with at the end of the play was unsatisfactory. And I think [this role was also unsatisfactory] for the actress[es] reading Cleopatra. I can't do that. No woman has "infinite variety."

Although Sinéad Cusack had doubted her capacity to play Cleopatra (as Harriet Walter later said of her Cleopatra), Cusack felt empowered after having performed an older woman in another play.

> I had to find a way [of playing Cleopatra]. I couldn't see a way through until very recently. And then I played a part of an older woman in *Our Lady of Sligo*,[11] which was another impossible role, and which when I first read it, passed it up entirely. When I first read *Our Lady*, I thought, "This can't be done. This *simply* can't be done in theatrical terms or in acting terms. It can't be achieved." But I did it. And not only did it give me pleasure, but I thought to myself, if I can play that woman in *Our Lady of Sligo*, if I can play her, then maybe, just maybe, I have the capability to play Cleopatra.

For Sinéad Cusack, it was vital to play Shakespeare's Cleopatra as a mature woman.

> When she was with Caesar, he was *so* much older than her. She was a kid. Whereas Cleopatra and Antony are older. You know, it's much more a meeting of minds and bodies, of two mature people who have *lived* their lives and who find each other.

In this production, Cleopatra did not make the famous declaration to her court: "Think on me, / That am with Phoebus' amorous pinches black / And wrinkled deep in time" (1.5.27–29).

> You noticed. I regret the cut. I don't know why it was taken out. It was a difficult few lines. He [director Michael Attenborough] thought it was too difficult to play. I pleaded for that line.

Cusack drew heavily for the role on her personal experience of age. The years between the forties and fifties have had a profound effect on her playing.

> I suppose one grows up. I suppose I've learned a great deal the last ten years. I grew up. My children have been growing, so I worry about that. But the relationships shift and change, but then there's marriage and sickness of one's parents, loss of parents; all sorts of things come into being in your forties, between your forties and your fifties. And so I've lived through that decade, age forty to fifty, and, yes, a great deal happened to me during that time and maybe that happened for my work—who knows? You see that in your skills, you know?

She mused about women and age:

> Women of a certain age, with regrets, with fears…I find all that very rich. I mean, infinitely richer than some of the women I played in my early twenties.

Cusack would like to play Juliet now that she understands her and has "knowledge"—but the staging of age bars her.

> I'll tell you what—I would give *anything* to play Juliet now. Anything! Because I *could* play her now. And I certainly couldn't play her when I played her. You know, I was twenty-four and I could not play the complexity of that woman. I couldn't play it! I had no knowledge, I had the skills, of course, but I had no knowledge. So I was completely ill-equipped.

Cusack expressed eagerness to explore the profundities of staging age.

> I think the parts I play in all these years, like the woman in *Our Lady of Sligo*, like Cleopatra now, and the two Chekhov women who I do really want to play, are extraordinary and you must get hold of their richness and I would give anything to explore them. I certainly loved exploring Cleopatra because she's so conflictory, capricious, confusing, captivating—all those things. You know, she's all those things. Oh, God, I'll never get bored with her. You can't. She's certainly of another color every night. I'm terrified of that play.

Spurred by her personal desire to search out intricacy, Cusack deplored a tendency in many actors to iron out ambiguity. For her, age has brought fuller understanding of the resonances of language and of the diversity of human behavior. In performing Cleopatra, for instance, she needs to switch abruptly from witty to warm to horrific. The view of life Sinéad Cusack takes to the stage is that volatility applies to all people.

> Years ago, John Barton[12] said to me to play the *ambiguity*. Yet I don't believe any person on the face of the earth is logical. They contradict themselves within a minute, an hour, a day—constantly. So we mustn't be frightened of really loving, really [being] passionate, and two seconds later being vile beyond belief. We do it to our husbands, our lovers, our children, our sisters, our brothers.

Interestingly, Cusack now feels ready to portray a complex younger woman such as Juliet, but still expresses apprehension about playing a complex woman nearer to her own age: Cleopatra. Rather than concerning herself with the appearance of the character—playing great beauty and maturity simultaneously—she addresses the challenges of playing Cleopatra's inner life. Even the minor characters she may play are fascinating to her, are rounded, not in spite of being older, but precisely because they have passed midlife.

Harriet Walter
The Older Female Body and Complex Sexuality: Cleopatra

Janet Hill interviewed Harriet Walter twice. The first time was in 2002 during a production by the Royal Shakespeare Company (RSC) at the Shakespeare Memorial Theatre (SMT), of *Much Ado About Nothing*.[13] In this production, Walter's personation of Beatrice was a feisty, intellectual, at times painfully vulnerable, *older* single woman. The following review captures the intelligence of how Walter and the director, Gregory Doran, chose to represent Beatrice:

> As views on sexuality and gender relations change and novels and soap operas are peopled with "thirty-something" professionals who are reluctant to adopt traditional role models, it has become possible to imagine a Beatrice in her forties, assertive and eloquent, perhaps awkward in her helpless rage, but nonetheless sexually attractive to both Benedick and the audience. In 2002 Gregory Doran directed a very successful RSC production in which Beatrice was the fifty-two-year-old Harriet Walter, who already had such heavyweights as the Duchess of Malfi and Lady Macbeth under her belt and who had earlier been described as a "tomato [...] precisely ripe for eating, not for squashing." (Stock 55)

The second interview took place during the RSC's 2006 run of *Antony and Cleopatra* at the Swan, again directed by Gregory Doran. The production as a whole was lauded in the press reviews, which unanimously praised Walter's performance of Cleopatra as an *older* woman. Some examples:

> Harriet Walter inhabits her role as the "serpent of old Nile" to perfection: the bewitching middle-aged woman still given to adolescent temper tantrums that, bafflingly, only add to her allure. (Hart)
> No Cleopatra can have shown so clearly the feeling of ageing: as Walter talks of being wrinkled deep in time, she snatches off her gloss boy—which suits her angular intelligent face so well that it's easy to forget it's a wig—and shows beneath it a wispy mop. She looks smaller, vulnerable and no less beautiful. (Clapp)
> [In an extraordinary moment when Walter takes off her wig,] you suddenly glimpse the emotional vulnerability and the fear of age that haunts her. (Spencer)

Walter met Hill the day after she had seen the play. Walter opened the meeting with the remark, "Yes, Cleopatra is, in the canon of women's parts, the peak." When asked whether Walter could have played Cleopatra earlier in her career, she responded that she would have lacked a vital maturity: "I doubt if I could have played it sooner, really. I mean it would have lots of elements missing, I think." She added that in earlier years she would not have been aware of what these elements are, especially a revelation that sexy is not necessarily gorgeous:

> And in a way it is a character who has to be partly judged on her sexiness, on the power she has over men, and that's why I was very daunted. I wanted to play, but maybe I couldn't have played her before now. Or thinking now in the last five or six years, one feels more confident to play her, which is a paradox because when I was younger I wouldn't have understood that women are sexy for all sorts of reasons other than being conventionally gorgeous.

In *Antony and Cleopatra,* the Roman contingent defines Cleopatra as a dangerous exotic who drains Antony of his Roman masculinity; for them, she is a siren luring a soldier from his natural self. During rehearsal and performances, as Walter engaged with the role, she said that she became aware of how past productions of the play had similarly oversimplified Cleopatra, propagandizing her as a luxurious, oversexed beauty. Walter refuted such theatrical and critical perspectives, considering them unsupported by the script. She and Hill agreed that Shakespeare's play script has Cleopatra openly identifying herself as being well worn and aging. In some productions, these aspects are underplayed or cut altogether (see Sinéad Cusack's complaint about her lost lines), a move that reduces the script's subversion of stereotypes about female age and sex appeal. In this RSC version, the audience saw a fascinating, but much used, older woman. Walter stated, "With age (both of actress and character) comes strong awareness of the complexity of 'sexiness.'"

Cleopatra has a long history. All her life, she has moved in a universe of politics and sex, with people of all ranks dependent on her for their comfort and survival. The character is acutely aware that, for women, sexual appeal is closely related to obtaining and maintaining power. Walter sees that Cleopatra makes disastrous mistakes (politically, militarily, and in reading people's intentions), yet she also thinks that a lifetime's experience of managing politics and men has taught Cleopatra to be canny and, wherever possible, to play an ambiguous game: "I think her power, her mental chemistry, the speed and the challenges she throws out to people—there's that little bit where she declares that she's just going to be contrary and that's the way to keep a man interested and she's developed these devices over a long, long period of time dealing with great men in history: Caesar, Pompey, and now Antony, her own family."

As they followed up on a discussion of the "infinite variety" of talk by Cleopatra, Hill observed to Walter the frequency with which Shakespeare's characters who are men of all ages and young women—think of Iago, Hamlet, Macbeth, or Viola and Imogen—speak openly to audiences, sharing their inner turmoils, desires, hopes, and plans with the playgoers. (This technique is what Hill calls elsewhere "open address.")[11] Antony and Enobarbus soliloquize, but Cleopatra does not do so: She talks to Antony, to her women servants—to everyone around her—and she confides very trustingly in Enobarbus. Cleopatra talks incessantly in this play, but essentially she voices "overheard" comments from which audience members are forced to *infer* the veracity and genuineness of her words. As Cleopatra maintains political power in conjunction with maintaining sexual power, she does not let down her guard onstage but remains a consciously performed self, never removing the public mask to reveal the more privately constructed sense of self.

This production played heavily on Cleopatra's deep need to talk. There was an astonishing moment when Antony, after his botched suicide, is hauled aloft to the monument. Now dying, he tries to convey his last words to Cleopatra, but Cleopatra simply will not shut up. Hill mentioned to Walter that she came in quickly on a lot of Antony's lines. She agreed that this represented a vital decision for the production. "Absolutely. Thank god for Patrick [Stewart], who's got a wonderful sense of comedy, and he noticed that and he said, you know, he's got about two gasps of breath left in his body and he says, 'Let me speak,' and she says, 'No, let me speak.' And then he says, 'One word, sweet Queen.'" Acted this way, the unique nature of their mature relationship—passion cut with banter—endured into their final encounter.

One advantage of being older is the self-knowledge and capacity to draw on such a specific kind of humor. Walter and Patrick Stewart played all their love scenes with warm, self-mocking humor. Walter noted, "That's what I think makes—you know when you're talking about playing older women, that's what makes you more or less fill your boots with contradictions and ups and downs. You can be idiotic." While deeply loving one another, Antony and Cleopatra laugh at themselves, knowingly playing mature love games, and consequently sharing these jokes with the audience.

Walter's final comment summed up her deeply held attitude of playing older women, in which the actor's responsibility is to focus on "learning, not comparing yourself to others, on honing what you do best, and on knowing this might be the last role.... there is a point where you have to accept the fact that things will thin out or go downhill, and possibly once you've played Cleopatra, there's a certain end to something. It's in your head that you're not going to have that kind of challenge often again."

Walter's interview reveals an actor who is solidly aware that she is both embodying and performing age. As Cleopatra, she removes her wig, the outward sign of performing a youthful self, and performs a more aged, vulnerable character—and actor. She acknowledges the guarded inner life of a character such as Cleopatra, for whom performing the allure associated with youth is integral to maintaining power. Walter also recognizes in the plays the humor necessary to the success of long-term relationships, and the blows delivered to relationships when one lover witnesses the decline of the other. Finally, she confronts the fact that performers must deal not only with the relative lack of importance of older women in Shakespeare, but also with the basic decline in the number of available roles throughout the theatrical field.

Conclusions

This chapter began by suggesting that although we are presently witnessing a surge of interest in female age, many older women lament that the theatre offers them few roles that are seen as worthwhile opportunities. Nevertheless, in their discussions of playing the Shakespearean roles available to mature women, all of these performers found a new understanding and power in those roles, as well as in roles that they played earlier in their careers. With their personal experience and development, they find that the available roles are more valuable, satisfying, and challenging than they had thought, and than audiences and critics tend to think. The observations of the seasoned performers demonstrate that the relative lack of critical attention to Shakespeare's older female characters—indeed, to older female characters in the media in general—obstructs a more complex understanding of women who have gone beyond their salad days to reach "a certain age."

One major complaint of the interviewees was that the Shakespeare canon and subsequent plays, right up into the twenty-first century, yield a very small number of parts for women over fifty. Harriet Walter voiced a frustration encountered by many older actors, that the pleasure of playing age is thwarted by finding few satisfying roles: "Since I was forty, I've had to find vehicles. I want to play characters who are bigger than me. Most of the time, writers and actors eliminate, reduce pieces of me. I like being older. I like older women, but the nature of drama, the rich discussions don't easily lend themselves to dramatic representation. I'm sick of playing people who are afraid of being old. I love getting older, but drama is conflict."

As Shakespeare's works are foundational to English-language drama, the lack of challenging roles for older women created a sad precedent. While the performers find as much depth and range as possible in the roles, they are frustrated by the irony of bringing decades of acting experience to diminished opportunities. Walter notes the major stereotype about aging presented in many of the roles created for older women: the narrative of decline that stems from youth's fear of age. These stereotypes come as no surprise, as youth dominates the mainstream theatrical world, from playwrights to production teams. However, the aging performers themselves offer unique perspectives on performing age that rewrite this narrative of decline. Walter, for example, asserts, "I love getting older," which contradicts the typical rejection of the aging self in Western culture.

Kathleen Woodward's concept of a mirror stage of old age, a response to Jacques Lacan's theories, outlines this rejection and has become a mainstay of age studies. In *Aging and Its Discontents*, she posits a stage of aging that is similar to the mirror stage of infancy, when the child sees and internalizes a (false) understanding of itself as the whole, pleasing, unified image in the mirror, in contrast to the partial, disjointed image that the child experiences. However, the aging person does not recognize— rejects—the older body reflected in the mirror. If the aged person were to accept this bodily image, then he or she accepts entering "the social realm reserved for 'senior citizens' in the western world" (67). Denying the body, focusing on the inner sense of a younger self, is the older person's reaction to cultural prejudice against old age. The aged person may then claim a younger self than the body indicates; the performances of that person's body then reflect the tension between the claimed younger self and the embodiment that is the older self.

Professional actors provide critical insights into our understandings of the performances of age, as they make a living by "inhabiting"— enacting—a different, aged sense of self. While the women interviewed must be able to envision themselves as older characters, in doing so, they seem able to accept the benefits of aging, even as they enter the roles fully understanding the social prejudice that accompanies older ages. The tensions are many: Our culture values youth more in women than in men, and more parts are available for younger women; however, these performers, who have played Shakespeare's younger women, cannot continue to perform youth indefinitely. They must accept an older bodily image in order to continue working, and face the roles that Shakespeare offers—roles that are seen as diminishing, but that these performers come to understand as texts of depth and strength.

Unlike the average older person, though, these performers have long ago embraced the separation of their physical appearance from a sense of "real" self; this separation is inherent in acting. Their ability to connect to the "not me" on an emotional plane expands their performance range, and the women interviewed here demonstrate impressive capacities for relating to a wide range of characters. The physical reality differs significantly from the emotional range; physical markers of age are easier to add to a performance than to subtract. These performers navigate their own mirror stage of old age while walking the minefield of professional performance: needing to appear as young as possible to continue working, and needing to be able to play older characters convincingly. All of the performers interviewed agreed that a woman's age can create a problem in finding roles in Shakespeare's plays. Nonetheless, in their post-fifty years, they found life and breadth in roles originally written for and played by boys and men; every one of them unearthed significant complexity in Shakespeare's depiction of female age.

Shakespeare's older female characters may be few, but, as the interviews indicate, opportunities for critical explorations of them are many. The crucial move is to build on what the interviews of these women have opened up for further discussion. In literary and theatrical studies, much remains to be said about staging age in Shakespeare. Dozens of aspects of how Shakespeare constructs female age await interrogation. For example, the actors here have talked about their notions of playing older female sexuality. But their comments, such as Harriet Walter's explicit observation, "Sex goes on forever, but it's shocking," open up a host of queries about eroticism and age, particularly onstage. Other facets of Shakespeare's depictions of female age ripe for investigation include mature women and work; mature women and class; single, married, or widowed older women; the language of Shakespeare's older women— its vocabulary, syntax, rhythms, wit, length, and frequency of speeches; older women's relationships with young females and men; the treatment of older women by the other sex and by youth; life opportunities open or closed to them; and the pressures in age of infirmity, madness, and death, or of health, energy, and strength.

In addition to considering these topics, we need to think about how we discern the connection between older female characters and their audiences. When we reflect on the stage positions assigned to this group, we find even major older female roles, such as Cleopatra and Volumnia, speak through dialogue, not soliloquy—a puzzling lack of close contact with the theatre as a whole because it is so uncommon in Shakespeare's technical repertoire. How does Shakespeare employ his stage strategy known variously as "soliloquy," "direct address," "open address," or simply as "talking to the audience" for older female characters? Are the inner lives of Shakespeare's older women held back, sheltered from playgoers? If so, why, and what effect does this concealment have on the plays? This area and many others await investigation by scholars and performers. Additional conversations with older women playing Shakespeare today may not supply definitive answers; however, they should provoke fresh insights—ideas unique to the practitioners—into an important but hitherto neglected critical and theatrical arena: Shakespeare's staging of female older age.

Notes

1. There are a few exceptions. For instance, in 2000, Barbara Jefford was seventy when she played Volumnia alongside Ralph Fiennes in the *Coriolanus*, presented at London's Almeida Theatre; in 2006, Judi Dench was seventy-three when she played Mistress Quickly in the Royal Shakespeare Company's musical version of *Merry Wives of Windsor.*
2. Also see Holland and Orgel (119–32).
3. *Romeo and Juliet* 1.3.16–48.
4. April 2000. Directed by Michael Attenborough.
5. April 2004. Directed by Peter Gill.
6. Under director Michael Bogdanov.
7. This company's controversial productions are lauded by Scott MacMillan: "*1 Henry IV*'s combination of iconoclasm and intelligence provided something that sentimentality can never approach, however—an opportunity to think beyond the staged moment to other parts of the production, and beyond those to other royal families, other rebellions, other authorities whose power is based on insecurity and the use of force" (*Performance* 122).
8. Directed by Nancy Meckler.
9. Some of what Sinéad Cusack said in 2002, she is also quoted as saying in John O'Connor's *Shakespearean Afterlives.*
10. Directed by Michael Attenborough.
11. *Our Lady of Sligo* by Sebastian Barry, directed by Max Stafford-Clark. For her performance, Sinéad Cusack won the 1998 *Evening Standard* Drama Award for Best Actress.
12. John Barton, the noted director and teacher.
13. In 2002. Directed by Gregory Doran.
14. For a full account of this dramatic strategy, which stretches back to English medieval theatre, see Hill.

Works Cited

Belsey, Catherine. *The Subject of Tragedy: Identity and Difference in Renaissance Drama.* London: Methuen, 1985.

Clapp, Susannah. "'Tis a Far Better Fang: Patrick Stewart and Harriet Walter Are a Mesmerising Antony and Cleopatra." *Observer,* Apr. 23, 2006 <Guardian. co.uk/stage/2006apr/23theatre>.

Gay, Penny. *As She Likes It: Shakespeare's Unruly Women.* London: Routledge, 1994.

Gullette, Margaret Morganroth. *Declining to Decline.* Charlottesville: UP of Virginia, 1997.

Hart, Christopher. "The World Will Love These Lovers: The RSC's Complete Works Promises a Glorious Summer." *Sunday Times,* Apr. 23, 2006. <http:// entertainment.timesonline.co.uk/tol>.

Higgins, Anne. "Reinventing Women: The Example of Cleopatra." The Renaissance Society of America Annual Meeting for Medieval and Renaissance Studies. Scottsdale, AZ. Apr. 12, 2002.

Hill, Janet. *Stages and Playgoers: From Guild Plays to Shakespeare.* Montreal: McGill-Queen's UP, 2002.

Holland, Peter. "The Resources of Characterization in *Othello.*" *Shakespeare Survey* 41 (1988): 119–32.

Holland, Peter, and Stephen Orgel, eds. *From Script to Stage in Early Modern England.* Basingstoke: Palgrave Macmillan, 2004.

Howard, Jean E. *The Stage and Social Struggle in Early Modern England.* London: Routledge, 1994.

Jardine, Lisa. *Still Harping on Daughters: Women and Drama in the Age of Shakespeare.* Sussex: Harvester Press, 1983.

Kastan, David Scott. Introduction. *King Henry IV Part 1.* By William Shakespeare. London: Arden, 2002.

Korda, Natasha. "Labours Lost: Women's Work and Early Modern Theatrical Commerce." *From Script to Stage in Early Modern England.* Ed. Peter Holland and Stephen Orgel. Basingstoke: Palgrave Macmillan, 2004. 195–230.

MacMillan, Scott. *Shakespeare in Performance: King Henry IV Part One.* Manchester: Manchester UP, 1991.

———. "The Sharer and His Boy." *From Script to Stage in Early Modern England.* Ed. Peter Holland and Stephen Orgel. Basingstoke: Palgrave Macmillan, 2004. 231–45.

Mares, F.H. Introduction. *Much Ado About Nothing.* By William Shakespeare. Cambridge: Cambridge UP, 2003. 1–47.

Newman, Karen. *Fashioning Femininity in Renaissance Drama.* Chicago: Chicago UP, 1991.

O'Connor, John. *Shakespearean Afterlives: Ten Characters with a Life of Their Own.* Thriplowe: Icon Books, 2005.

Orgel, Steven. *Impersonations: The Performance of Gender in Shakespeare's England.* Cambridge: Cambridge UP, 1996.

Rutter, Carol. *Clamorous Voices.* London: Women's Press, 1988.

Shakespeare, William. *Antony and Cleopatra. The Riverside Shakespeare.* Ed. G.B. Evans. Boston: Houghton Mifflin, 1974.

———. *Coriolanus.* Ed. Reuben Brower. New York: Signet, 2002.

———. *Romeo and Juliet. The Riverside Shakespeare.* Ed. G.B. Evans. Boston: Houghton Mifflin, 1974. 1055–99.

Smith, Alistair. "Ian McKellen Joins Call for More Older Female Roles." *The Stage,* June 4, 2009. <http://www.thestage.co.uk/newsstory.php/24608>.

Spencer, Charles. "Middle-aged Passion Goes to the Heart." *Daily Telegraph*, Apr. 20, 2006 <http://entertainment.timesonline.co.uk/tol>.

Stock, Angela. Introduction. *Much Ado About Nothing*. By William Shakespeare. Cambridge: Cambridge UP, 2003. 48–59.

Van Dyke, Joyce. "Making a Scene: Language and Gesture in *Coriolanus*." *Coriolanus*. Ed. Reuban Brower. New York: Signet, 2002. 244–54.

Werner, Sarah. *Shakespeare and Feminine Performance*. London: Routledge, 2001.

Wilders, John. Introduction. *Antony and Cleopatra*. By William Shakespeare. London: Arden, 1995.

Woodward, Kathleen. *Aging and Its Discontents*. Bloomington: Indiana UP, 1991.

CHAPTER 5

MEDIATING CHILDHOOD: HOW CHILD
SPECTATORS INTERPRET ACTORS'
BODIES IN THEATRICAL MEDIA

Jeanne Klein

While many adults endeavor to remain young against biological odds, the overarching work of childhood calls for reaching adulthood against the socializing (and highly politicized) forces of mediated culture. In strident debates and moral panics over mass media consumption, adults position themselves in relation to children in two basic ways. Protectionists believe that they should protect youngsters from adults' secrets and keep them innocently pure for as long as possible by regulating or censoring their media diets via parental and governmental policies. Nurturers, on the other hand, believe children should negotiate these secrets openly in compassionate conversations that nurture their rights and responsibilities as democratic citizens. Between these two camps lie children themselves, who make and control many of their own decisions about media preferences no matter what adults think. While media content contains countless messages about human conditions, how actors communicate these dramatized messages matters greatly as age-identified bodies perform and mediate child-adult constructs on stage and screen.

Over the past twenty-five years of U.S. culture wars, protectionists have focused their attentions on the dangerous and debilitating effects of mass-mediated messages, while neglecting the far more pernicious problems lying hidden beneath presumably innocuous entertainments that actually serve to mock childhood itself. By manipulating children's minds and emotions, these diversionary entertainments literally divert attentions away from adults' discriminatory acts of ageism. Therefore, in this chapter, I will explore why nurturers need to expose these adult secrets of adverse ageism by addressing two central questions: Whose bodies do theatrical producers employ to perform childhood on stage and screen, and how do child spectators interpret these embodied performances?

To answer these questions, the first section of this chapter provides a brief history of how childhood came to be performed for past generations of spectators—that is, the people who went on to produce embodied performances for subsequent generations of child spectators. Based on this cultivation of child-oriented performances, the second section compares stage- and screen-mediated content in recent decades by analyzing characterizations of actors' live and animated bodies. The third section spotlights children's own preferences for these embodied performances by detailing how they perceive, interpret, and evaluate age-identified bodies by age and gender throughout the developmental stages of childhood. Given children's preferences for humorous entertainments, the fourth section exposes adult actors' underlying mockeries of childhood in performance by explaining how children interpret so-called innocuous forms of adults' humor. Finally, I explain why protectionists and nurturers alike need to take childhood seriously by acting upon these dramatized dilemmas on and off the stages and screens of mediated culture.

A Brief History of Childhood in Performance

Children have watched and read the performances of actors' live and animated bodies ever since theatre and then books provided modes of dramatized and literary storytelling. However, the recognition of children as a distinct audience deserving of performances uniquely suited for their aesthetic pleasures did not arise in Western culture until the mid-seventeenth and eighteenth centuries, when their own bodies came to be included in private performances at home and then school and other public venues. With the appearance of child actors on public stages throughout the nineteenth century, children's bodies began to activate spectators' normative images of childhood itself. As each subsequent generation of theatrical producers imitated and reproduced what they had experienced as young spectators, they increasingly marketed family entertainments to women and their children.

Not until the establishment of psychology as a specialized discipline near the start of the twentieth century did children's minds come to play contested roles as both interpreted actors of childhood and interpretative spectators of adult-mediated performances. As Richard Butsch documents, after the mid-twentieth century, child spectators became an "endangered group" as film, television, and computerized media shifted public performances to the privacy of their homes and transformed mediated processes into "a cause-effect chain" of events that sparked today's cultural debates over mass media (6–9). The following brief history of childhood in performance reveals how age constructs both caused generational reproductions of embodied performances with the appearance of each new medium and subsequently effected governmental restrictions on commercial entertainment intentionally produced for child spectators.

Literature published specifically for children began during the eighteenth century's Age of Reason as a means of "delightful instruction," and enduring classics rose to prominence with increasingly artistic pictorial images for young readers. In the same century, theatre with children began when Countess de Genlis and other women wrote original plays and "dramatic dialogues" enacted by their charges. Child performances in schools and home parlors moved to public stages as early as the 1820s, when child actors, such as eight-year-old Louisa Lane, trouped with their families across the United States in such popular plays as *The Spoiled Child*. In 1852, four-year-old Cordelia Howard stole hearts as Little Eva in an unfaithful adaptation of Harriet Beecher Stowe's *Uncle Tom's Cabin* and toured with her family before "retiring" at age thirteen. Thereafter, the "infant phenomenon" swelled as profit-driven managers recognized how small, angelic bodies could heighten pathos in melodramatic situations. Although few plays required leading child roles (e.g., Meenie in *Rip Van Winkle*), Frances Hodgson Burnett expanded the repertoire considerably by dramatizing her children's novels, starring nine-year-old veteran Elsie Leslie, who initiated the *Little Lord Fauntleroy* craze in 1888 as the embodiment of Burnett's son.

From the 1870s through the 1920s, however, a campaign to banish child performers from the stage shifted the public's rage for child stars to film (Zelizer 85–96)—just as a new wave of immigrant children flocked to nickelodeons and moving pictures that visualized stories for nonnative listeners. When J.M. Barrie dramatized *Peter Pan* in 1905 as an extravagant British pantomime, his U.S. manager, Charles Frohman, cast an adult actress, Nina Boucicault, in the lead role in time for the Christmas season because British law forbade boys under age fourteen from performing on stage after 9 p.m. (Birkin 103–105). Although girls and women had been playing young males' "breeches" roles for some time, the tradition of employing adult actors to play child roles on stage began at that point.

Nevertheless, women still saw how theatre could nurture children's innate "dramatic instincts" and introduce them to literary canons while keeping them off professional stages. Theatre for and with young people shifted from an artistic endeavor to an educational enterprise for "stage-struck" girls and "delinquent" boys when Alice Minnie Herts founded the Children's Educational Theatre in 1903 at a New York settlement house. As Daniel Frohman, Charles's brother, remarked:

> I think the "Educational Theatre" an excellent name. It at once differenti-
> ates your work from that of the commercial theatre, and if your plays are
> interesting you cannot keep people away no matter what you call it. If,
> however, your plays happen at times not to be interesting, as is the case
> with us all, people will say, "Well, this is only educational; it is not sup-
> posed to be interesting." (Herts 79–80)

With this newly incorporated identity, Herts sought to advance an "evolv-ing theory" of her educational practices by seeking "far greater authority" (86) from such male experts as G. Stanley Hall, who had recently defined "adolescence" as a separate stage of childhood. From then on, child psy-chology became the "scientific" means of studying media effects, as Dr. Elnora Whitman Curtis first reported in her 1914 investigation of how young people utilized storytelling, theatre, puppetry, civic pageantry, dance, music, and moving pictures. As industrialized child labor declined and compulsory education laws forced young people into public schools, theatre with youth became subordinated as an amateur recreation and extracurricular activity primarily with high school thespians by 1929.

Meanwhile, the ongoing practice of adapting children's literature, particularly romanticized fairy tales, for the stage transferred to the screen. It began when a 1912 stage version of *Snow White and the Seven Dwarfs* was captured on silent film in 1917 and recalled by a young man who animated it as a colorful Broadway musical in 1937—after introducing a mouse cartoon in 1928 (Schickel 60). Walt Disney's sanitized branding of grim tales with happily-ever-after endings met the public's compelling need for escapist humor during the Depression and firmly established Disney-brand films as "safe" family entertain-ment thereafter. Although caricatures of humans as animals had long been the province of editorial satire in early newspapers, episodic strips known as "the funnies" blossomed into full-fledged comic books during the 1930s, allowing superheroes to fly and achieve oth-erwise impossible human-defying feats in order to fight and resolve violent crimes. Early cinematic techniques also permitted stop-motion animations of puppets and clay (e.g., Gumby) before the computer age would come to mechanize human actors as well. In these ways, animated bodies became the prevailing symbols of childhood and its performances.

When television entered homes in the 1950s, children's programs, staged with live actors and puppets, initially were broadcast to entice parents to purchase TV sets. Within the next decade, an explosion of cartoons, offering less expensive and more highly controlled means of production, gradually superseded actors as food and toy manufacturers discovered profitable child markets on weekend mornings. As a racialized war on poverty raged, Joan Cooney established the Children's Television Workshop in 1968 to educate disadvantaged preschoolers through *Sesame Street* with Jim Henson's Muppets on public television (PBS). Likewise, in 1985, Geraldine Laybourne began to develop Nickelodeon into a "kid-branded" cable network as educational programs waned on other channels.

As rampant amounts of violence, sex, profanity, and advertising increased on the public airwaves, media psychologists intensified their investigations and pressured Congress to enact new regulations. During the 1990s, children's television underwent seismic shifts as a result of new federal policies and deregulated corporate mergers sparked by the 1996 Telecommunications Act. By 2005, the four major networks (ABC, CBS, NBC, and FOX) had all but abandoned over 13 million young viewers whose families could not afford basic cable subscriptions, leaving PBS to fulfill their educational and informational (E/I) programming needs.

With the 2009 switch to digital television and the convergence of televised performances on the Internet, debates over children's "free" access to limitless information have intensified as a "digital divide" threatens to exclude 39 percent (or 28 million) of all children and adolescents who live in economically impoverished and low-income households. As with any new medium, the educational promises of the Internet have proven to be especially false and illusory, as critics find children using computers more for personal entertainment than for educational purposes, regardless of socioeconomic class (e.g., Seiter). Time will tell what future federal regulations may affect the Millennial generation's access to mediated performances, now readily available and mobilized in their private bedrooms and public classrooms. Nevertheless, it is important to keep economic class contexts in mind when considering how children use and interpret any adult-produced media content today.

The Content of Characters on Stage and Screen

Regardless of medium, theatre and media investigators agree that the fictional content of performed stories matters far more than artistically realized forms or delivery systems (e.g., Sauter). When analyzing the cultivated effects of story content, critics often emphasize characters' identities by age, gender, race, and ethnicity, because they theorize that role models are most responsible for socializing young identities (e.g., Harwood; Hust and Brown; Greenberg and Mastro). Yet descriptive characterizations of stage and screen role models tend not to analyze more important plot events—that is, the dramatized conflicts and resolutions that situate characters in their fictional contexts. Nevertheless, a brief review of characterized bodies found on stage and screen suggests some general cultural themes contained within plotted content.

At this writing, only four corporate giants (Disney, Viacom, Time Warner, and News Corporation) control the production and distribution of the vast majority of children's entertainment and licensed merchandise, with content that reflects Hollywood's white, upper- to middle-class, male-dominated producers (Alexander and Owers 62–65). Content analyses consistently reveal the devaluation of child and teen characters on television and film, with largely male-oriented stories that promote ongoing gender and cultural stereotypes in stark contrast to the actual social realities of young lives (e.g., Heintz-Knowles; Signorielli). Media psychologists continue to dwell on the short- and long-term effects of these cultivated messages on the physical, cognitive, and social health of youth, as media ratings signal graduation rites from child to adult content (e.g., Calvert and Wilson; Bushman and Cantor).

Within this vast mass mediated landscape, Theatre for Young Audiences (TYA) remains but a blip on the map, with an estimated 100 professional, nonprofit companies reaching roughly 2 percent of the entire U.S. population. Unlike Herts, who scorned commercialization, today's TYA producers embrace commercial markets in order to survive in their local economies. An average season of seven plays includes largely dramatized adaptations from popularized children's literature, biographical histories, and Broadway-inspired musicals to support the commissioning of lesser-known original plays. Since the mid-1970s, fairy and folk tales have given way to more "social issue" plays ever since Suzan Zeder spotlighted a child's socially realistic struggles to accept her stepmother with imaginary playmates in *Step on a Crack*. As a result, content analyses of TYA plays reveal child protagonists using their dreamlike imaginations to resolve their intra- and interpersonal conflicts alone or with peers, given a preponderance of absent or deceased parents, with an equitable number of female and male characters (e.g., Dezseran; Bloom; Stroud).

Although children's literature lacks a balanced number of multicultural characters in proportion to respective populations (Gangi 243), directors strive to cast actors of color, regardless of human, animal, and inanimate roles, to reflect their local communities. For animal roles, full-body animal suits have given way to ears, tails, masks, or simply human clothing. While adult actors still dominate professional TYA stages, "age-appropriate" casting often admits child actors from the companies' own extensive educational theatre programs. Thus, in comparison to mass media, TYA offers far more gender-balanced and diverse characters in "safer" stories that routinely censor sex, violence, and profanity, given requisite partnerships with local schools.

Despite these local theatre and mass media offerings, what young people want in their aesthetic diets differs from what producers presume they want (or need) for artistic and educational purposes. Invariably, studies find children preferring literary stories, theatre productions, and television programs least approved by librarians, theatre critics, and educators (e.g., Hall and Coles 138; Schonmann 128–136; Calvert and Kotler 317). Children's own aesthetic values need to be taken into account to help determine whether mediated content cultivates their cultural tastes and/ or whether children's preferences drive their parents and teachers to purchase media entertainment based on their desires to please and gratify their offspring and students.

Children's Preferences for Embodied Performances by Age and Gender

Across industrialized nations, when six- to twelve-year-olds from all socioeconomic classes are asked to identify and explain their story preferences, they use seven main criteria in the following order of priority: (1) comprehensibility, (2) involving dramatic action, (3) humorous entertainment, (4) informative child characters, (5) realism, (6) innocuousness of violence or romance, and (7) aesthetic qualities (Valkenburg and Janssen; Davies, Buckingham, and Kelley). These criteria constitute the inductive principles by which children justify their preferential tastes to let adults know what they most appreciate from adult-produced performances as cross-cultural spectators (Klein and Schonmann; Valkenburg 15–38).

Children involve themselves vicariously in dramatized actions because they are driven by a passionate desire to comprehend personally relevant meanings in performances. They want interesting, suspenseful, and action-filled events to arouse their emotions and engage their minds in predicting and finding out what goal-directed actions may happen next. In other words, they pay close attention to what characters are doing visually and how they perform each dramatic action moment to moment. For these reasons, long-winded conversations in dramas and "talking heads" on news and documentary programs are often rejected outright as utterly "boring." How children comprehend performances depends on the physical neuro-machinations of their developing brains, as marked by their biological ages, as well as their culture-specific experiences with all forms of media.

During their preschool years, youngsters compare their physical similarities with others, first by age and gender (at age three) and later by discernible races (by age five). As they segregate themselves into same-age and same-sex play groups, they use pretense to perform their own scripts and thereby learn to conceptualize—and blend—the differences between actors and characters. Boys learn to overcome their fears by confronting frightening situations, while girls tend to avoid dangerous situations. These characteristics set the stage for ongoing gender differences.

When viewing others' fantasized stories, preschoolers explore immediately observable physical features sequentially and learn to distinguish central activities from incidental details in order to connect causal actions within episodes. For these reasons, media producers offer them bite-size chunks of information in the form of episodic structures (like *Sesame Street*), often with puppets and animated characters that show them how to master new abilities, behaviors, and activities. While watching cartoons and educational programs, they rely upon facial expressions to identify basic emotions and assume that characters think and feel the same thoughts and emotions as themselves in similar situations until they recognize others' differing perspectives. Knowing full well that puppets, cartoon characters, and human actors are fictional entities who feign emotions, they revel in both realistic and unrealistic pretenses. These factors explain why three- to seven-year-olds are most prone to imitating both pro-social and antisocial behaviors, especially after viewing fantasy violence in cartoons that justify physical aggression as resolutions to conflicts.

Media producers know that once children enter school, they are no longer interested in viewing E/I programs during their leisure hours at home. Between the ages of five and eight, primary grade students search more selectively for comprehensible stories by connecting causal events both within and across episodes of longer narratives. Having mastered basic story schemas for linear structures, they prefer more adventurous, suspenseful, and faster-paced stories that allow them to predict characters' destinies, especially in fantasies between good and evil forces. Media connote gender content via pacing; boys focus on how mechanical objects operate in relation to themselves (fast pacing), while girls focus on how living entities work in interpersonal relationships (slow pacing). At this stage, girls and boys alike tend to avoid "tainted fruit" media in favor of "innocuous" or G-rated content that presumably contains no violent realism, sexual themes, or other parent-forbidden behaviors that young-sters (other than themselves) might imitate.

By age eight, as children distinguish their self-concepts from those of others, they focus less on characters' physical appearances and facial expressions and more on what characters are doing and saying in plot-driven situations to compare themselves with characters' pro-and antisocial behaviors and activities. Most important, they now realize that they need to imagine or infer characters' intentions from their role-play-ing perspectives in order to comprehend more fully what characters are actually thinking and feeling. This pivotal ability to make speculative inferences also aids them greatly when evaluating media producers' and advertisers' intentions.

At intermediate grade levels, as cognitive competencies develop fur-ther, nine- to twelve-year-olds (or "tweens") aspire to achieve more inde-pendent, authorial power and self-regulated control over their identities like adults whom they see valued for their fame and fortune. They lose interest in "childish" role-playing toys and now want fashionable cloth-ing, popularized music, sports equipment, and the latest media technolo-gies to conform with and remain loyal to their peers. They now grow more interested in the "forbidden fruits" of media by watching PG-to R-rated programs with better production values intended for adults. Boys are attracted to physically aggressive violence and sexually titillat-ing action-adventures with athletic heroes who win competitive power struggles, especially in electronic games. In contrast, girls are drawn to emotionally nurturing and serialized romances with attractive celebrities who negotiate popularity through fashions, sexuality, and music. These gender scripts also play out online in same-and opposite-sex pairs when children dramatize avatars in multiuser domains (Calvert et al. 627).

When choosing to use stories for "educational" purposes, children seek informative child characters by using age and gender as normative constructs to distinguish content intended for "babies," "kids," "cool" teenagers, parents, or "old-fashioned grannies"—the latter being least vis-ible and most stereotyped in animated media (Robinson and Anderson). Powerful protagonists show children how to achieve goals despite physi-cal and social obstacles and how to behave in social situations as they negotiate fairness and justice in caring relationships with siblings and peers. Throughout early and middle childhood, viewers prefer and pay more attention to same-sex characters in media, whether portrayed as puppets, animations, or human actors. Media producers know that most boys refuse to watch female characters, unless they behave in masculine ways, but girls are willing to engage with both genders, perhaps because male characters tend to be dramatized in more interesting and exciting adventures than female characters. This rationale explains why male characters dominate mass media, especially cartoons that allow superheroes to take flight and rescue weaker creatures (Thompson and Zerbinos 415). Given the dearth of child and teen actors in prime-time television (Harwood and Anderson 88), tweens turn to young adult programs (e.g., *Friends*) that feature more exciting roles and realistic situations they expect to encounter in their future lives.

Realism surfaces repeatedly as an artistically charged criterion during middle childhood as viewers scrutinize and increasingly criticize audio-visual images for their physical authenticity, psychological possibilities, and social violations of character decorum within realistic and fantasy contexts. Children define physical realism by the ability of stage and screen technologies to create the most hyper-real simulations possible in comparison to phenomenal reality. Likewise, they judge social realism by believable, plausible, and honest portrayals of genuine characters and situations in comparison to their individual social experiences. While screen media afford young viewers ready access to a variety of realistically embodied performances, children cannot access theatre unless their caretakers transport them to local venues. If child spectators could choose freely between the types of realism offered in live and mediated performances, would they prefer living or animated bodies, and for what reasons?

Theatre studies reveal that six- to twelve-year-olds prefer live actors over televised renditions three to one, in part because, as one girl notes: "It just feels like you're really in the play." Another observes, "You have much more feeling of real life, and you can see how it really happened. On stage, you're actually seeing the living and the dying and the faces" (Klein "Processing" 12). When comparing live actors and computer-animated dinosaurs, mediated forms do not matter because dinosaurs are, after all, extinct, necessitating "realistic" animations (Klein "Dinosaurs" 47). No other studies, to my knowledge, have compared preferences between live actors (on stage or screen) and animated bodies directly, although two television studies offer indirect and mixed results.

Out of thirty most-admired characters televised during the 1991–92 season, seven- to twelve-year-olds favored live actors (67 percent), primarily in situation comedies, more than animations (33 percent). They estimated characters' ages as children (34 percent), teens (47 percent), and adults (19 percent), affirming tweens' preferences for "realistic" teenage models (Hoffner 400–401, n. 4–6). During the 1999–2000

season, out of thirty-two E/I programs airing, children's top preferences included five animations dealing with socially realistic issues and
one live-action program featuring a boy and his puppet (*Cousin Skeeter*),
mostly on Nickelodeon. Although animations held sway over actors with
no significant age differences, Calvert and Kotler noted that girls preferred live-actor programs, given their predominant social and emotional
themes, more than boys did, suggesting that human actors may arouse
emotions more effectively than animations.

Children have seldom been asked directly to evaluate actors' age-spe-
cific acting abilities in theatrical media. In television studies, six- to
twelve-year-olds find performers who do not "act their age" to be "unrealistic," "unbelievable," and worthy of ridicule for their "bad acting"
(Sheldon and Loncar; Gunter, McAleer, and Clifford). In one longitudinal theatre study, Saldaña found largely same-sex preferences for "best"
(or favorite) college-age actors on the basis of their physical appearances,
competencies (i.e., able to sing, dance, speak with a British dialect, and
memorize lots of lines well), and their abilities to evoke believable emotions. For example, in *Big River*, a musical adaptation of *The Adventures of
Huckleberry Finn*, most fifth graders chose Jim, in part, because the actor
made them believe he was "really a slave." In *Great Expectations*, sixth
graders chose Pip, the protagonist, performed by two actors. Drama students chose Young Pip, played by a fourth-grade boy, for they were more
aware of his acting challenges than non-drama students who chose Adult
Pip, a college student, as their role model.

Debates over age-appropriate casting in TYA have intensified over
the past decade as directors question whether and how adults should play
child roles (Nolan). To address this dispute, Grady and her colleagues
double-cast the child protagonist in *Step on a Crack* and divided nine-
to twelve-year-old spectators into three conditions. One group saw an
eleven-year-old play Ellie, another group saw a twenty-three-year-old in
her role, and four nine-year-old drama students attended the play twice
to see both performers. When questioned afterward as to whether children or adults should play child roles, most children (71 percent) preferred
child actors because "kids know what kids are thinking" and they "know
how children act right now," whereas with adults "the size would be
weird" (84–85). The drama students who saw both actresses had evenly
divided opinions, in part because they thought the adult actress looked
to be around thirteen years old. When asked which actress "could play
Ellie most realistically or believably," most (66 percent) chose the child
actress again, especially if they had only seen her performance; and one
drama student perceived the child actress as more "realistic," but the adult
actress felt more "believable" (86–87). Their casting advice to directors

included physical and behavioral criteria, acting capabilities, and "good" personalities.

Children's transparent desires to see their bodies on stage and screen warrant appreciable public attention. Yet national accolades are rarely granted to young actors, despite their tremendous followings among cyber-fans. At age six, Shirley Temple sparked the creation of the "honorary" juvenile Academy Award in 1934 (for nine movies in that year alone)—a miniaturized trophy handed out sporadically until 1961, when Hayley Mills (age fourteen) won acclaim as Disney's *Pollyanna*, adapted from Eleanor Porter's 1913 novel. Since then, child nominations have been folded into adults' awards, most recently to Haley Joel Osment (age eleven) for *The Sixth Sense* in 1999 and Keisha Castle-Hughes (age thirteen) for *Whale Rider* in 2003. No child "stars" have been awarded an Emmy for television, especially given their expulsion from prime-time slots in recent years.

Not until 1991 did a child stage performer win a Tony Award—Daisy Eagan (age eleven), for Best Featured Actress as Mary Lennox in Burnett's *The Secret Garden*. In 2009, Tony accolades were showered upon three rotating, teenage actors for their "triple-threat" performances in a staged musical adaptation of the film *Billy Elliot*. Finally, in 2003, the Children's Theatre Company in Minneapolis received the Regional Theatre Award in lieu of their Tony nominations for *A Year with Frog and Toad*—notably with adult performers—the first TYA company to be so recognized.

In sum, adults' artistic standards regarding age-embodied performers appear to trump children's aesthetic criteria and their age- and gender-specific actor preferences. More notably, this combined evidence explains why children seldom call attention to aesthetic qualities in media (other than noting "beautiful" imagery), because their embodied minds remain focused on comprehending the informative subject matter and social realism of characters' dramatized actions (see Parsons 59–93). By blending character and actor constructs, they don't yet differentiate characters' content-specific intentions within fictional representations and actors' performance-specific intentions within theatrical presentations. These key conceptual differences arise most significantly in regard to humorous entertainments, wherein actors' overt intentions and actions designed to please their audiences actually contain covert and pernicious deceptions that serve to mock and denigrate their viewers' very childhoods.

How Actors Mock Childhood in Humorous Entertainment

Whether on stage or screen, comedy reigns supreme among all age groups who value humorous entertainment as an emotional diversion and ready-made escape from daily preoccupations, primarily because comic escapism requires little mental effort. Everyone needs a good guffaw every once in while as a brief respite from personal problems, and there is nothing inherently wrong with offering some fun-filled entertainment for everyone to enjoy. Children under age eight take great delight in cartoons and animated actors for their exaggerated facial expressions, clownish gestures, surprising movements, and other forms of physical humor. Tweens relish situation comedies for their humorous, quick-and-easy resolutions to otherwise serious and challenging conflicts. Adults tend to dismiss "childish" comedies altogether as "innocuous" entertainment not worthy of any critical evaluation—and there lies the rub.

Regardless of physical embodiments, comic characterizations depend on directors' interpretations of scripted texts, actors' performance styles, and theatrical conventions within various kinds of comedy. For instance, a farcical moment can be subverted into a grave threat, a lighthearted game can stop cold with deadly silence, and a slapstick gesture can be treated as a surreal, macabre mystery. Performance styles vary along a continuum between psychologically realistic acting, usually adopted for serious and semi-comic subjects in representational frameworks, and nonrealistic acting, most often employed for zany animations and other presentations that imitate two-dimensional media. However, all too often directors choose the latter approach to hyperactivate young audiences, due to widespread falsehoods about children's so-called short or weak attention spans and the cultivation of animation as the prevailing province of performances intended for child spectators.

Like anyone, children evaluate actors' performances primarily by their abilities to arouse authentically honest emotions with believable vulnerability. Having performed everyday roles since age three, they often project themselves into actors' situations by imagining how it feels to perform in public, especially live on stage. Whether actors are playing human or animal characters in realistic fictions or nonrealistic fantasies, children want to believe that even Peter Pan's fairies are true—as long as actors believe with them. When actors stop believing and start playing the audience rather than the dramatic texts, they start deceiving children in insidious ways. As a result, actors and spectators manipulate each other without the other even knowing it, for the following reasons.

In stage performances, when adult actors in child roles do not "act their age," adults need to realize that children are most likely writing them off, not only as physically unrealistic characters in otherwise believable social roles, but as actors worthy of ridicule for their unrealistic laughing, fake crying, and generally improbable acting behaviors. When children laugh uproariously, they may be laughing at (not with) the "childish" adult actors (not characters) who do not know how to behave like children as they make physically incongruous fools of themselves in public. After performances, if asked to explain the reasons for their laughter, they may point out an actor's "funny" behaviors but feel reluctant to call him or her a bad actor outright on the basis of age alone for fear of hurting the actor's personal feelings. After all, they know that adult actors cannot possibly change their physical attributes, so instead, they praise actors for succeeding in making them laugh.

Children's laughter, I argue, likely stems from feeling superior to and far more mature than these ludicrous adults who do not know any better, especially when foolish adult villains suffer defeat at the hands of child protagonists—all of which raises children's self-esteem and releases their tensions, albeit for brief moments. When insecure actors hear these vocally loud responses, they have a natural tendency to exaggerate their facial expressions and buffoonish gestures even further to raise their own self-esteem—at the expense of children's. Children find visual forms of physical humor, sudden surprises, and innocent misunderstandings hysterically funny; however, parody, slapstick, satire, and irony involve far more cognitively complex and deceptively antagonistic forms of "adult" humor (see Buijzen and Valkenburg).

Full appreciation of parody requires historical knowledge of the dramatic genre and theatrical style that is being parodied (e.g., camp in drag). Children do not know that cross-dressed actors are a common theatrical convention that dates back to the nineteenth century when male actors mocked "dames," like Mother Goose in British pantomimes, and female actors played males' breeches roles. Their lack of historical knowledge also explains why they keep wondering why stage directors cast women in men's roles, because they know nothing about Greek and Elizabethan theatre history. Likewise, they do not know the origins of slapstick in commedia dell'arte wherein Harlequin, a servant, used a slapstick to degrade Pantalone, his master, to cut his wealthy status down to size. Therefore, when stage and screen actors use slapstick humor to create comedic hysteria, they are actually degrading the status of children by cutting them down—to infant size. In other words, while animated actors think children are savoring their parodies of cartoons, they are actually mocking childhood quite aggressively and maliciously— without children realizing that they themselves are being ridiculed as wholly ignorant and immature. In effect, each misunderstands the other's highly manipulative and underlying motivations, as comic escapism diverts everyone's attention from thinking more deeply and reflectively about these respective subtexts, especially during rapid-fire rates of slapstick comedy.

In addition to parody and slapstick, irony is another sophisticated form of verbal and psychological humor that child audiences do not fully comprehend. Irony relies on verbal incongruity, so when actors say one thing but mean something else or exactly the opposite of what they are saying, children do not laugh. As Ellen Winner makes clear, "misunderstanding irony appears to reflect a genuine conceptual confusion about why someone would knowingly say something false yet not intend to deceive his listener" (146). Another ironic way to deceive child audiences while entertaining adults is to rely on puns that play with word meanings, especially vocabulary words that children have not yet learned. In effect, puns exclude children from laughing with adults around them, which can make children feel ignorant and inferior to adults for not getting the verbal jokes that adults alone get to enjoy.

One final form of so-called humor includes children extremely well because they have learned it from so many older bullies in their lives. Put-downs, such as calling someone a hostile name, allow children to feel superior to their victims—a devious trap of comic cleverness that adults often fail to notice and fully realize. Given that males of all ages prefer more aggressively hostile and malicious forms of comedy than females, ironic and satiric humor directed at girls and women to assert male superiority is particularly pernicious, because girls (as audiences and actors) may not always realize they are actually being sexually harassed. As Lynn Phillips points out, "harassment occurs while other people watch; it is indeed a public performance conducted primarily by boys toward girls" (48).

No studies, to my knowledge, have asked child actors directly to explain their comprehension of parody, camp in drag, slapstick, and various ironies in performances. Although they may ask their directors to explain these forms of humor to them during rehearsals, I doubt very much that directors would point out or expose any "unintentional" mockeries of childhood. Instead, child actors may be thrilled for any all too infrequent opportunity to perform in public on stage and screen—even if it means participating in parodies that satirize otherwise serious situations in their own childhoods. While many securely self-confident performers may not mind laughing at themselves and subjecting themselves to public ridicule, I maintain that directors who employ children under age twelve for satirical and campy parodies are, in effect, exploiting their inabilities to fully understand and appreciate these antagonistic forms of humor.

In short, producers' desires to please and entertain all spectators, with the myriad forms of humor they so love, keep everyone's attentions happily diverted from the economic powers and political controls firmly clenched in corporate hands. Selling happiness through action-ridden and -riddled escapism sells everyone short, as theatre and media producers and their hired performers teach generations of consumers to never mind the wizard behind the curtain. For example, when college students study critical assessments of Disney films, they are often amazed to discover cultural stereotypes they never recognized as children. Still, they question whether these dripping streams from one man's flood actually affect children in the long run, even as they encounter deceptively insidious forms of racism and sexism. For their part, elementary teachers often fail to see how contemporary plays about poverty, menstruation, homophobia, and AIDS could possibly assist girls and boys living with these physical, social, and economic conditions. While protectionists argue over characters' identities and "educational" messages from on high, children down below have already spoken loudly and clearly, as if to say, "It's the story, stupid!"

Taking Childhood Seriously

If theatre and media producers were to take children seriously by performing children's roles as those roles are seen from inside children's hearts and minds, the adults would learn some incredible lessons as children's students, particularly if producers treated tweens as teenagers-to-be instead of large young children. Children yearn to get out of their constrictive homes and schools to explore the world at large—which is why the Internet offers such a glorious playground to those who have "free" access. Seriously treated performances on stage and screen bring the outside world in and dramatize multiple truths about young lives—which is why boldly serious, risk-taking dramas threaten those protectionists who want the world's woes kept away from children at all costs. Comically treated performances keep children insulated from the outside world by distracting them from the very problems that adults created in the first place, thereby ensuring that children will not notice how these dramatized dilemmas impinge upon their lives. Simultaneously, keeping children happy through riotous laughter and making fun of their otherwise serious childhoods also distracts adults from taking exclusive responsibility for resolving these problematic conflicts off stages and screens.

As for childhood conflicts dramatized in fictional plots, whether child characters should be forced to solve their own problems alone and/or with peers by escaping into their dramatic imaginations remains the artistic choice of stage and screen writers. When adult characters abandon child protagonists, even for perfectly justifiable reasons such as divorce, disabilities, drugs, diseases, dementia, death, and other destabilizing desertions, leaving them to their own devices, what else is left but their imaginative minds? In such cases, their abiding dramatic instincts and playful impulses allow them the creative freedoms of self-expression to restore their basic human dignities and to survive whatever debilitating obstacles may come their way.

As I hope this chapter has amply demonstrated, theatre for and with young people offers nurturing performance spaces for imaginative child actors and audiences to wrestle directly with innumerable intergenerational conflicts that hold no easy solutions, but hopeful possibilities. Deeply embedded metaphors within many contemporary and original TYA plays offer subversive opportunities to deceive those protectionists who do not want children to know adults' dirty secrets about life's realities. Knowing how children's embodied minds perform in these arenas may be the best step toward providing everyone with more meaningful entertainment that enlightens as it educates, regardless of age.

Works Cited

Alexander, Alison, and James Owers. "The Economics of Children's Television." *The Children's Television Community.* Ed. J. Alison Bryant. Mahwah, NJ: Erlbaum, 2007. 57–74.

Birkin, Andrew. *J.M. Barrie and the Lost Boys: The Love Story that Gave Birth to Peter Pan.* New York: Potter, 1979.

Bloom, Davida. "Feminist Dramatic Criticism for Theatre for Young Audiences." *Youth Theatre Journal* 12 (1998): 25–35.

Buijzen, Monica, and Patti M. Valkenburg. "Developing a Typology of Humor in Audiovisual Media." *Media Psychology* 6 (2004): 147–67.

Bushman, Brad J., and Joanne Cantor. "Media Ratings for Violence and Sex: Implications for Policymakers and Parents." *American Psychologist* 58.2 (2003): 130–41.

Butsch, Richard. *The Making of American Audiences: From Stage to Television, 1750–1990.* New York: Cambridge UP, 2000.

Calvert, Sandra L., and Jennifer A. Kotler. "Lessons from Children's Television: The Impact of the Children's Television Act on Children's Learning." *Journal of Applied Developmental Psychology* 24.3 (2003): 275–335.

Calvert, Sandra L., and Barbara J. Wilson, eds. *The Handbook of Children, Media, and Development.* Malden, MA: Blackwell, 2008.

Calvert, Sandra L., Brian A. Mahler, Sean M. Zehnder, Abby Jenkins, and Mickey S. Lee. "Gender Differences in Preadolescent Children's Online Interactions: Symbolic Modes of Self-Presentation and Self-Expression." *Applied Developmental Psychology* 24 (2003): 627–44.

Curtis, Elnora Whitman. *The Dramatic Instinct in Education.* New York: Houghton, 1914.

Davies, Hannah, David Buckingham, and Peter Kelley. "In the Worst Possible Taste: Children, Television, and Cultural Taste." *European Journal of Cultural Studies* 3.1 (2000): 5–25.

Dezseran, Catherine. "Form and Content in Plays for Youth Dealing with Serious Subject Matter." *Youth Theatre Journal* 2.2 (1987): 3–11.

Gangi, Jane M. "Inclusive Aesthetics and Social Justice: The Vanguard of Small, Multicultural Presses." *Children's Literature Association Quarterly* 30.3 (2005): 243–64.

Grady, Sharon. "Asking the Audience: Talking to Children about Representation in Children's Theatre." *Youth Theatre Journal* 13 (1999): 82–92.

Greenberg, Bradley S., and Dana E. Mastro. "Children, Race, Ethnicity, and Media." *The Handbook of Children, Media, and Development.* Ed. Sandra L. Calvert and Barbara J. Wilson. Malden, MA: Blackwell, 2008. 74–97.

Gunter, Barrie, Jill McAleer, and Brian R. Clifford. *Children's Views about Television.* Aldershot, UK: Avebury, 1991.

Hall, Christine, and Martin Coles. *Children's Reading Choices.* London: Routledge, 1999.

Harwood, Jake. "Viewing Age: Lifespan Identity and Television Viewing Choices." *Journal of Broadcasting and Electronic Media* 41 (1997): 203–13.

Harwood, Jake, and Karen Anderson. "The Presence and Portrayal of Social Groups on Prime-Time Television." *Communication Reports* 15.2 (2002): 81–97.

Heintz-Knowles, Katherine E. *Images of Youth: A Content Analysis of Adolescents in Prime-Time Entertainment Programming.* FrameWorks Institute. April 2000. Web. Jan. 9, 2006.

———. *Reflections on the Screen: Television's Representation of Children.* Oakland, CA: Children Now, 1995.

Herts, Alice Minnie. *The Children's Educational Theatre.* New York: Harper, 1911.

Hoffner, Cynthia. "Children's Wishful Identification and Parasocial Interaction with Favorite Television Characters." *Journal of Broadcasting and Electronic Media* 40 (1996): 389–402.

Hust, Stacey J.T., and Jane D. Brown. "Gender, Media Use, and Effects." *The Handbook of Children, Media, and Development.* Ed. Sandra L. Calvert and Barbara J. Wilson. Malden, MA: Blackwell, 2008. 98–120.

Klein, Jeanne. "Children's Interpretations of Computer-Animated Dinosaurs in Theatre." *Youth Theatre Journal* 17 (2003): 38–50.

———. "Children's Processing of Theatre as a Function of Verbal and Visual Recall." *Youth Theatre Journal* 2.1 (1987): 9–13.

Klein, Jeanne, and Shifra Schonmann. "Theorizing Aesthetic Transactions from Children's Criterial Values in Theatre for Young Audiences." *Youth Theatre Journal* 23.1 (2009): 60–74.

Nolan, Ernie. "What Adults Sometimes Forget When Playing Kids." *TYA Today* 21.2 (2007): 12–16.

Parsons, Michael J. *How We Understand Art: A Cognitive Development Approach of Aesthetic Experience.* New York: Cambridge UP, 1987.

Phillips, Lynn. *The Girls Report: What We Know and Need to Know About Growing Up Female.* New York: National Council for Research on Women, 1998.

Robinson, Tom, and Caitlin Anderson. "Older Characters in Children's Animated Television Programs." *Journal of Broadcasting and Electronic Media* 50.2 (2006): 287–305.

Saldaña, Johnny. "A Quantitative Analysis of Children's Responses to Theatre from Probing Questions: A Pilot Study." *Youth Theatre Journal* 3.4 (1989): 7–17.

———. "'Significant Differences' in Child Audience Response: Assertions from the ASU Longitudinal Study." *Youth Theatre Journal* 10 (1996): 67–83.

Sauter, Willmar. "Fiction, Mainly Fiction: Some Surveys on the Theatrical Experience of Young Audiences." *The Theatrical Event: Dynamics of Performance and Perception.* Iowa City, IA: U of Iowa P, 2000. 187–98.

Schickel, Richard. *The Disney Version: The Life, Times, Art and Commerce of Walt Disney.* 3rd ed. Chicago: Dee, 1997.

Schonmann, Shifra. *Theatre as a Medium for Children and Young People: Images and Observations.* Dordrecht, Neth.: Springer, 2006.

Seiter, Ellen. "Children's Reporting Online: The Cultural Politics of the Computer Lab." *Television and New Media* 5.2 (2004): 87–107.

Sheldon, Linda, and Milica Loncar. *Kids Talk TV: "Super Wickid" or "Dum."* Sydney: Australia Broadcasting Authority, 1996.

Signorielli, Nancy. *Reflections of Girls in the Media: A Content Analysis.* Menlo Park, CA: Kaiser Family Foundation, 1997.

Stroud, Cynthia D. "Sexism and Gender-Typing in AATE Award-Winning Plays, 1990–1993." *Youth Theatre Journal* 12 (1998): 19–24.

Thompson, Teresa L., and Eugenia Zerbinos. "Television Cartoons: Do Children Notice It's a Boy's World?" *Sex Roles* 37.5/6 (1997): 415–33.

Valkenburg, Patti M. "The Development of a Child into a Media Consumer." *Children's Responses to the Screen: A Media Psychological Approach.* Mahwah, NJ: Erlbaum, 2004.

Valkenburg, Patti M., and Sabine C. Janssen. "What Do Children Value in Entertainment Programs? A Cross-Cultural Investigation." *Journal of Communication* 49.2 (1999): 3–21.

Winner, Ellen. *The Point of Words: Children's Understanding of Metaphor and Irony.* Cambridge, MA: Harvard UP, 1988.

Zeder, Suzan. *Step on a Crack.* New Orleans: Anchorage, 1976.

Zelizer, Viviana A. *Pricing the Priceless Child: The Changing Social Value of Children.* Princeton, NJ: Princeton UP, 1985.

CHAPTER 6

"WHAT AGE AM I NOW? AND I?": THE SCIENCE OF THE AGED VOICE IN BECKETT'S PLAYS

Ruth Pe Palileo

Samuel Beckett's dramatic works are known for aged and ageless characters—from the "eighty-nine, ninety"-year-old Voice in *Footfalls* (Beckett, *Complete* 400), to the elderly Nagg and Nell in *Endgame*, to Krapp, the "wearish old man" of sixty-nine in *Krapp's Last Tape*, hereinafter *Krapp* (Beckett, *Complete* 29). Various performance strategies, particularly makeup and lighting, are typically used to accentuate the age of younger actors playing these characters; these strategies may be perceived as necessary to age a younger actor for these roles. However, just as Beckett's texts designate physical constraints for a given character (such as May's characteristic footsteps in *Footfalls* or Nagg and Nell's confinement to ashbins), so, too, do they provide vocal restraints. Over the past fifteen years, gerontological studies in vocal aging have described the aging voice in terms of pitch, breath-pause length, and fundamental frequency variability. Such qualities, when examined in the scripting and delivery of Beckett's dialogue, demonstrate that Beckett creates a score for aged voices using words and pauses. Moreover, examining Beckett's physical stage directions in light of the physiological bases of vocal aging reveals that these physical cues also create vocal restraints—means by which certain vocal qualities are induced so that the audience perceives the actor's voice as having an aged sound, whatever the age of the actor.

Since the advent of gerontological studies about the aging voice, scientists have been just as concerned with determining why a voice is *perceived* as aged as they have been with studying the physiological characteristics that occur in a person whose voice is aging. That is, scientists posit that a person's voice sounds aged because certain physiological events are taking place. James Harnsberger and his colleagues at the Institute for the Advanced Study of Communication Processes in Florida summarize the events that age the voice: The oral cavity lengthens; pulmonary function decreases; the cartilage of the larynx ossifies; the vocal folds stiffen; vocal fold closure is reduced; and, in elderly women, less estrogen is produced.[1]

These physiological changes manifest as changes in a person's voice. For example, reduced pulmonary function results in increased number of pauses for breath as well as reduced loudness. This contributes to a drop in speaking rate, from an average of 150 words per minute at age forty to fewer than 125 words per minute at age seventy-five (Boone 162). Ossification of the larynx and stiffening of the vocal cords increase harshness and strain while lowering control over pitch and pitch breaks. Vocal fold closure results in increased breathiness and less precise articulation. Lowered estrogen levels reduce the pitch of a woman's voice. All of these factors can contribute to increased strain, more vocal breaks, and more vocal tremor.

However, physiological changes do not necessarily mean that a listener will perceive the speaker's voice as aged. Therefore, scientists have also concerned themselves with the qualities that listeners perceive as connoting an aged voice. The *Journal of Voice* catalogued listeners as perceiving a voice as aged if it has lower vocal pitch, increased hoarseness, increased strain, higher incidence of voice breaks, vocal tremor, increased breathiness, reduced loudness, slower speech rate, hesitancy, less precise articulation, and longer duration of pauses.[2] Some scientists have also worked to ameliorate these qualities so that the voice loses its aged sound.[3]

However, Beckett's stage directions for aged characters include words and pauses that emphasize qualities that make a voice sound aged. Beckett's plays are not only a physical challenge to actors but also a vocal challenge, because, within the plays, Beckett scores certain characters to speak with an aged voice rather than a young or middle-aged instrument (what I call a "non-aged" instrument). Thus, scientific studies of the aging voice enrich our understanding of the way that Beckett's pacing and staging achieve an aged sound for a character's voice.

Some scientists, such as Robert Sataloff and his colleagues at the American Institute for Voice and Ear Research, argue that aspects of the aging voice—such as huskiness and tremolo—can appear desirable, acceptable, or, at the very least, do not have to be perceived as signs of irreversible deterioration (Sataloff et al. 157). The aged voice is not necessarily one that is less robust, although it may be perceived as such. A voice perceived as aged may have more frequency variation in its sustained vowels; a richer, deeper pitch; or simply a tone that marks it as aged. Gerontological studies of the voice are still working to define these terms with precision. Moreover, scientists now realize that the vocal aging process may be quite gradual. Thus, the aged voice may not have drastically different characteristics from a middle-aged voice. On stage, however, the differences between a non-aged voice and an aged voice should be readily discernible by an audience. Thus, Beckett has scripted some of his characters to be played with voices that are aged rather than voices that are non-aged or even rather than voices that are highly trained.

Many who have worked intimately with Beckett and his plays, such as French actor Pierre Chabert, have described the plays as "a score, auditory and visual, textual and spatial" (qtd. in Knowlson 86). Donald Davis, who created the role of Krapp in the United States, called Beckett's sense of timing "almost a musical sense; the contrasts of silence and speech, bursts of speech, different kinds of speech" (qtd. in Knowlson 63). Alan Schneider, who worked closely with Beckett whenever directing Beckett's plays, called them "a kind of theatrical chamber music. In them, sounds and silences, cadences and rhythms, are selected, arranged, pointed and counter-pointed" (qtd. in Harmon xvi). It is not, therefore, unusual to perceive Beckett's plays in terms of a musical score wherein each actor's voice serves as an instrument.

Moreover, Beckett is not necessarily writing these scores to be performed using the voice of a trained actor. Studies by Sataloff and his colleagues and by Daniel Boone at the University of Arizona reveal that often the voice of the trained actor and singer ages differently from the voice of a typical speaker. In trained speakers, vocal exercises, which condition muscles such as the diaphragm, can counteract the loss of elasticity that occurs as lungs age. Regular vocal technical training can counteract the increased hoarseness as well as the strain and vocal tremor that may come with age (Sataloff et al. 156). Thus, a trained voice may remove the very characteristics that Beckett scripted. However, a trained actor who is willing to follow Beckett's vocal and physical cues will be able to attain an aged voice.

Theatre essayists James Knowlson, Martin Esslin, and Michael David Fox have extensively discussed the physical restrictions that Beckett scripted for particular characters. Esslin suggests that these physical restrictions exist to deny Beckett's characters individualized facets of humanity, precluding the audience's empathy (89–90). Fox, on the other hand, argues that the physical restraints "ensure that the fictional suffering of his stage figure is existentially present as the real physical and spiritual suffering of the actor" (370). Fox even mentions the rumor that Beckett created these physical restraints to deliberately torture actors (364).

However, I suggest that, in certain cases, Beckett is guiding actors to attain the desired character voice through physical restraint so that, in performance, the voice of the performer is perceived as aged. Walter Asmus, who was Beckett's assistant director for the majority of the German productions that Beckett directed, reports that in rehearsals for *Footfalls*, Beckett did not explain to the actor why she should speak her lines in a certain way. Instead, he concentrated on showing the actor "the position of the body" that would enable her to speak in the manner he desired (qtd. in Kalb 198–99). As Chabert said when working with Beckett on *Krapp*, in Beckett's plays, "speech is never conceived as being separate from gesture, movement, place, physical position and bodily posture" (qtd. in Knowlson 86). The physical restraints and bodily postures contribute to aging the performers' voices. I now provide examples of this use of physical restraint to influence vocal quality.

I limit this discussion to four plays: *Come and Go* and *Footfalls*, because recent productions in Dublin facilitated my in-depth study of the performed text; *Endgame*, because I directed a production in which I based some of the vocal strategies for aging Nagg and Nell on scientific studies into the aging voice; and *Krapp*, because the text and stage directions of this play definitively show that Beckett was aware of the challenges that actors face when attempting to perform age with their voices. These performative challenges can be correlated somewhat to scientific terminology for the characteristics of the aged voice, so I now briefly provide additional detail for these terms.

Voice production, the physiological act of speaking, involves three processes: breathing, phonation, and articulation. In breathing (breathiness), air is expelled through the lungs. In phonation, the larynx generates an audible sound. In articulation, the movement or nonmovement of the vocal cords, as well as the movement of air past the glottis (the gap between the vocal cords) further affects this sound.

For the purposes of voice production, the lungs supply outward-going air that conveys the voice. The larynx, an arrangement of several cartilages, controls the flow of air between the lungs and the mouth and nose. The vocal cords comprise muscle and ligament that are stretched horizontally between the cartilages of the larynx. The vocal cords may vibrate during phonation, producing one set of sounds (typically called voiced sounds), such as most English vowel sounds. The vocal cords may also be relaxed or partially relaxed during phonation, producing another set of sounds (typically called voiceless sounds), such as most English consonant sounds (McCallion 67–74). Whatever the speaker's age, he or she will be capable of voice production; however, breathing, phonation, and articulation change in the aged voice—and these changes are perceived by listeners. For example, listeners notice those changes as increased breathiness, or breathing in which the listener hears more air being expelled through the lungs; as decreased phonation, in which the loudness of the speaker's voice is decreased; and as decreased articulation when the sounds generated seem less distinct.

Speaking fundamental frequency (SFF) is the basic audio frequency at which a speaker speaks—in other words, pitch.[4] Studies have found that SFF in men lowers from young adulthood to middle age and then rises in old age. In women, SFF tends to remain constant or decrease with age. A change in SFF has been linked to reduced laryngeal control, which in turn may result from stiffening of the vocal cords and ossification of the larynx (Linville, "Sound" 192).

Speaking rate is the rate at which a speaker generates segments of sound, typically measured in words per minute. Whether researchers time a speaker's paragraphs, sentences, words, or segments (such as syllables), speaking rate has been documented as slowing with age. This change in speaking rate has been linked to reduced pulmonary function, which in turn may result from lungs losing their elasticity (Sataloff et al. 156).

Fundamental frequency perturbation is variation in the fundamental frequency (the oscillation of the vocal sound waves) of a speaker's voice production. This can be perceived as a rougher or harsher voice or a voice with more vocal tremor. Studies have found that in both men and women, fundamental frequency perturbations occur more often with age (Ferrand 480–87). Scientists have not completely linked these perturbations to physiological changes, but they may result from loss of laryngeal control, which in turn may result from stiffening of the vocal cords and ossification of the larynx (Ferrand 480–87).

Harmonics-to-noise ratio (HNR) is the measure of how much additive noise there is to a voice signal; additive noise arises from turbulent airflow in the glottis during phonation. An increase in HNR may be perceived as adding a husky, grainy (even rough) quality to the voice signal; sometimes it is even perceived as a susurration around the voice signal (McCallion 67–84). A lower HNR has been found to differentiate the aged female voice from younger female voices (Linville, "Source" 472). Physiologically, this may be attributed to differences in the configuration of gaps in the glottis: In young women, the gaps tend to occur in the posterior glottis; in elderly women, the gaps occur in the anterior glottis. Moreover, elderly women achieve total closure of the vocal cords. Thus, elderly women are actually likely to have less breathy voices rather than more breathy voices, which is contrary to most listeners' perceptions; that is, most listeners indicated that they perceive a woman's voice as "older" if it is breathy, whether or not the woman speaking is actually aged (Ferrand, 482; Linville, "Source" 474).

Using these terms, I argue that, to indicate the age of his characters, Beckett exploits restrictions to the voice to the same extent that he explores physical restrictions. As Chabert states of *Krapp*:

> The text as it is written remains to be deciphered: a score with all its variations, nuances, repetitions, internal echoes, broken rhythms and so on.... It is important to stress...Beckett's meticulous care in this area, his constant search for a particular intonation, a particular way of emphasizing a word, by accentuating or lengthening one of its syllables, preceding it by or following it with a pause, the way he has of dropping the voice on the last syllable of a word to suggest the action involved and so on. (qtd. in Knowlson 91–92)

I do not necessarily suggest that Beckett himself thought of his voices as "aged voices" or "non-aged voices." However, when we examine certain Beckettian roles in light of the vocal aging studies, I believe that for Beckettian drama, it is more appropriate to cast an actor based on ability to perform an aged voice rather than based on physical age.

I begin with the case of *Come and Go*, which is in some ways a negative example, because the script does not specify the ages of Flo, Vi, and Ru, the play's characters, all of whom are female. It has been the trend in recent productions to cast women who are over fifty in these roles. Based on the vocal clues that Beckett scripts, it is possible that the characters are not in fact elderly, but are intended to be ambiguously ageless. As Beckett himself writes, their ages should be "undeterminable" (Beckett, *Complete* 353).

This ambiguity regarding a speaker's age is achieved via the physiological characteristics of a whispered voice. Several studies in the *Journal of Voice*, including those by Linville, prove conclusively that listeners are capable of making reasonably good estimates of a speaker's age from taped voice samples. However, a study by T. Shipp and H. Hollien in the *Journal of Speech and Hearing Research* showed that listeners have more difficulty in perceiving accurately the age of a speaker who whispers words, particularly vowel sounds. Further studies by Linville and by Ludo Max and Peter Mueller indicated this is even truer when the speaker is a woman. By directing that the women's voices be "as low as compatible with audibility. Colourless except for three 'ohs' and two lines following," Beckett ensures that listeners will be unable to determine the women's ages from their voices (Beckett, *Complete* 353). In fact, by naming the women as he does—Flo, Vi, and Ru—ending in the vowel sounds of "o," "eye," and "oo," he is inviting the speakers to efface their ages even within their own names. This is because, according to the work of Linville, vowel sounds, when whispered, do not help a listener to perceive the age of the speaker's voice ("Sound" 192).

In letters to Schneider, Beckett estimated that *Come and Go* should have a playing time of four minutes (qtd. in Harmon 185). He also indicated that the delivery of all the dialogue should be "very formal" and that the women should have the "same toneless voices save for 'Oh!'" (qtd. in Harmon 417).

My analysis of the aged voice in *Come and Go* compares two productions in which the actors are from two significantly different age cohorts. Irish director Conor Hanratty directed Beckett's plays in Dublin, London, and most recently in Tokyo. In 2002, Hanratty directed *Come and Go* for Beckett Week at Trinity College in Dublin. He cast three women who averaged nineteen years of age. Hanratty said in an interview that he was interested in exploring whether the "aesthetically pleasing diminutive heights of the actors would add to the perception of the Beckettian dramaticule as an animated miniature photograph." Thus, he based his casting completely on physical attributes. He found that by "following every stage direction precisely, and letting Beckett's words do most of the work," everything in the piece became "measured and quiet"; the piece was eventually six minutes in playing time. Hanratty recounts that most of the work he did was to get the actors to speak as softly as possible; once they had achieved the right levels, youthful pitch and tone were "not problems," and "nearly disappeared" from the final performance. Thus Hanratty's experience appears to confirm that Beckett's stage cues aid in creating the appropriate voice of the characters. This conclusion is further substantiated in Annie Ryan's production.

Director Annie Ryan of Corn Exchange Theatre Company is renowned for plays performed in a highly physical style of what she describes as "renegade commedia." In 2006, Ryan directed a production of *Come and Go* for the Beckett Centenary Festival at the Gate Theatre, also in Dublin. The three actors averaged sixty years of age. Despite the fact that Ryan's trademark theatre is quite physically based, she paid a lot of attention to voice when casting this production. Ryan observed that the three actors "had all done the show before as well as other Beckett plays with the Gate," and suggested this as the reason why all three women initially lapsed into a "Beckettian slow deep, kind of posh accent." Ryan began by asking them for a "more old Proddy [Protestant] Irish accent." Eventually she also pushed them to "go as slow and low as possible" because it was "more effective that way." She did state that when the two characters whisper about the third character, who has left the scene, it made her "think of how we treat older people." Certainly when the piece went to the Barbican, Aleks Sierz's review on *The Stage* website stated that it "conveyed powerful images of old age and female solitude." Thus, connotations of old age found their way into Ryan's production. This is because Ryan's directions to the actors slowed the speaking rate of their voices and reduced the harmonics-to-noise ratio of their voices through whispering. Both of these effect a change in a woman's voice that causes her voice to be perceived as aged. Again, Beckett's cues as to the women's slow speaking rate and whispered voices contribute to creating an age effect for Flo, Vi, and Ru's voices.

I do not intend to state definitively that either the Hanratty or the Ryan production "got it right" in terms of the ages of the cast. When Beckett directed *Come and Go* in Berlin in 1978, he cast three women in their early sixties (Harmon 417). Beckett also approved Schneider's casting choices for both Schneider's 1970 Toronto production, in which the women averaged twenty-seven years of age, and Schneider's 1983 New York production, in which the women were even younger; in fact, one was only twenty-three (Harmon 417). It can be seen that the women of *Come and Go* may be any age at all, so long as their voices are rendered "ageless" by following Beckett's text and stage directions. When the production follows those directions, any age attributed to the actors in *Come and Go* is based on the listener's perception of the women's voices.

From *Come and Go*, we move to *Endgame*, for which Beckett's directions specify the relative ages of Nagg, Nell, and Hamm. The textual cue that indicates old age for Nagg and Nell is simply that the two are Hamm's parents and, therefore, must be older than he is. Roger Blin, who created the role of Hamm, was fifty when the play debuted in 1957. P.J. Kelly was seventy-five years old when he played Nagg in this production; Christine Tsingos, who played Nell, was also in her seventies.

In February 2006, I directed a production of *Endgame* for the Samuel Beckett Centre School of Drama at Trinity College in Dublin. Our Hamm was portrayed by Dr. Matthew Causey, whose robust speaking voice is in the forty- to fifty-year-old range. My original casting choices were based on facial and vocal features; because of this, I ended up with a Nagg and Nell who were younger than Hamm—John-David Johnson and Holly Maples, both in their twenties. Our Clov was in his early twenties.

Though I knew that lighting and makeup would suitably age all four actors, I intended to use the actors' voices to convince our audience that Nagg and Nell were older than Hamm. Beckett's plays are an opportunity to present to an audience a vocal symphony accompanied by gray, barely living pictures seen almost through half-closed eyes. When I first listened to the actors read through the script, I actually closed my eyes and found that Johnson and Maples both had voices full of character and odd music. I was certain that Johnson and Maples could find what I thought of as their "old voices," despite their physical youth. To help them do so, I reviewed several scientific articles that described listeners' perceptions of aging voices. Meanwhile, Johnson and Maples diligently sought out older acquaintances and watched older actors in films to listen to their voices. I constantly stressed to them that most of the acting would be in their voices because the play is staged with their characters confined to a bin.

In rehearsal, the two tried voice after voice after voice. After I found the B.J. Benjamin studies indicating that the fundamental frequency in the voice of very old men rises, Johnson gamely performed the entire Nagg monologue in falsetto. It was patently obvious that this did not make his voice seem aged so much as false. Meanwhile, the earlier Linville studies indicated that listeners perceived older women as having huskier voices. For a few sessions, Maples delivered a very good Bette Davis version of Nell, but it also rang a little false.[5] Though Johnson and Maples have good ears and thus did credible impressions of older individuals, the voices were just that—impressions. Eventually, we realized we had to discover how Johnson would sound when he was old and his breath shorter and his vocal cords elongating; we had to simulate how Maples' voice would sound when her vocal cords stiffened and her lung capacity decreased.

Both Johnson and Maples are quite physical actors; Maples in particular has extensive dance training. They found the constraints of Nagg and Nell's kneeling position quite challenging, even chafing, in rehearsal. In many of our sessions, they would require time to "break out" of the kneeling posture. In every rehearsal, we usually did a few line-throughs, during which they would move freely around the rehearsal space in an extremely physical manner. The only constraints I ever gave them during these sessions were that they were never allowed to touch each other or to gaze directly into each other's eyes, even when they came quite close to each other. These moments gave them a background of intimacy, which, over several weeks, added a physical back story to Nagg and Nell's story—a body remembrance of when the two characters used to be able to move and touch. However, it did little to age their voices—until we finally put the two actors into the bins.

We discovered that, if the two did some highly physical work just prior to crouching into the bins, their voices retained shortness of breath. The limited space inside the bin physically restrained Johnson from fully getting his breath back during the duration of the performance. Johnson would take a brisk jog around the space before every performance to maintain this breathless quality to his voice. While in the bin, he kept himself crouched low and his chest pressed firmly against the bin's front, again restricting the lungs that provided power to his voice. He also decided to keep any saliva he generated during the performance in the back of his throat. In order to do this, he kept his head slightly tilted back part of the time; this resulted in a slightly higher pitch to his normal tone. Thus, through physical constraints, Johnson increased his fundamental frequency slightly and reduced his speaking rate.

Maples, who is a little over five feet tall, was not physically constrained in the manner that Johnson was. The bins were, of course, the same size, as Beckett indicates in his stage directions—large enough to accommodate a kneeling Johnson, who is well over six feet tall. This meant that the bin in which Maples sat was quite roomy. She, too, leaned her chest forward against the front of the bin to restrict her lung capacity, but it did not produce the desired effect. Instead, Maples used her dance training to elongate her neck and hold it stiffly, mimicking the stiffened vocal cords and vocal passageway of an older woman. She called this the "birdlike" posture, similar to the stances of some of the eighty-and ninety-year-old women she had observed. She kept her head movements small and quick. Rather than extreme physical exercise prior to the performances, which was Johnson's technique for Nagg, Maples, who is a talented singer as well, used her extensive repertoire of breathing exercises to control her breathing and keep her delivery of words "chirped," though slow in tempo. Her chirped words were delivered in a breathy but clipped tone, as if she could not sustain words for long without having to take another breath.

Although I will not list them in detail here, Nagg and Nell's dialogues contain a high occurrence of directions for intrasentence pauses. The work of Hoit and Hixon indicates that "elderly men and women require more intrasentence breaths than do their younger counterparts" (355). Moreover, each pause in Beckett's script was emphasized; actor Klaus Herman reports that in *That Time*, Beckett did not want any pauses except those he specifies in the text and that the text between the pauses should be delivered as much as possible without breathing (Kalb 203). Thus, there is a Beckettian precedent for Johnson and Maples' delivery of alternating pauses and breathlessness.

Originally, Hamm's opening monologue also contained a high occurrence of intrasentence pauses, but we discovered that a significant number of these pauses were cut in Beckett's Revised Text, thereby making Hamm's voice less aged in contrast to Nagg's and Nell's voices (Beckett,

Theatrical 50–53). Both Johnson and Maples used the moments when Nagg or Nell would echo one of Hamm's lines to redeliver the line with a slower speaking rate, thereby creating a contrast of their aged voices to Hamm's younger one. Johnson particularly used this technique when he echoes Hamm by saying to Nell, "I thought you were going to leave me" (Beckett, *Complete* 101). Maples used the technique to great comic effect when she echoed Hamm's "Perhaps it's a little vein" (Beckett, *Complete* 101).

Did the actors' use of physical constraints successfully age their voices? The show was sold out every night of the run and received standing ovations, but the most striking moment for me was on opening night. When Johnson and Maples stepped out of the bins to take their curtain calls, emerging out of dim lighting into the house lights, there was a gasp of surprise from the audience. I believe it was because, outside of the bins, they are obviously young and physically fit, although their voices coming out of the grayness did not sound that way.

I turn now to Beckett's *Footfalls* to demonstrate that, based on perceived age of vocal characteristics, the characters of May and Voice are much closer to each other in age than the two characters reveal. In other words, based on Beckett's vocal score, May might be older than Voice tells us she is. *Footfalls* was first performed in May 1976, at the Royal Court Theatre in London. Billie Whitelaw played May; she was forty-four at the time. Rose Hill originated the role of Voice; she was sixty-two. Traditionally, *Footfalls* has been performed with Voice as an older character than May, most probably on the basis of two textual cues. First, May calls out at the play's beginning, "Mother [pause. No louder] Mother," and Voice answers (Beckett, *Complete* 399), implying that Voice is May's mother. Second, Voice asks May, "What age am I now?" and May answers "Ninety…Eighty-nine, ninety." A little bit later, May asks Voice, "What age am I now?" and Voice replies "In your forties" (Beckett, *Complete* 400).

Despite these seemingly straightforward textual cues to the age difference between May and Voice, Beckett still tells us that the voices of the two characters should be quite similar—"both low and slow throughout" (Beckett, *Complete* 399). Again, by lowering the audible vocal quality, Beckett reduces the listener's ability to perceive age accurately. In addition, the low speaking tone reduces breathiness in both women's voices. SFF is the same for both women—"low." Thus, only speaking rate remains as a characteristic for distinguishing the two characters' ages.

In the pause-to-line ratio, as measured by pauses, ellipses, and dashes in the script, the score for May's prolonged monologue is nearly the same as that for Voice's prolonged monologue. Voice's monologue comprises approximately thirty-five lines, and there are twenty-eight pauses within these lines, an average rate of one and two tenths per line. Meanwhile, May's monologue comprises approximately sixty-three lines, and there are fifty-four pauses within these lines, an average rate of one and one tenth per line. Every pause causes the actor to take an intrasentence breath and to slow the tempo of the delivery. I have already discussed the work of Hoit and Hixon, who discovered that "elderly men and women require more intrasentence breaths than do their younger counterparts" (355). Based on pause-to-line ratio alone, May and Voice have nearly the same number of breath-pause occurrences, and thus a similar tempo or speaking rate.

Moreover, regarding the physical restraints, May's pacing can contribute a breathless quality to her voice, which further ages it and thereby further reduces any vocal difference between a middle-aged May and an aged Voice. This contributes to the mystery of *Footfalls*, for an audience cannot conclusively determine whether Voice is a real voice or simply another Voice in May's head.

In 1980, Schneider wanted to do a version of *Footfalls* with one actress playing May and responding to a "recording [of] her [i.e., May's] mother's voice" (Harmon 290). Beckett vehemently disliked this idea of having Voice as a recording, because a recorded voice did not give Voice the quality he was looking for in the character (Harmon 290). This could be attributed to Beckett's wanting May and Voice to be two clearly separate characters. It could also be attributed to Beckett's awareness that, in terms of perceived age, the recorded voice of an individual can sound younger than the live voice of the same individual (Benjamin 722). Beckett would have been aware of this perception, whether or not he thought of Voice in terms of aged or aging, because more than fifteen years before he wrote *Footfalls*, he had seen the effects of placing a recorded voice side by side with the live originator of the voice in *Krapp's Last Tape*.

No analysis of the aging voice in Beckett is complete without a look at *Krapp*, which Patrick Magee first performed at the Royal Court Theatre in London in October 1958. Magee was thirty-four at the time of his first performance as Krapp. In one sense, I have saved the most obvious example for last because this play is a comparison between the voice of the same actor at older and younger stages in his life, although in a typical theatrical twist, the actor is actually the same age for both recorded and live performance. One could say, though, that *Krapp* treats the audience to the phenomenon of a voice as it ages over time. Knowlson notes that, since the play's publication in 1959, there are few records that Beckett made any changes to the actual words spoken by Krapp, either recorded or live. Rather, Beckett changed some of Krapp's actions. These changes, which Beckett made to the notes on set, costume, lighting, props, and stage business, were based on the four productions he directed himself and on productions with which he was associated, such as those of Schneider Thus, our analysis of the aged voice is based appropriately on examining Krapp's younger voice against Krapp's older voice or, if you will, Krapp's recorded voice against Krapp's live voice. As Roy Walker wrote in a review of *Krapp*, it "is a solo, if that is the word for one voice with two organs, one human, one mechanical" (qtd. in Knowlson 48).

In his beginning stage directions, Beckett sets the parameters for the older voice in terms that are as precise as his directions for costume; Krapp is described as having a "Cracked voice. Distinctive intonation" (Beckett, *Complete* 215). Beckett wrote this play with Magee's voice in mind. In an interview, Donald McWhinnie, who directed Magee in the first performance of *Krapp's Last Tape*, said he noticed "that Pat Magee had this curious voice, which could somehow speak these old men's lines...[in] this curious cracked voice" (qtd. in Knowlson 46). Beckett first learned how to operate a tape recorder, still a relatively new technology in 1958, in order to finish writing the monologue for Magee. Beckett's guidelines for Krapp's voice on the tape were also fairly stringent: "strong voice, rather pompous, clearly Krapp's at a much earlier time" (Beckett, *Complete* 217). The text informs us that recorded Krapp is thirty-nine at the time of recording. In McWhinnie's production, the opportunities for stage business (i.e., actions on stage) and lighting to age Krapp were minimal. Thus, both live and recorded, Krapp's age was largely revealed through his voice, although makeup was also used (Knowlson 46).

In a 1960 production of *Krapp's Last Tape*, Schneider cast Donald Davis, who was only thirty-two at the time. "Schneider had really wanted an older man for the part, but he knew that Davis...would be able to portray old age and had, besides, a rich and flexible voice that would work well on tape" (qtd. in Knowlson 53). Preproduction recording of the tape took longer than the actual rehearsal period. Says Schneider, "We were trying to capture the character, timbre and tempo of the voice of a thirty-nine-year-old man as it would resemble and differ from the voice of the same man at seventy. So we had Davis read the lines over and over, with varying pitches and inflections, and made about ninety tapes before we were satisfied" (qtd. in Knowlson 54). Schneider rehearsed Davis's live, aged performance for a much shorter period of time before he was satisfied that live Krapp's voice was age appropriate.

In 1975, seventeen years after he had played Krapp, Patrick Magee directed a production of *Krapp*. Max Wall, who portrayed Krapp in Magee's production, was in his sixties, roughly the age of live Krapp. Wall had the reverse difficulty to Davis, that of trying to portray a younger voice on tape. Sir Ian McKellen writes that it is extremely difficult to make one's voice younger on stage (137); it would seem that Wall would have more difficulty than Davis, who was in essence only recording his own voice at the appropriate age. Yet Wall says it took only two or three tries to create the voice of younger Krapp—"once we got…the right timbre, the right joyousness and the right arrogance in the younger voice, that was done" (qtd. in Knowlson 64).

Beckett and Schneider originally believed that Cyril Cusack, who was fifty at the time of casting, would be "vocally…all right" (qtd. in Harmon 98). In production, however, Beckett declared the "recording inaudible" and "synchronisation unspeakable," with little distinguishing Cusack's live Krapp from his recorded Krapp (qtd. in Harmon 105). Perhaps rather than being completely attributed to mechanical failure, this could also be due to the fact that Cusack's voice was in an age midway between that of recorded thirty-nine-year-old Krapp and live sixty-nine-year-old Krapp. The Linville studies show that, on tape, middle-aged voices are often indistinguishable from younger voices ("Source" 475).

Chabert also worked to overcome the difficulties of having a middle-aged voice when Beckett directed him in *Krapp's Last Tape* in April 1975; Chabert was in his fifties at the time. Knowlson said of this performance, "One is too conscious that beneath the rather over-vigorous figure of an old man dressed in a grey dressing-gown, black skull-cap and white, untied plimsolls (yet another change, of course) there lies not far from the surface a young actor playing a role which is extremely difficult for him" ("Review"). Knowlson concedes, however, that Chabert understood the "musical harmonies and rhythms of this text" ("Review"). Chabert himself summarizes the process that he and Beckett used to overcome the difficulties faced by any actor playing Krapp:

> The first stage in working with Beckett consisted in seeking to establish a musical difference between the two voices. The problem rests in finding either one or the other, depending on the age of the actor who is playing the part. In our case, it was a matter of finding the correct voice for the old Krapp without falling into the traditional trap involved in portraying an old man's voice. (qtd. in Knowlson 89)

Chabert does not elaborate in any of his writings what this "traditional trap" is, but it appears to be the trap of faking an aged voice rather than trying to age one's voice according to Beckett's script.

Of course, even after the "correct" voice is found for either the old, live Krapp or the younger, recorded Krapp, the audience still is listening to a recorded voice of a live actor—and this live actor is the same age as when he recorded the tape, give or take a few months. So why do audiences perceive that the taped Krapp is younger than the live Krapp we see?[6] As discussed earlier with *Come and Go*, the vocal studies of such scientists as Linville established that listeners are capable of making reasonably good comparative estimates of speaker age from taped voice samples (i.e., a listener can reasonably guess which taped voice is older than another taped voice) (Linville, "Sound" 190). Listeners are particularly accurate when the recording of a vocal passage is played straight through—which is exactly how Krapp's tape is played on stage. So why does the audience not perceive that the voices of the live Krapp and the taped Krapp are the same age?

It is not just suspension of disbelief; once again, Beckett provides theatrical and physical restraints, which not only cause us to think of recorded Krapp as a "past," implicitly younger voice, but also cause us to perceived live Krapp's voice as aged. First, we must remember that studies conducted into vocal performance use state-of-the-art equipment. Machines such as the Tektronix Visipitch continuously monitor and record fundamental frequency contours, and the Honeywell Visicorder records voices with extreme clarity. Thus, the listeners in these studies are judging the age of the speakers using machines that reproduce the voice as clearly as possible. In contrast, the tape recorder in *Krapp* is nearly a character itself. It is a specific type of recorder that requires "reels of recorded tapes"; this is not a state-of-the-art machine, but rather one that evokes a bygone era of technology (Beckett, *Complete* 215). Upon seeing such a machine, even if the sound quality of its recordings is crystal clear, the audience will assume the tape is aged and replaying a voice from the past.

Beckett also slyly interrupts the straightforward playback of the tape several times during the play. This disrupts the story on tape, bringing the audience back to the present Krapp and reminding them of his physical aged presence. When the playback begins again, the recorded voice is a ghost of the voice we have just heard in the present, so we subconsciously interpret it as a past voice—though not necessarily a non-aged voice.

Beckett also uses Krapp's recorded voice to comment on an even younger Krapp "from ten or twelve years ago" (at approximately twenty-seven or twenty-nine years old): "Hard to believe I was ever that young whelp. The voice! Jesus! And the aspirations!" (Beckett, *Complete* 222). First, this serves as a classic Beckettian pun on the aging voice. The *Oxford English Dictionary* defines *aspiration* as "the act of aspirating," and *to aspire* as "to pronounce with a breathing; to add an audible effect of the breath to any sound; to prefix H to a vowel, or add H or its supposed equivalent to a consonant sound" ("Aspiration"). The thirty-nine-year-old Krapp is commenting on the "young whelp's" aspirations and desires during his twenties. Krapp is also alerting us to how that voice has aged from twenty-seven: The "H" sound becomes harder to pronounce as one ages, since it requires more breath behind it than other sounds (Linville, "Sound" 190). Second, by making this reference, Beckett again establishes that the machine is aged, a thing from the past.

It is not just the tape recorder that Beckett renders dated, however. As he has done in the other plays, Beckett adds physical restraints to Krapp's performance. If the actor is willing to work with the physical actions set by Beckett rather than use training to overcome them, Beckett's directions age the voice of live Krapp. Before he first speaks, Krapp consumes a banana very quickly, paces meditatively, nearly slips on the banana peel, paces again, heaves a great sigh, and retrieves a big ledger from backstage. All these physical actions affect the actor, causing a certain constriction to his breath and, therefore, aging his delivery of the lines. In particular, eating the banana will coat the actor's tongue, thickening the saliva in the actor's mouth. Eating causes complete glottal closure, which reduces loudness (McCallion 69). There is also a fair amount of stage business, with Krapp bending down to get tapes, lifting boxes, and bending over the recorder. When Krapp goes backstage a second time, then comes forward and assumes a listening posture, he typically constricts his chest somewhat. He also carries an "enormous dictionary" onstage (Beckett, *Complete* 219). Carrying this huge tome causes a shortness of breath (because, as Boone indicates in his study, carrying anything causes a slight shortness of breath in individuals), which again mimics the reduced lung capacity of the aged voice.

Supplementing the physical restraints are textual restraints, which Chabert catalogued extensively based on the directions that Beckett gave him. These directions correlate quite closely to vocal aging studies, such as those published in *The Journal of Gerontology* by B.J. Benjamin. The Benjamin acoustic studies examined the variations in fundamental frequency within the aging populations. Most of these studies proceed by having a group of young adults and a group of older adults reading the same passage into a tape, just as happens in Krapp. Krapp's younger recorded voice has very few pauses in comparison to Krapp's live speaking voice. The first portion that is played of thirty-nine year-old Krapp's voice comprises approximately 520 words. It is interrupted by twenty-nine pauses, if we include the hesitations and dashes in that category (a ratio of approximately one pause every twenty words); only one line is delivered "vehemently" (Beckett, *Complete* 215). However, sixty-nine-year-old Krapp's latest entry comprises approximately 440 words and thirty-nine pauses (in the form of pauses, hesitations and dashes), a ratio of approximately one pause every ten words. For the older Krapp, Beckett also scripts shouting, singing, speaking with relish, and gasping—all activities that interrupt the flow of words and, in some cases, contribute to breathlessness. Again only one line is delivered "vehemently," thereby establishing that we are, after all, listening to the same old Krapp, whatever his age (Beckett, *Complete* 223).

Chabert describes the difference that these pauses make in the flow of the two voices:

> The general tone [of recorded Krapp] corresponds to the voice of memory, distance and contemplation. This voice is contained, concentrating, unchanging, monotonous even in its delivery, with an even, continuous level of sound. The text glides and flows, quite swiftly but with something distant and obsessional about it; a kind of litany. This arises from the regularity of the tempo, the accentuation and the intonation (and from the removal of intonation)…this narrative tone…is heavy, contained (with a note of underlying threat), solemn, simple, regular, unbroken with weak accentuation and intonation reduced to a minimum. (qtd. in Knowlson 64)

Meanwhile, the tone of live Krapp's voice is "obtained by slowing down the tempo, using a stronger accentuation, lengthening the syllables, and varying considerably the intonation" (qtd. in Knowlson 64). The higher occurrence of pauses in live Krapp's monologue forces the actor to take more frequent intrasentence breaths and to slow the tempo of the delivery. As noted in the discussions of *Endgame* and *Footfalls*, elderly men and women require more intrasentence breaths. Furthermore, Beckett has scripted (and in the case of Chabert, directed) a slower speaking rate, more frequent breath pauses of longer duration, and more variable intonations—all characteristics associated with an aged voice.

In addition, Krapp's younger voice does not change from the "strong, rather pompous voice" that it opens with, apart from a few brief laughs (Beckett, *Complete* 215). In contrast, when Krapp sits recording his latest entry, his delivery veers erratically from "a shout" to "weary," from speaking "with relish" to "vehemently," from singing and coughing to "almost inaudible" and "gasping" (Beckett, *Complete* 222–23). Chabert says,

> these breaks in style also reveal themselves in the articulation, timbre and level of the voice. After the solemn, middle register of the [recorded Krapp] narration (with the voice well-placed) there follows the transformations of the [live Krapp] voice used in exclamations: a raucous, rather husky voice, full of sarcasm (which is clearly articulated but comes from the throat) and a voice of rapture (which is higher and slightly breathy). (qtd. in Knowlson 92)

Results of the Benjamin studies showed that older speakers produced lower pitches, larger intonational ranges, and greater numbers of inflections in reading than did younger speakers. Live Krapp has a "raucous,... husky voice"; listeners often perceive an aging voice as having "increased harshness or hoarseness" (Linville, "Sound" 190). Live Krapp's sarcasm should be clearly articulated but coming from the throat; this effect adds a higher harmonics-to-noise ratio and breathiness (McCallion 73). Finally, live Krapp's rapturous voice is higher and slightly breathy, evoking the higher fundamental frequency and strained voice quality of an aged voice. We see again that Beckett's written text, as confirmed by his directions to Chabert, creates a score for a live aged voice and a recorded non-aged voice.

Finally, the Benjamin studies indicated that frequency perturbation found in the sustained vowel production of older speakers was significantly greater than that of younger speakers. Beckett provides the live Krapp with a premium opportunity to present a "cracked" or perturbed delivery of a sustained vowel in the word "spool" (note the sustained vowel, /oo/) that Krapp repeats several times at the play's beginning. Krapp first says "Spool!" with relish, pauses, says a more sustained "Spoool!" and then later an even more sustained "Spoooool!" (Beckett, *Complete* 216). By sustaining the vowel several times and lengthening the sustainment with each repetition, Beckett is winding down the actor's voice to deliver the ultimate "ooooo" sound in an aged manner. And Beckett directed Chabert to deliver these lines in just such a manner: "Krapp... explores [the word *spool*] musically and gesturally, so that by the third repetition all that he is left with is the vocal gesture—very exaggerated in its articulation, mimed, outlined by the mouth, sculpted and barely audible" (qtd. Knowlson 92). The vocal gesture for the ultimate "spoooool" is one in which the vowel sound itself is barely audible—once again Beckett scripts an aged voice whose lung capacity is spent; at the same time, we neatly return to the "age undeterminable" whisper which Beckett also scores within his texts.

Of course, greater knowledge of the perceived vocal characteristics of younger and older individuals, combined with today's technology, makes it entirely possible that the voice of a sixty-nine-year-old Krapp will be recorded and then digitally modified in pitch, frequency, and breathiness so that it sounds thirty-nine on tape. Yet it is unlikely that any digitally modified Krapp would vary greatly from the pauses and pacing implicit in Beckett's text; Beckett gives precise directions for the recorded Krapp's voice. Furthermore, as discussed, these directions from Beckett create a voice for recorded Krapp that are likely to be perceived as younger than live Krapp's voice. As was the case with May, Voice, and the other characters, Beckett's directions provide a score in *Krapp*, using physical constraints to help one of Krapp's voices sound aged while keeping the other younger-sounding.

The examples I have discussed illustrate that Beckett's panoply of characters—Flo, Vi, Ru, May, Nagg, Nell, and Krapp—may be aged not just by makeup and changes to physical appearances, but also—perhaps even more so—through the deliberate use of vocal strategies that change the pitch, frequency, and speaking rate of the actors' voices. Beckett's texts clearly specify physical constraints that create vocal restraints for the actors. These vocal restraints, in turn, create a vocal age for a given character. Although I only examined the restraints that create an aged voice, in light of gerontological studies in vocal aging, it seems clear that scientific studies of voice might prove helpful in using pitch, frequency, and speaking rate to create other desired theatrical effects.

Beckett's theatrical texts have so often served as a guide to directors and theatre makers on how to obtain a specific effect onstage through lighting, physical constraint to the actor's body, and use of props. Certainly, in the cases of *Come and Go*, *Endgame*, *Footfalls*, and *Krapp's Last Tape*, Beckett's texts also prove a guide for obtaining a desired aged voice by simply following the vocal constraints that Beckett details in his stage directions. Thus, the actor's attainment of the appropriate vocal quality relies less on physical appearance or actual age and more on the actor's skill at following Beckett's text. Furthermore, having learned the techniques of "aging" a voice through the works of Beckett and the age-modulation effects of speaking rate, pitch, and frequency, actors should be able to use these techniques to age their voices in other productions. As Donald Davis says of performing *Krapp's Last Tape*, Beckett's "sense of that balance between sound and silence, between speed and slowness was far more accurate and telling than our own" (qtd. in Knowlson 64). The additional evidence from scientific voice studies testifies to Beckett's ability to successfully create on stage voices that at once evoke a certain age for their characters, yet are timeless.

Notes

1. Harnsberger et al.'s work provides the most recent summary of the terms. However, these same terms have been used fairly consistently in most scientific articles on the aging voice, as in the studies conducted by Linville and by Ferrand.
2. See, in particular, the works of Linville.
3. See, in particular, Boone's and Sataloff's work.
4. Technically, SFF can be measured precisely, whereas pitch is actually the perceived correlate of this frequency.

5. Linville's later studies as well as those studies by Ferrand report that, in fact, elderly women have less breathy voices than younger women.

6. Although I have not yet had the pleasure of seeing a production of *Krapp*, I base my audience perceptions on an extensive discussion I had with Joanne Dolan, a PhD student in language and linguistics at Trinity College Dublin. Dolan kindly summarized the reactions of several audience members who attended the Gate Theatre's 2006 version of *Krapp* featuring John Hurt, who was sixty-six at the time he played Krapp.

Works Cited

"Aspiration." *Oxford English Dictionary* online. Jan. 15, 2007. <http://www.oed.com>.

Beckett, Samuel. *The Complete Dramatic Works*. London: Faber and Faber, 1986.

———. *The Theatrical Notebooks of Samuel Beckett: Vol. 4. Endgame*. Ed. S.E. Gontarski. London: Faber and Faber, 1992.

Benjamin, B. J. "Frequency Variability in the Aged Voice." *Journal of Gerontology* 36.6 (Nov. 1981): 722–26.

Boone, Daniel R. "The Singing/Acting Voice in the Mature Adult." *Journal of Voice* 11.2 (June 1997): 161–64.

Esslin, Martin. *The Theatre of the Absurd*. London: Penguin Books, 1986.

Ferrand, Carole. "Harmonics-to-Noise Ratio: An Index of Vocal Aging." *Journal of Voice* 16.4 (Dec. 2002): 480–87.

Fox, Michael David. "There's Our Catastrophe." *New Theatre Quarterly* 17.68 (Nov. 2001): n.p.

Harmon, Maurice, ed. *No Author Better Served: The Correspondence of Samuel Beckett and Alan Schneider*. Cambridge, MA: Harvard UP, 1998.

Harnsberger, James D, Rahul Shrivastav, W.S. Brown, Jr., Howard Rothman, and Harry Hollien. "Speaking Rate and Fundamental Frequency as Speech Cues to Perceived Age." *Journal of Voice* 22.1 (Jan. 2008): 58–69.

Hanratty, Conor. Personal interview. Nov. 20, 2006.

Hoit, J., and T. Hixon. "Age and Speech Breathing." *Journal of Speech Hearing Research* 30 (1987): 351–66.

Kalb, Jonathan. *Beckett in Performance*. Cambridge: Cambridge UP, 1989.

Knowlson, James. "Review: La Derniere Bande at the Greenwood Theatre." *Florida State University* May 1976. Dec. 30, 2006 <http://www.english.fsu.edu/jobs/num01/Num1Knowlson3.html>.

Knowlson, James, ed. *Theatre Workbook 1: Samuel Beckett, Krapp's Last Tape*. London: Brutus Books, 1980.

Linville, Sue Ellen. "The Sound of Senescence." *Journal of Voice* 10.2 (June 1996): 190–200.

———. "Source Characteristics of Aged Voice Assessed from Long-Term Average Spectra." *Journal of Voice* 16.4 (Dec. 2002): 472–79.

Max, Ludo, and Peter B. Mueller. "Speaking Fo and Cepstral Periodicity Analysis of Conversational Speech in a 105-year-old Woman: Variability of Aging Effects." *Journal of Voice* 10.3 (Sept. 1996): 245–51.

McCallion, Michael. *The Voice Book*. London: Faber and Faber, 1988.

McKellen, Ian. "Ian McKellen on Acting Shakespeare." *Shakespeare Quarterly* 33.2 (Summer 1982): 135–41.

Rubin, Adam D., Veeraphol Praneetvatakul, Shirley Gherson, Cheryl A. Moyer, and Robert T. Sataloff. "Laryngeal Hyperfunction during Whispering: Reality or Myth?" *Journal of Voice* 20.1 (March 2006): 121–27.

Ryan, Annie. Personal interview. Nov. 11, 2006.

Sataloff, Robert, Deborah Caputo Rosen, Mary Hawkshaw, and Joseph R. Spiegela. "The Aging Adult Voice." *Journal of Voice* 11.2 (June 1997): 156–60.

Shipp, T., and H. Hollien. "Perception of the Aging Male Voice." *Journal of Speech and Hearing Research* 12.4 (Dec. 1969): 703–10.

Sierz, Aleks. "*Footfalls/Come and Go*." *The Stage* Apr. 4, 2006. Jan. 15, 2007. <http://www.thestage.co.uk/reviews/review.php/12150/beckett-on-stage-footfalls-come-and-go>.

Verdonck-de Leeuw, Irma M., and Hans F. Mahieu. "Vocal Aging and the Impact on Daily Life: A Longitudinal Study." *Journal of Voice* 18.2 (June 2004): 193–202.

CHAPTER 7

MOLIÈRE'S *MISER*, OLD AGE, AND POTENCY

Allen Wood

Molière's miser is old. In fact, Harpagon is one of the oldest characters in all of the thirty or so plays by the seventeenth-century French dramatist.[1] He keeps precise count of his age as well as his money, boasting to the matchmaker Frosine that he is sixty years old (*j'en ai soixante bien comptés* [I am sixty well-counted years old]). A widower, he plans to remarry at the same time he arranges marriages for his two children still living at home. Within the world of Molière's theatre, Harpagon is one of the obsessed, authoritarian father figures, along with Orgon in *Tartuffe*, Monsieur Jourdain in *Le Bourgeois Gentilhomme*, and Argan in *Le Malade Imaginaire*. The character type comes from the *senex* (old man) of Roman comedy, whose function is to try, unsuccessfully, to block the wedding plans of a child. In addition, Harpagon seems to be a *senex amans* (amorous old man), in that he is in love with a woman young enough to be his daughter, and the play encourages the audience to view his "passion as contrary to nature and ridiculous in its appearance" (Sweetser, 115, my translation). In Molière's plays, the ages of the other fathers remain unspecified, and usually they are portrayed as being in their late forties or early fifties, about the age of Molière when he played the parts. This study examines the relationship between Harpagon's age and issues of power and desire. The play shows that Harpagon loses social value and power for his foolishness on three fronts: because he desires money more than human love, because he seeks amorous affection across the generations, and because he tries to control the loves of his children. Critics often connect Harpagon's debasement to his age, but in contrasting Harpagon with the character of Seigneur Anselme, Molière makes it clear that Harpagon departs from the stock character of the *senex amans.* Harpagon's narcissism, reverse ageism, and avarice—rather than his absolute age—cause his downfall.

A brief review of historical and demographic data from the period is useful to provide the context in which to understand the play's references to age, as well as family life and marriage. Although statistical records were not kept with our current expectations of scope, frequency, or reliability, the documentation that surviving parish registers and other sources provide allows us to determine some general patterns. To say the least, life was very difficult in seventeenth-century France. The ravages of war, famine, and disease quickly wore out the body and often brought death to people in their fifties, if not before. Molière himself fell gravely ill with tuberculosis in 1666 at the age of forty-four, and died seven years later, almost a decade short of Harpagon's age, sixty.[2] Other notable playwrights of the period enjoyed greater longevity, although this was uncommon. Pierre Corneille died at the advanced age of seventy-eight, and Jean Racine died just months before his sixtieth birthday. Although the usual life span was shorter than our current expectations, middle-class people such as Molière, his acquaintances, and his characters often did not marry until they were financially established, in their thirties for men and for women in their mid-twenties.[3] Harpagon and his children (whose ages are not stated in the text, but who are often portrayed as young adults) may well be on the upper end of the age ranges for a family whose children are still at home, but their situation would still not seem too far outside the conventional.

In seventeenth-century France, then, Harpagon is indeed old at sixty. In the play, his family considers him to be despotic and thoroughly disagreeable, but this has less to do with his advanced age than with his character flaw: a neurotic and narcissistic obsession with money that controls his words and deeds throughout the comedy. His obsession is clearly manifest throughout the play and affects the entire plot, which is an intertwining of the wedding plans for himself and his children at a time when he fears he will lose money, either through a bad marriage arrangement, marriage expenses, or the theft of his buried money.

In one of Harpagon's rare absences from the stage, in the opening two scenes, his children reveal their true, hidden love interests. The daughter, Elise, loves Valère, who keeps his past vague and who works as a servant in Harpagon's house in order to be near her. The son, Cléante, loves a poor, beautiful young woman in the neighborhood, Mariane, who is closely guarded, and whom he has seen only while passing beneath her balcony. Harpagon does not know and could not care less what his children desire, but informs them that he intends to marry Mariane, while marrying his daughter to Seigneur Anselme, a wealthy older neighbor (he is fifty), and his son to a rich widow. The children and those they love plot to undo Harpagon's plans, to little avail, and the miser's various financial dealings and thrifty household management provide many farcical scenes.

Harpagon is clearly in charge, central to the action, and mostly aware of events surrounding him. He thwarts his children's disobedient behavior although he is unaware of their plans or desired partners. His repeated visits to the spot where he buried his money (in the garden offstage) draw the attention of a wronged servant, who steals it. The theft devastates Harpagon, having lost the only thing that truly mattered to him. In the legal process of recovering his money, the truth comes out and all identities are revealed.

The basic plot indicates that despite Harpagon's advanced age, he is a force to be reckoned with, as he is mentally lucid, verbally sharp, and physically engaged in the action. He refuses to accept his advanced years and the image others have of a frail, dependent old age. However, his plans are ultimately doomed to failure, due to the convention in comedy for the younger generation, the children, to triumph. Northrop Frye elaborates on this master plot:

> The obstacles to the hero's desire, then, form the action of the comedy, and the overcoming of them the comic resolution. The obstacles are usually parental, hence comedy often turns on a clash between a son's and a father's will. [...T]he older members of almost any society are apt to feel that comedy has something subversive about it. (164)

The miser is also doomed to failure due to Molière's social satire of avarice. Yet Harpagon's efforts are nonetheless persistent and intricate; he is a formidable opponent to his children's plans. Until the very end of the play, he is the master; he is in control.

As we consider Harpagon's age, we must remember that a character in a play is not merely textually defined, but also interpreted in performance. This play contains few stage directions that might suggest character depiction, and we lack information as to how the seventeenth-century playwright/actor performed the role himself. Actors have portrayed Molière's miser in vastly different ways. For example, in 1989, the play was presented in Paris in two theatres, and differing, even contradictory interpretations of Harpagon were represented. Some critics and actors see the miser as a dark, almost tragic figure, and this is how Michel Bouquet portrayed him at the Atelier, "like a marionette whose every gesture [was] meditated" (Hilgar 23). Dressed all in black, Harpagon expended energy as he spent money—in other words, barely at all. His steps were small, his arm gestures limited, combining to make him appear, among other things, as old and frail. At the other extreme, Jacques Mauclair in his Théâtre de Ville d'Avray gave audiences a Harpagon of slapstick comedy, with boundless energy, who often ran all around the stage, gesticulating wildly. He seemed to act like a man half his sixty years, and also got lots of laughs.[4] With such divergent staged versions stemming from the same text, critics must be very careful as to how they read the play's constructions of Harpagon's age. In this chapter, the examination will be textual in nature, not based on any particular performance of the role.

The play provides few indications about the physical prowess and vitality of the miser, but it is a demanding role. Harpagon is on stage and actively involved in twenty-three of thirty-two scenes and has the most lines of any character. He does comment to Frosine about his *fluxion* (2.5), the tubercular cough that the author/actor Molière could not disguise, but the matchmaker solicitously reassures him that he coughs gracefully. Harpagon seems to have no other physical ailments or defects, other than being old, unattractive, and dressed outlandishly. When the servant La Merluche accidentally knocks him down, he is quick to recover (3.9). Although it is not clear how much force Harpagon has to give to physical, slapstick violence, he threatens to slap La Flèche (1.3), beats his cook Maître Jacques (3.1), and calls for a stick to beat his son (4.3). While lacking the vigor of youth, he is certainly not passive or decrepit.

A clear sign that Harpagon is mentally alert is found in his ability to calculate monetary sums swiftly and accurately. This was no easy matter in seventeenth-century France, as the standard unit of account, the *livre* (pound), was not one of the several kinds of coins, *écus*, *pistoles*, and *louis d'or*, that actually circulated (paper money was not yet used). As a businessman and financier, Harpagon must be able to establish monetary value independently of the actual coins of varying denominations. Throughout the play, the miser, who does not trust safes, is afraid that somebody will discover and steal the money he had buried the day before, an enormous sum of 10,000 gold *écus* (or 100,000 pounds), about which he talks to himself in the first act. Yet when he describes this money to the Commissioner in the final act, it turns out that the 10,000 gold *écus* were composed of *louis d'or* and *pistoles* (5.1). However it is calculated, Harpagon's treasure is always on his mind; unlike other misers who are portrayed counting out their hoards of money, even at home he must keep his hidden away.

Harpagon does freely and accurately talk about other monetary figures, however. Very displeased at the expensive clothes his son Cléante wears (1.4), Harpagon does a quick inventory and determines they must be worth about twenty *pistoles* (about 220 pounds). He advises his son to invest this money instead, noting that at just over 8 percent interest this would yield eighteen pounds six sous a year. This impressive mental calculation reveals the sharp mind of the old moneylender.

Because both father and son use an intermediary, Maître Simon, they are unaware that Cléante, reduced to borrowing money to maintain his lifestyle, had sought a loan from his own father. When the terms of the loan for 15,000 francs (the same as pounds) are revealed, Harpagon's underhanded business practices are apparent. As lender, he claims not to have the money on hand, and requires the borrower to pay interest on the loan and also the interest the lender must pay. When all is totaled, this amounts to 25 percent. Furthermore, the lender claims that only 12,000 pounds can be delivered in cash, and Cléante is forced to accept a ridiculous assortment of old clothes and furniture that supposedly are worth 1,000 silver *écus* (3,000 pounds). It is an intricate, usurious scheme that immediately falls apart when the lender and borrower—that is, father and son—meet to conclude the deal. The old man proves himself to be a shrewd and experienced moneylender, quite different from the foolish senex stock character.

Harpagon is also quick to realize when somebody tries to take financial advantage of him. He wants to marry Mariane but is troubled by the fact that her impoverished mother is unable to provide her with a dowry, despite the fact that he is quite happy to promise his own daughter Elise to Seigneur Anselme *sans dot* (without a dowry). The opportunistic Frosine hopes to convince the miser to marry Mariane because she will bring to the marriage 12,000 pounds a year. The matchmaker enumerates all the various expenses Mariane will not cost him, since she does not gamble and her needs are simple regarding food, clothing, and cosmetics. Harpagon is not duped for a minute and complains that none of these supposed savings represent a real dowry.

Frosine is more successful in flattering Harpagon about his age and how youthful he appears in a scene (2.5) that explores at length the issue of Harpagon's age. At first the miser is a little surprised at Frosine's praising his fresh complexion and healthy look. She continues by claiming, "*Je vois des gens de vingt-cinq ans qui sont plus vieux que vous*" [I see young men of twenty-five who are older than you], and predicts that he will live to be one hundred. After examining lines in his forehead and his palm, she revises her prediction to 120 years of age. He replies to each flattering comment with some skepticism but he seems pleased by what he hears. When he is told he will live so long he will bury his children and their children, his brief comment, "*Tant mieux!* [So much the better!]" reveals his highly narcissistic attitude.

While somewhat encouraged that he might live many more years, Harpagon is concerned that Mariane will find him too old to marry at his current age. In fact, he admits to wanting to be younger. Of course, Frosine is quick to invent a reassuring response, which becomes more elaborate as Harpagon shows his growing satisfaction. According to the matchmaker, Mariane does not like young men at all, but prefers old men with flowing beards. Supposedly, she once even broke off an engagement because the man, who had claimed to be sixty, was only fifty-six and did not wear glasses. Both Harpagon and Frosine seem to agree that it can only be madness for a young woman to fall in love with a young man. Frosine admires the ridiculously old clothes the miser wears, such as his *fraise*, a kind of ruffled collar that was at least forty years out of date. But despite the volume of Frosine's praise for the old suitor, which the audience usually finds comic in its delusional irony, her words do not have the immediate effect that Frosine seeks. Harpagon does not give her a *sou* for all her troubles.

In short, Frosine feeds his fantasies of a prolonged youth as she fictitiously tries to fulfill his wish to be considered young. The mirror she holds up to him is distorting, producing the image he wants to see rather than the reality of what the rest of us see. Simone de Beauvoir speaks of becoming old in terms of an alienation, which is not internally perceived: "Since it is the Other within us who is old, it is natural that the revelation of our age should come to us from outside—from others. We do not accept it willingly" (288). Because Frosine wants to be paid eventually— she lives by her wits and flattery—she will not be the one to acknowledge any physical indications of Harpagon's advanced age to him. She has no trouble, however, giving a much more realistic appraisal of his age to Mariane. Hoping to convince the young woman to the match, Frosine advises Mariane to stipulate in the marriage agreement that she soon become a widow, and within three months at that (3.4). Cléante had also predicted Harpagon's imminent demise while seeking his loan, claiming that he would inherit money upon the death of his father within eight months (2.2). However, Harpagon does not show signs of frailty that would portend death within the year.

The miser seems to draw some of his physical virility and longevity from his buried treasure. According to Goux, gold is a monetary equivalent of phallic potency, of "the *paternal metaphor* (money, phallus, language, monarch), the central and centralizing metaphor that anchors all other metaphors" (21). Indeed, Harpagon's money is his greatest desire, and the guarantor of his social potency, which Frosine reflects to him as a continuation of the vitality of his youth. If money is equivalent to virility, Harpagon's fear of being robbed is a displaced fear of castration.

Additionally, Freud asserts that "aging is associated with castration" (Woodward 29).

The sexual symbolism of money is evoked throughout the play, start ing with Harpagon's first act of searching the servant La Flèche (1.3). He asks the servant to show him his hands, and then asks for *les autres* (the others). At first it seems nonsensical, as though the old man has lost his reason. In modern productions, sometimes the servant turns his hands over, shows his empty pockets, or something similar. But the line is a slight modification of one found in one of the source plays, Plautus's *Pot of Gold*, and probably indicates a somewhat obscene double entendre. Plautus's miser asks the servant to show his "other hand," his penis, to make sure the treasure is not in the servant's pants. Satisfied finally that he has not been robbed, the miser in both the Latin and French plays lets the servant go.

Harpagon's strict control over La Flèche's actions is one early indica- tion that his position as head of the household is analogous to that of a warden in a prison, as he practices surveillance, examination, and pun- ishment over his children and servants. The miser accuses La Flèche of being an *espion* (spy) (1.3). Harpagon is projecting this onto La Flèche, for the servant informs us that it is the master who *faites sentinelle jour et nuit* (acts like a sentinel day and night). Foucault's comments on objecti- fication are pertinent: "*Au coeur des procédures de discipline, [l'examen] mani- feste l'assujettissement de ceux qui sont perçus comme des objets et l'objectivation de ceux qui sont assujettis*" (At the heart of penal procedures, the examination indicates the subjugation of those perceived as objects and the objec- tification of those subjected) (187). Harpagon's inhumane treatment of others arises, at least in part, from his objectification of people. He has spent his lifetime quantifying his experiences and relations in terms of monetary interactions, considering only the material side of the nascent capitalistic society. In other words, as Albanese analyzes the miser's char- acter, "*il se laisse gouverner exclusivement par des valeurs d'échange qui relèguent les êtres humains au stade d'objet inerte*" (he allows himself to be governed exclusively by exchange values that relegate human beings to the level of inert objects) (43).

Harpagon structures his world so that he is able to maintain con- trol over all the "objects" in his life. Since Harpagon lacks trust in safes, which just call attention to themselves, he keeps his money buried, hid- den but close at hand. Throughout the play his interactions with others are primarily financial, and this includes even the marriages he arranges. His domination over others is powerful and absolute, as he keeps a tight hold on the family's *bourse* (money pouch)—a term with clear sexual sym- bolism. However, Harpagon cannot control his own anxiety and must frequently check to make sure the fruit of his moneylending livelihood, symbolically his manhood, is still intact. His actions only draw attention to the spot, making the private cache more public, and finally La Flèche robs him at the end of the fourth act.

Many critics have characterized Harpagon's behavior as paranoid, and it is true that the miser imagines enemies all around him, even (and especially) the members of his own family. In the final analysis, however, Harpagon is his own worst enemy. He recognizes this even at the beginning of the play, when talking to himself about his 10,000 écus, only to see that his children had entered. He exclaims that he may have betrayed himself and then ineptly, suspiciously tries to deny repeatedly having a lot of money. His words would only betray him further and make matters worse if not for the basic indifference of his children, who are more concerned with their own love interests, and with wanting to free themselves from Harpagon's many tight constraints.

Fearing his own symbolic castration and dwindling youthful vigor, the miser indicates early in the play that he mocks and despises young men. He tells Frosine that if he were a woman he would not fall in love with a young man. She immediately feeds into his self-serving, unconventional views by calling young men beaux morveux, de beaux godelureaux (handsome little snots, good-looking fops). When Cléante chokes upon hearing his father's plans to wed Mariane, his father makes fun of him for being like the flouets damoiseaux (skinny, effeminate dandies) who have no more strength than a chicken (1.4). He repeats the term damoiseau in reference to his son when planning for the dinner party he will host for Mariane (3.1). Harpagon's depreciation and hatred of young men, and especially his son, crystallize into a variation of the Oedipal conflict when he finally learns in the fourth act that his son is a rival for Mariane's hand in marriage.

Rather than the traditional action of a son vying with his father for the mother's affection, this somewhat burlesque, comic form of the Oedipal conflict involves the father contending for the young woman who should be his daughter-in-law. Although Harpagon claims her by paternal authority and by the priority of his intentions, Mariane clearly finds the miser abhorrent and loves only his son.[5] Father and son quarrel bitterly, and, since neither will renounce his intent to wed Mariane, the miser renounces his son, disowning him and walking out on him with a curse. Harpagon displays the height of his frightening power in this scene, indicating a social, symbolic castration of his son.

Just after this point La Flèche enters, having unearthed Harpagon's treasure and taken from the old man that which is both his object of affection and the source of his power/youth. Upon discovering the theft of his money, Harpagon mentally collapses, losing his will and power to live. He finally acts like an old man and undergoes a symbolic death, which unfolds in a way that is both grotesquely comic and tragically pathetic. Suffering from shock, Harpagon at first calls out that he has been murdered; then, simultaneously immobilized with panic and frenetically active, he cries out: *Où courir? Où ne pas courir?* (Where should I run to? Where shouldn't I run to?) (4.7). In his psychic disintegration, he searches around for the money and mistakes one of his hands for somebody else's, that of his thief. He grabs at it, only to realize it is his own hand, *Rends-moi mon argent, coquin...Ah! c'est moi* (Give me my money back, rascal...Oh, it's me).[6] He verbalizes his mourning, lamenting the loss of his money, his only "joy" in life. Because he has no reason to go on living, he lies down and stages his death: *...je n'en puis plus, je me meurs, je suis mort, je suis enterré* (I can't go on, I'm dying, I'm dead, I'm buried).

Harpagon cannot will himself dead, and the reality of his continued living becomes clear to him. His distress is so forceful that he breaks the theatrical convention of the fourth wall and asks the audience for help, while suspecting the spectators of complicity in the theft. His suspicions reveal the extent of his paranoia, which at the same time is accurate, since the audience does know who took his money and remains silent. Harpagon does not regain even partial composure or any sense of control until he decides to appeal to an authoritative social force, the law, in order to recover his beloved money. He decides to call in all the lawmen, see to it that all suspects are questioned and tortured, and, in the end, have them all hanged. If all that fails, he vows to hang himself, and achieve the death he wishes for but is denied in this scene. He is still desperate, but focused now on finding somebody other than himself to blame.

His references to instruments of torture are not isolated here, but recall his initial entry onto the stage, chasing the servant La Flèche and calling him a *gibier de potence* (gallow's bird) and a *pendard* (hanging man) (1.3). Both in the beginning and at the end of the play, Harpagon allies himself closely with the penal function of the law; his enemies are those of the state and will be punished severely. Throughout the final act, however, the Commissioner acts more like a bumbling bureaucrat than a menacing authority figure of the Lacanian Law, and Harpagon is more of a blustering buffoon than ever before. The investigation loses its force and focus, as Valère is unaware of what the miser has lost and confesses to having taken the "treasure," that is, as he sees it, Elise. When Seigneur Anselme arrives and realizes Valère and Mariane are his children whom he had supposed drowned in a shipwreck, he takes on the role of the Good Father to that of Harpagon's Bad Father. The miser relinquishes financial responsibility to Seigneur Anselme and thereby loses control over all the children, including his own. Furthermore, he renounces his claims on Mariane, all so his money will be returned. He is no longer a father or a suitor, and he is marginal to the new family configurations. However, his financial power is restored, and since his secret cache has been revealed, he can publicly be united with his money, a condition that he had constantly desired. The play ends with Harpagon wanting to see and caress his *chère cassette* (dear moneybox) in a rather implausible but satisfying comic denouement.

Harpagon is indeed old, but his disagreeable character is related less to advanced age than to longstanding character flaws. He is old, but he is not slow, being quick of both mind and speech as he displays a great mental agility. Yet he ultimately fails in his plans as a father because he tries to control the uncontrollable, the erotic desires of his children.

Notes

1. Géronte in *Les Fourberies de Scapin* and Ariste in *L'Ecole des Maris* are about the same age as Harpagon, while only *Tartuffe*'s Mme. Pernelle, Orgon's mother and hence a grandmother to Damis and Marianne, is clearly of an older generation.
2. Goubert refers to the 1660s in France and notes that "Only about ten [out of one hundred people] ever made their sixties" (21).
3. William Roosen discusses the phenomenon of "late marriages" and ascribes it to obtaining "economic resources necessary to provide for their own subsistence before they married" (14).
4. In December 1989, I attended the performances by Bouquet and Mauclair on successive nights. The differences between the two interpretations were astounding.
5. It is not really clear which of the two may have "seen" the closely guarded Mariane first. A passing reference, however, is made to visits that Cléante paid to her and her sick mother (3.4), which is more than anything Harpagon did.
6. This is one aspect of the scene not found in Plautus's play. It is hard to make the action believable, even given Harpagon's frantic state of mind. It has been staged with his hand caught up in folds of his coat, sticking out from under and beyond a chair, and so on.

Works Cited

Albanese, Ralph. "Argent et réification dans *L'Avare*," *L'Esprit Créateur* 21.3 (1981): 35–50.

Beauvoir, Simone de. *Old Age*. Trans. Patrick O'Brian. London: André Deutsch and Weidenfeld and Nicolson, 1972.

Foucault, Michel. *Surveiller et Punir: Naissance de la Prison*. Paris: Gallimard, 1975.

Frye, Northrop. *Anatomy of Criticism*. Princeton, NJ: Princeton UP, 1957.
Goubert, Pierre. *Louis XIV and Twenty Million Frenchmen*. Trans. Anne Carter. New York: Pantheon, 1970.
Goux, Jean-Joseph. *Symbolic Economies: After Marx and Freud*. Trans. Jennifer Curtiss Gage. Ithaca, NY: Cornell UP, 1990.
Hilgar, Marie-France. *Onze Mises en Scène Parisiennes du Théâtre de Molière, 1989–1994*. Paris: Biblio 17, 1997.
Molière. *Œuvres Complètes*. Ed. Georges Couton. Paris: Gallimard, 1971.
Roosen, William. "The Demographic History of the Reign." *The Reign of Louis XIV*. Ed. Paul Sonnino. Atlantic Highlands, NJ: Humanities Press International, 1990. 9–26.
Sweetser, Marie-Odile. "'Docere et Delectare': Richesses de l'*Avare*." *Convergences*. Ed. David Lee Rubin and Mary B. McKinley. Columbus, OH: Ohio State UP, 1989. 110–20.
Woodward, Kathleen. *Aging and Its Discontents: Freud and Other Fictions*. Bloomington: Indiana UP, 1991.

SECTION III

DANCE

CHAPTER 8

OLD DOGS, NEW TRICKS: INTERGENERATIONAL DANCE

Jessica Berson

> *Age is opportunity no less*
> *Than youth itself, though in another dress,*
> *And as the evening twilight fades away*
> *The sky is filled with stars, invisible by day.*
>
> —Henry Wadsworth Longfellow

> *Old age is no place for sissies.*
>
> —Bette Davis

More than any other medium, dance can seem to neglect and even abhor the aging body. A major factor in the neglect of the elderly by concert dance[1] is the tendency to think about older bodies as being in a process of decay. Expectations of physical infirmity are a part of the "degrading, even contemptible myths" about old age, as Anna Halprin enumerates in her introduction to Liz Lerman's *Teaching Dance to Senior Adults*:

> Old people should be dignified and circumspect.
> Old dogs cannot learn new tricks.
> Old people are closed minded, set in their ways, slow, and senile.
> Old people are ugly.
> There is no future for old people, so why teach them?
> Old people don't want to touch or use their bodies.
> Old people aren't interested in sensual or sexual experiences.
> Old people like to sit and be quiet. (vii)

Conventional dance productions often depend on the energetic and virtuosic movements of performers, who dazzle audiences with leaps and
turns, and the muscular displays of youthful, finely honed bodies that can
seem to bear little relation to our own. In this world, there is no room
for aging bodies, with their decreasing powers and increasing physical
constraints. The exclusion of older bodies also means the absence of the
maturity, artistry, and history that older people might have to offer theatrical dance. However, the inverse is not always true: Including older
dancers does not mean that the full range of their abilities and characters
will be utilized. Presenting the elderly in performance can serve to reify
some of the myths of old age that Halprin describes, offering audiences
a different kind of spectacle from that created by technical prowess, but
a spectacle nonetheless. Similarly to the possibility for saccharine-soaked
depictions of childhood in productions by youth dance companies, performances by older dancers can present maudlin portraits of old age.

Intergenerational performances deal with many of the issues that
surround other kinds of community-based performance: modes of
employing nontraditional performers, democratic creative processes and
pedagogies, and perhaps most cogently, means of assessing and evaluating artistic merit. When asked to review *Still/Here*, Bill T. Jones's work
exploring life-threatening illness, Arlene Croce famously refused: "I can't
review someone I feel sorry for or hopeless about" (54). A similar reticence might hinder our approach to performances by older people—how
can we critically engage productions by people whom we are taught to
perceive as "dignified and circumspect," infirm and pitiful? How can we
understand dances that refute our expectations of athleticism and technical expertise?

In this chapter, I examine works by two contemporary choreographers who incorporate a broad range of age groups in their work, and
I reflect on my own experiences working with older dancers[2] as a way
to begin to address these questions. Liz Lerman, a 2002 recipient of a
MacArthur Fellows "genius" award, is widely recognized as a leader
in both intergenerational performance and, more broadly, community
dance. Lerman, who has been working with older dancers since 1976,
has become a prominent advocate for teaching dance to senior citizens.
Stephan Koplowitz, recently awarded a Guggenheim Fellowship for
his large-scale, site-specific work, choreographed a number of intimate
intergenerational pieces in the 1980s and 1990s. A comparison of their
work provides a means to explore differing approaches to creating intergenerational choreography and a lens through which to interrogate some
of the broader concerns of performances by older adults and other traditionally unrepresented groups. While both Lerman and Koplowitz make

use of the rich performance qualities that older dancers can offer, the way in which those qualities are deployed can either support or subvert stereotypical ideas about age.

I have worked with older dancers as both a performer and choreographer, and a brief account of this experience may be useful in highlighting some of the issues under consideration. For "Atavism," a piece focused on family history, which I choreographed in Seattle, Washington, in 1996, I felt it important to work with dancers from a range of age groups, and I gathered a "pick up" company that included children, young adults, and a colleague in her early fifties. All were accustomed to performing before an audience: The children were members of Kaleidoscope, a children's dance company; the young adults were local professional dancers; and Alison, the oldest member of the group, had had a long career as a dancer and teacher. However, the children were also used to working with people their own age, and it took a while to establish a sense of cohesion within the group. Initially, they often seemed to operate according to a familial model, which had the unexpected effect of mirroring the subject of the dance; while they explored intergenerational patterns and power dynamics as part of the process of making the piece, they were also enacting some of those patterns (consciously and unconsciously) as members of an intergenerational company.

Although vestiges of this feeling remained, over time the dancers came to see each other as equal partners. From her work with intergenerational dance troupes, Lerman writes that performing with older dancers hones younger dancers' ability to "sustain an internal/external focus" (*Teaching Dance* 144), to be especially aware of the older dancers' needs while maintaining their own sense of presence in the choreography. In my group's "Atavism" rehearsals, Alison was not old enough to require quite such attuned attention—she was only somewhat more at risk for injury than the traditionally aged dancers and capable of knowing her own limitations—but certainly the younger performers developed a different sense of possibility for the ways they could interact with older people. Rather than simply looking to Alison for guidance, the younger dancers began to realize that they could also offer her their perspectives, and that they could teach the older dancers as well as learn from them.

It was important to me that the dancers perform choreography with which they felt comfortable, and that there not be an attempt to dilute their differences. At the same time, I did not want to encase anyone in rigid roles. For example, despite her maternal sentiments toward the younger dancers, I did not want to consistently cast Alison as motherly. In one section, Alison lay on her side on the floor, and an eleven-year-old dancer rocked her forward and backward, soothing her—the younger nurturing the older. Concerns about stereotypical representations come into play in many choreographic efforts that make use of the performers' personalities, but they become heightened when working with dancers about whom audiences can make easy assumptions. In utilizing older dancers, choreographers can risk capitulating to dominant perceptions of old age, limiting agency alongside range of motion. However, older dancers also offer choreographers possibilities for resisting these perceptions and challenging social constructions of aging and the aged.

Most concert dance tends to reify dominant notions about the body, including the aging body; thus, it is likely not coincidental that both choreographers examined in this chapter came to prominence in dance through unconventional channels. Though both trained as dancers and choreographers, neither did a great deal of professional work for other choreographers before embarking on choreographic careers of their own. Instead, both Lerman and Koplowitz began—and continue—to work in dance as teachers. After she graduated from the University of Maryland, Lerman taught history at Sandy Spring Friends School, where she also started a dance program (Slaughter 32). Lerman soon left full-time teaching, but her choreographic process and community-based projects depend on her continuing development of creative pedagogical strategies. Koplowitz, on the other hand, taught children at the Packer School in Brooklyn.[3] He believes that teaching grounds his artistic practice and informs his process:

> My sensibility about working with people of different ages of course came out of the fact that I was teaching full-time, K–12. That's the other thing—that kind of teaching keeps you honest—you cannot lie to those kids, you cannot put on airs, you cannot bullshit, you cannot intimidate them—or you can, but you're not going to get very far. It's also why I do things the hard way. I guess maybe I know the difference. (Koplowitz, Interview)

What Koplowitz calls "the hard way" cuts to the heart of some of the central debates within intergenerational and other community-based dance projects. As opposed to a kind of "Kumbaya" approach that often characterizes community performance, the hard way means acknowledging and embracing the frictions produced by difference rather than simply "celebrating diversity"; recognizing a range of individual perspectives and identities, rather than exclusively showcasing those that easily align with the sensibilities of the lead artist(s); accepting the ephemerality of the communities that community dance invokes. It entails challenging the "myth[s] of authenticity"[4] implicit in the ideologies surrounding many community performance projects. In work with older dancers, the hard way also demands confronting our own list of myths about aging—and frequently our concerns about growing older ourselves.

Liz Lerman, like Koplowitz, began working with senior citizens because of the particular demands of a specific artistic project. When her mother became terminally ill in 1975, Lerman spent hours by her bedside, listening to her tell family stories (McCleod 19). Lerman began to imagine creating a piece in which her mother's remembered relatives could surround and comfort her, and decided this:

> The piece, by its very nature, had to have older people in it. When I returned to Washington, I began working with a class of about 60 people at the Roosevelt Hotel, which was a downtown residence for senior adults.... Some of the residents agreed to be in this piece. My students from George Washington University also were in it, as were some professional dancers from the area. So I was beginning to pull together this notion of professionals and nonprofessionals working together, young and old, trained and untrained. (*Liz Lerman Dance Exchange [LLDE] press packet*)

"Woman of the Clear Vision," the piece that grew out of this process, was enthusiastically received by audiences and affirmed Lerman's creative and personal instincts about the possibilities generated by including older dancers. In her MFA thesis, *Making Dance that Matters: Dancer, Choreographer, Community Organizer, Public Intellectual Liz Lerman*, Lisa Traiger writes:

> The piece became a means of personal healing for the choreographer, who even used one of her mother's nightgowns and a pair of her eyeglasses as costumes during the performance. The five older women from the Roosevelt were gray-haired and lumpy, their bodies nothing like the lithe, lean, trained dancers audiences were accustomed to seeing at a dance concert. But they had something more important than technique for Lerman; they had life experiences, they had honesty. (134)

Lerman "soon became smitten with the older dancers' impact on an audience, their incredible openness to learning, the beauty of their movements, and what they had to teach [her] about dancing" (Cohen-Cruz, "Speaking" 223). Following the success of "Woman of the Clear Vision," Lerman launched her company Dancers of the Third Age, a group of senior dancers that she directed alongside her traditionally aged company. In 1993, she reorganized her company to include a range of ages—as well as races, ethnicities, and nationalities—and renamed it the Liz Lerman Dance Exchange.

Lerman's work has three components: concert productions, community work,[5] and educational workshops. Lerman sees these elements as closely entwined: "We keep insisting that the work in the community is not separate from our formal concert work. Most people have an either/or mentality, but for me it is not a dichotomy" (*LLDE press packet*). Just as Lerman choreographed "Woman of the Clear Vision" partially through classes taught at a senior citizen center, much of her intergenerational work seems rooted in the methods she has developed for teaching older adults. Her book *Teaching Dance to Senior Adults* describes her teaching methods and outlines numerous exercises and improvisational structures, while providing guidelines and rationales for artists considering working with older populations. A number of these exercises can be seen in videotapes of a 1986 workshop in Lee, Massachusetts, that was part of the Jacob's Pillow Dance Festival. The first procedures, led by Lerman and Don Zuckerman, one of her company members, are likely familiar to anyone who has taught children or worked in a collaborative dance setting: The students are arranged in a circle and take turns developing movement motifs individually, which then get incorporated into a group phrase. However, the students in this case are elderly men and women, they are sitting in chairs rather than standing, and their range of motion is sometimes constrained by aging joints and ligaments.

After warming up in the circle, the group begins an exercise Lerman calls "Introductions." Participants say their names and tell brief stories about themselves through words and gesture. Lerman's response to each solo reveals something about her insistence on the maintenance of aesthetic criteria (even) in nonprofessional work. One woman named Marguerite tells of her experiences as a delivery room nurse, saying, "My most rewarding position was working in the labor room. I'd rush to the patient, reassure her, help her onto the table, take her vital signs, listen to the heartbeat—sounds like a boy." The dance that she executes while recounting this story is entirely pantomimic and largely evenly paced, punctuated only by a pause before the line "sounds like a boy." Lerman coaxes Marguerite toward a more abstract way of interpreting her text: "'Vital Signs' is a rich moment for more movement. You say you're taking the pulse, but you can't see it. What if you take that pulse into your whole body? What you want to do is bring to life what you're talking about." Lerman works with Marguerite to change her action from miming listening to a stethoscope into a stylized pulsating movement. She stands in a low stance with her feet spread wide, arms reaching out to the sides in mid-reach space. Beginning with her breath patterns, the rhythmic expansion and contraction of her torso resonates throughout her body. In the move from "make-believe" gesture to full-body expressive movement, Marguerite's solo grows from a pedestrian recitation into an unexpectedly dynamic, visceral account. With Lerman's guidance, both Marguerite's story and her movements amplify and celebrate her age and experience.

Lerman's suggestions to another woman in the workshop are even more direct: "Use the dance technique of repetition." The student is working on a dance about milking cows, and Lerman advises her to repeat the milking movement, but with different qualities for each cow: each cow is named in the woman's story, and each should have its own way of being milked. After watching Lerman and Zuckerman help shape several pieces, the students break into pairs to watch and direct each other. Later in the video, we see Zuckerman teaching a dance phrase in much the same way combinations are taught in any dance class, but in this case the phrase is made up of moments from the students' solos. At every stage of developing material, Lerman has coached the seniors not only in how to refine their choreography, but also how to help others do the same. In her workshops, Lerman claims, "My primary goal is to transmit dance-making tools, and to teach seniors about dance as an art form...my contract with my students is not to make them feel better, but to make dances. Of course, along the way people do feel better because the process is so life-affirming" (Slaughter 33). Like community dance pioneer Anna Halprin,[6] Lerman believes in dance as an agent for healing, but Lerman positions herself more clearly as an artist and teacher rather than a healer. For Lerman, older dancers not only benefit from the opportunities for self-expression and reflection that dance training affords, but also bring much-needed nuance and character to an idiom she perceives as being overtaken by a focus on technique. However, Lerman remains committed to dance as an art form, and to choreographically shaping the contributions of older dancers.

This is not to say that Lerman accepts the bifurcation between art that is meant to have a use-function, such as "'outreach programs, children's projects, access for the handicapped and artists in schools,' and art that is validated through its 'creative contribution,'" as described by Robert Brustein (Cohen-Cruz, "Speaking" 220). However, for Lerman, the "usefulness" of community-based art comes through the art—through craft, making aesthetic choices, generating interesting movement vocabularies, and effectively moving bodies through space. This insistence on the primacy of art seems to mark a sea change from community dance models that focus more effort on the "delight of the shared experience"[7] of participants rather than on the product of their endeavors.

In an interview, Koplowitz echoes Lerman's adamancy in speaking about his first critically acclaimed community-based piece, "I'm Growing," which he cast with seven of his students from Packer: "That piece slapped me across the face, and said, look, you can make art out of your environment, out of community...But make ART, OK? Not just make everyone feel good, but actually make a work that people can say, that's a work of art" (Koplowitz Interview). The inclusion of nontraditional dancers—perhaps especially older dancers, whose bodies are usually unable to satiate audiences' thirst for virtuosic display—in concert choreography necessitates that we rethink what we mean by "a work of art," but not that we dismiss artistic criteria altogether.

In viewing Lerman's and Koplowitz's choreography, I was struck by the differences not only in the ways that they utilize older dancers, but also in the resulting kind of art: while both sometimes verge into sentimentality, Lerman's work often includes images that "make people feel good" about older dancers, while viewers often feel that Koplowitz's dances challenge comfortable modes of thinking about both art and aging. Writing this, I am somewhat uncomfortable criticizing Lerman's artistic work, because I find so much value in her pedagogy and advocacy, but I cannot help feeling that sometimes Lerman takes the "easy way." The older dancers in her work can seem to be on the stage for their affective rather than aesthetic value: utilized for their ability, just by their presence, to elicit emotional responses from audiences, including admiration and nostalgia. Rather than being integrated into the choreography, the older dancers in Lerman's work sometimes stand apart, unintentionally highlighting the vitality of the younger dancers.

Informed by her ideas about community, Lerman's choreographic structures often allude to communal relationships and reference tropes from folk dance. For example, in the opening sequence of "This Is Who We Are" (1993), six dancers execute a kind of circle dance, moving in simple phrases along intertwining pathways. They lean into and on each other, sharing weight in gentle partnerings, and the movement seems safe, both literally and figuratively. A reviewer for *Dance Magazine* compared the role of the older dancers in "This Is Who We Are" to that in an earlier Lerman work:

> Lerman has used older dancers, and sometimes older nondancers, to extraordinary effect in works such as her immigrant epic "Still Crossing" (1986), where they can be themselves as people, as members of a community. This aspect is missing from newer works, like "This Is Who We Are," which presents the "crossgenerational" cast simply as dancers. The gap between the young professionals and the seniors is as clear, and as false

a community, as it is in those productions of *Giselle* where everyone is either sixteen or sixty-six, and we have to politely pretend not to notice. (Tomalonis)

That gap is a sort of presence by virtue of absence: It makes itself felt through the lack of middle-aged or middle-ability dancers, and can be widened through choreography that may remind audiences of the limitations, rather than the potential, that older dancers bring to the stage.

In 1986, Lerman was commissioned to choreograph "Still Crossing" for a celebration of the centennial of the Statue of Liberty. Evoking the experiences of generations of immigrants who have passed through the statue's shadow on their way to a new life in the United States, "Still Crossing" incorporated performers from Lerman's Dancers of the Third Age as well as older nondancers from senior centers and workshops around New York City. Traiger describes the piece:

> The work begins in darkness, with nearly formless bodies rolling across the floor, a pair of standing shapes rising up like distant masts of ships, or landmarks in a vast open sea.... As the lights intensify, the rolling bodies continue, some dancers lifting their knees, some rising to sitting before they sink back into the rolling pulse that carries them across the stage. The sparseness of the simple human gesture becomes strikingly prescient.... [The older] dancers, clad in blues—sea blue, sky blue, deep navy—form a chain across the back of the stage holding hands as they walk across the space. The iconic image of one hand held above the head, the other stretching to the side, is a searchlight of sorts and it mimics the Statue of Liberty, bearing that great light of freedom, the torch she holds high as a beacon to all who enter the harbor. When each dancer lifts an arm straining upward or forward, it's an unadorned moment, but one rich with resonant power, of reaching higher, of moving forward and out, of striving toward the unknown. (141–43)

The performance of "Still Crossing" I viewed was from 1994, but the sense of a spare gestural vocabulary and rolling wavelike imagery remained. In an early section of the piece, dancers fall into each other's arms and onto the floor, utilizing a lovely interplay of the Laban Movement Analysis[8] Effort factors Weight, Flow, and Time: a combination known as "Passion Drive" for its evocation of strong emotions. The overarching movement qualities of Lerman's choreography in this period would be familiar to anyone who watched dance in the late 1980s and early- to mid-1990s: a sense of release, abandon, overlapping phrasing, virtuosic displays of speed and force, and occasional chaos. However, these qualities are almost exclusively the domain of the younger dancers. The older dancers

perform simple phrases that imitate aspects of the movement danced by
their whirling younger counterparts, but that lack its energy, speed, and
dynamic changes. This difference is not a function of the different skill
levels or vigor between the two groups so much as an artistic choice:
While, as noted earlier, there are obvious and numerous gaps between
trained, youthful dancers and dancers who are older and sometimes less
trained, there are many ways to address the questions those gaps raise.

Lerman's choreography complicates the rhetoric of inclusion and artistic agency that she invokes in her writing, teaching, and creative process. Lerman is extremely articulate in her calls to develop new artistic
standards and new ways for artists to respond to each other's work.[9] In
"Speaking Across Communities: The Liz Lerman Dance Exchange," Jan
Cohen-Cruz writes of Lerman:

> Incorporating older people into her work, in which the thrill, as she puts
> it, cannot possibly be seeing how high someone's leg is going to go, has
> had the salutary effect of weaning audiences from the habit of overvalu-
> ing technique.[10] So the inclusion of older people has also illuminated
> the richness of community art. Contrary to the stereotypic conception
> of community-based art as an oxymoron, this reflects one of Lerman's
> basic criteria for artistic merit—how committed and connected a per-
> son is to the movement: "and if I don't see THAT on stage I'm bereft."
> Thus, a deepening of the artistic experience—the emphasis on an aesthetic
> of commitment as well as technical prowess—takes place concomitantly
> with a focus on communal representation. (223)

In addition to the performer's "commitment" to the movement, Lerman
cites "a revelation of something about the mover and her world" and
a sense of the dancer "overcoming a hurdle in the process" as essential to the creation of an artistically satisfying product (Cohen-Cruz,
"Motion" 103). As a teacher, I find Lerman's criteria useful and inspiring. "Commitment to the movement" is an intangible, indispensable element of dance performance and choreography that is often described as
impossible to teach: You either have it or you don't. Lerman's pedagogical
work suggests that in fact commitment is a quality that can be nurtured,
and that participation by older and otherwise nontraditional dancers can
encourage audiences to appreciate commitment and connection as artistic ideals.

Based on her humanist belief in the universality of creative potential,
Lerman's pragmatic approach to commitment as something that can and
should be taught has radical repercussions for dance education and performance training. If all students can learn a feeling for movement—like
biologist Barbara McClintock's famous "feeling for the organism" she

studied under a microscope[11]—then a different kind of attention must be paid to teaching those students, including those not bound for careers in dance. A few years ago, I had an unexpected chance to experience the demands of this revised focus while teaching a class at Hunter College in New York City. As a guest teacher, I had little idea of what my students would be like and was very surprised when a young woman entered the studio in leg braces. Her ability to execute even the most basic technical maneuvers was compromised, but she was clearly determined to embody the movement phrases in her own way. My attention had to be as focused on this student as on her able-bodied, technically adept classmates. This kind of attention is not about altruism or a feel-good, paternalistic attitude toward disability, but about a change in the way we think about who can dance and why—which is exactly what Lerman claims as fundamental to her work and worldview.

As a viewer of dance, however, I cannot help feeling that there is something askew in Lerman's criteria. Many community dance artists argue for the inclusion of the performer's experience in our conception of aesthetic value, but in most cases we have to imagine what that experience is—our feeling for the movement must be in dialogue with the performer's. Lerman's shift toward a focus on the performers' experience can leave the audience unmoored, disconnected from the process of interpretation and analysis: If the performers are "connected to the movement," and this is how the viewers know the work is good, how can the viewers resolve their reactions if those reactions are not positive, or are not engaged by the performers' connection to the movement?

I was bemused by my own distraction while I was viewing recordings of Lerman's concert work at the Performing Arts Library at Lincoln Center. There, banks of monitors are lined up in a row. While the sounds of other people's selections are muted by headphones, it is easy to see what everyone else is watching. As one Lerman piece segued into another—older dancers moving slowly, sometimes almost supplicant as they rolled on the floor or walked in formations, all the while seeming fully engaged in the movement—my eyes kept wandering over to the monitor near me, on which a student was watching a production of Martha Graham's "Night Journey," which I had seen at least twenty times before. As much as I believe in Lerman's egalitarianism, I was seduced by the dated, hierarchical, choreographically rigorous dancing on the other screen—a demonstration that even those of us who study and participate in intergenerational dance have been trained to make aesthetic judgments based on technical virtuosity, which privileges and norms the abilities of youthful bodies rather than the engagement and the experience of aged bodies.[12]

The role of the choreographer similarly becomes confused when the responsibility for the performance is so weighted toward the performer's commitment. Lerman employs a collaborative creative model, eliciting movement and often text from performers through structured improvisations. This is a process similar to that of many community-based choreographers: Working with dancers, professional or not, to generate movement and words that are meaningful for them and resonate with their bodies can yield powerful, personal images beyond what any individual choreographer might create in isolation. There is also a risk, however, that if the variety of creative voices is unfiltered through the sensibility of the choreographer, the resulting dance will be diffuse; I find this sentiment consistently cited in reviews of Lerman's work. For example, in a review of the Los Angeles segment of Lerman's "Hallelujah" project, Lewis Segal noted that despite the "platoons" of talented dancers and musicians involved in the project,

> the result never held together, not nearly. Sprawling, half-baked, too obsessed with high-minded homilies and a generalized performance vitality, "Hallelujah" never managed to touch a spiritual or emotional core—not even in its death scenes.... Think of it as a cultural disaster epic with lots of talented artists running around desperately looking for artistic direction instead of lifeboats. (3)

If the performer's feeling for the movement is the guiding principle by which to evaluate dance, then the artistic direction Segal calls for becomes less valued. Clearly Lerman does not subscribe to this notion, at least not fully: Her coaching of seniors at Jacob's Pillow and her insistence that she is seeking to "transmit dance-making tools" point to her belief in the craft of choreography and her own authority as an artist. However, the conflict between that authority and her desire for others to claim their own creative powers may undermine the clarity of her work.

Lerman's goals for the social aspects of her work may be seen as similarly broad. When asked about connections between the realm of politics and her dance practice, Lerman responded,

> That depends on your definition of politics. There are two things here: one is the literacy aspect of it. We are teaching people how to understand and comprehend art so they can use it as a tool. The other aspect is how we change people's minds. What we do about changing people's minds is by asking: who gets to dance? Do you really think an old person can dance? Do you really believe it is possible for black, white, straight, gay, and Jewish to be in the same space together? Well, come and watch this

company. You go away with a different sense of what human beings can do. (McLeod 20)

Lerman, as well as other community artists, seems to assert that there is something inherently progressive about different kinds of people sharing space and telling their own stories, verbally and/or kinesthetically. A number of reviews remark on the diversity of Lerman's company, in terms not only of age but also race, religion, and sexual orientation:

> The company members range in age from their twenties through their sixties and are Puerto Rican, Filipino, African-American, Jewish, gay, and straight. The diversity of the company mirrors the diversity of the audiences that Lerman is committed to reaching. Indeed, the *San Francisco Chronicle* described the Dance Exchange as "an opportunity to see America dancing." (Cohen-Cruz, "Speaking" 215)

Representing difference is a laudable goal—but as Peggy Phelan so cogently noted in *Unmarked: The Politics of Performance*, "If representational visibility equals power, then almost-naked white women should be running Western culture" (10). Presenting older people on stage is a good start in challenging the myths of old age, but it is just that: a start.

Another review of "Hallelujah," a four-year, multicity project dealing with issues of faith that incorporated community-based productions and company concert work, reveals some of the difficulties that can arise within this kind of approach. Attending a performance of the project barely a month after the terrorist attacks of September 11, 2001, during which Lerman and her company asked the audience to perform a simple dance in unison, Tara Zahra experienced a sense of discord:[13]

> By including representatives from nine different faiths, Lerman surely thought the company was teaching us all a valuable lesson in pluralism, in the strength of diversity. Yet the experience effectively universalized spirituality itself: there was no one on stage to represent non-religious ways of understanding or coping with the September 11 attacks...community-oriented dance companies need to think hard about what it means to ask for "audience participation" in a moment when calls for "unity" threaten to spill into a gross chauvinistic nationalism. The dance we were asked to perform as an audience...left me with a hard choice. I feel that discussion, debate, and disagreement are more important than unity when lives are at stake...that there are many ways of grieving and coping, only some of which are religious. But to opt out of the dance, to opt out of participating, seemed almost impossible. Opting out was a forbidden expression of cynicism, a failure to grieve. (2–3)

Though claiming to celebrate diversity, this version of pluralism can actually serve to elide difference: It operates within an idealized construction of community that "privileges unity over difference, immediacy over mediation, sympathy over recognition of one's understanding of others from their point of view" (Young 300). This erasure of the particular is an unintended effect that subverts Lerman's artistic and political goals. The older dancers in Lerman's choreography sometimes similarly have their edges worn away, smoothed out into a generalized vision of old age as wise, triumphant, and poignant. These are different myths of aging from those Halprin disparaged, but they are still myths. While Lerman's teaching and choreographic processes empower seniors to create movement and find new modes of self-expression, the product of her concert work can generate stereotypical images and reaffirm dominant notions of old age.

If Lerman attempts to take on universal themes in her choreography, Stephan Koplowitz conversely deals in specificity. In the last ten or so years, Koplowitz has become known for large-scale, site-specific works,[14] but in the late 1980s and early 1990s he made a number of small chamber pieces in which spoken text, rather than music, served as the soundtrack. I first saw Koplowitz's choreography in 1992, while I was an undergraduate, and it made a big impression on me: I had not seen work in which people told such personal details of their lives in such an artfully orchestrated way. Looking at some of those pieces now, I can see occasional moments that seem pat, but at the time I was entranced by the rich way Koplowitz used text. I was also, sad to say, shocked to see both young children and senior citizens on stage. While "I'm Growing" was performed by middle-school boys, two other pieces on the program, "To My Anatomy" and "There Were Three Men," incorporated intergenerational casts. As with Lerman's initial work with senior citizens, Koplowitz began using nontraditionally aged dancers out of a desire to explore an artistic concept. When we met, I asked about the concepts he had been exploring. In our discussion, Koplowitz said that his motivation for working with older dancers such as Stuart Hodes and Alice Tierstein "wasn't my desire to work with older people and be inclusive, but it was really what's the most interesting way, the most creative way, for me to elucidate this idea—whatever idea it is." However, while Lerman came to focus on addressing aging populations and finding strategies to use dance as a means of community-building, Koplowitz continued to approach his work—even work that could be called "community-based"—from a resolutely artistic point of view.

"To My Anatomy," first performed in 1987, presents four women in different life stages. The women announce their ages at the beginning of the piece: "This is thirteen," "This is seventeen," "This is thirty-two," "This is fifty." Each dancer performs a brief solo that reveals something about her age, though not necessarily what we expect: the thirty-two-year-old's lyrical, sustained undulations give way to an unexpectedly athletic phrase executed by her older colleague. Each tells a story about her body, a story that reflects the individuality of the performer's experiences while echoing memories and feelings that are familiar to many women: emerging sexuality, expectations of childbearing, cancer. As the piece progresses, the juxtaposition of younger and older dancers yields a sense that they are simultaneously representing their own histories and offering glimpses of multiple moments in a single woman's lifetime. Koplowitz believes that the deeper implications of the piece grow out of the simplicity of the task he set himself and the performers, who are—as are most dancers he works with—listed in the program as "performers/collaborators." In an interview, he explained to me that "To My Anatomy"

> was a conceptual work, where every woman, young or old, would tell a story about their relationship to their body, but that became a sort of portrait of women. But the concept was very pure, and very simple. Talk about your memory, talk about a memory of your body. That can sound glib, but in a weird way it organized the piece without having to be heavy handed about it, without having to hit people over the head with it.

Simplicity can be a virtue, but it also can veer easily into the simplistic, and sometimes Koplowitz's work crosses that line. Unlike much postmodern choreography that begins with movement exploration, work that starts from a conceptual base can sacrifice innovative or inventive dance phrases to exposition. The urge to explain, to tell rather than show, can become more pronounced when the performers are not the age (or skill level, or physical ability) that we have come to expect from concert dance. "To My Anatomy," while it presents an unconventional age range of dancers, circumvents the potential pitfalls of explaining or justifying the dancers' presence by making their age differences the point of the piece, rather than the means to an end.

"There Were Three Men," which premiered in 1988, was Koplowitz's first collaboration with Stuart Hodes (b. 1924), who had been a soloist with Martha Graham in the 1950s. I met Hodes in 1992 at the Bates Dance Festival, where he was performing the piece, and he told me how thrilled he was to be dancing because, as he put it, "that part of my life was supposed to be over." Koplowitz told me that he was hesitant to approach Hodes, not because of his age, but because of his status as a prominent modern dancer, but the two went on to produce a number of pieces that challenged audiences to reassess the ways they imagined old age, masculinity, and sexuality. In "There Were Three Men," Hodes dances with two men in their thirties as they talk about what it means to be a man. Unlike "To My Anatomy," this piece leans on pedestrian loco-motion—running, walking, rolling—and gestural phrases, along with many unison movement sequences. While the older dancers in Lerman's work often perform different, gentler choreography from the younger performers, Hodes does the same phrases as the other dancers, from iron-ically executed ballet steps and ballroom partnering to fast-paced runs and turns. In a humorous section in which the men recount axioms about manhood delivered by their fathers, they mold each other into iconic stances as they declaim: "A man doesn't worry, a man decides. A man knows what to do and how to act. A man knows how to go places and what to do when he gets there." Assuming poses of boxing, saluting, and Superman-like strength, they take turns commenting on their state-ments through their movement. Watching this sequence, we hear echoes of some of the stories they have already told, especially of Hodes's nar-rative of flying fighter planes in World War II. This story of wartime combat could have been used to contain Hodes within a sentimental trope, as a member of "the greatest generation," distancing him from the other men, who speak about childrearing and coming out. However, Koplowitz instead utilizes Hodes's story to connect his experience to those of the other performers. Rather than exalting his service, Hodes compares his fear of death during the war to stage fright, and recounts his prayer before flying missions: "Please God, I've really only had one chance for fucking, and it's really important that I fuck some more, so please keep an eye out for me for the next few hours, okay?" In that one brief moment, Koplowitz violently undermines many of Halprin's myths about old age. If we expect that "Old people should be dignified and cir-cumspect, old people don't want to touch or use their bodies, old people aren't interested in sensual or sexual experiences, and old people like to sit and be quiet," then what are we to make of an old person who runs, jumps, and speaks of "fucking"?

Hodes and Koplowitz confronted these questions even more directly in "Dirty Old Man" (1995). More sophisticated in its choreographic and narrative structure than "To My Anatomy" or "There Were Three Men," "Dirty Old Man" uses a strategy of defamiliarization: Rather than letting us feel that we are overhearing conversations among people who could be our friends, the performers play stylized characters and seem to occupy a space within Hodes's imagination. The piece opens with Hodes's trying, and failing, to play "Happy Birthday" on the violin. As he walks an imaginary tightrope downstage, he is joined by a mysterious woman (Sarah Hook), who dances sinuously on a chair center stage in a dress from the flapper era. Hodes himself wears a dapper white suit, and their costumes evoke an indeterminate sense of time gone by. The fractured narrative of the piece careens from the present to multiple pasts to a hysterical science-fiction future, which also refers to the past. In a series of vignettes, Hodes and Hook perform "science-fiction dances" that invoke images from films such as *Alien* and Melies's *Voyage to the Moon*. Alluding to imagined filmic futures that lie far beyond either of their lifetimes, they note that although such movies do not contain scripted dance, "however far in the future you go, as long as there are people, they will dance." As in Koplowitz's other pieces, the performers speak, but in "Dirty Old Man" they offer up jarring, disjointed observations rather than self-contained stories, presenting an unsettling, nonlinear vision of the process of growing older.

A bitter humor pervades the piece and hardens moments that might otherwise become maudlin. Hodes talks about reading the obituaries and his fear of Alzheimer's disease: "Your soul dies, your body hangs on. If I ever find out I have Alzheimer's, I'll go find my friend Jack. Kevorkian." When Hook asks Hodes, "What's it like to be old?" he replies, "You really want me to tell you," and then he elaborates:

> When I was ten, I could chop the head off a chicken. I'd pull the axe out of a tree stump and chop its head off, watch the headless chicken run madly around the barnyard. I don't think I could do that now, I don't like to see things die…You know, I don't want to know any more theories about anything. I'm exasperated with egos, sick of sarcasm. I don't want to be unique! If I could only find one other person who liked to drink sauerkraut juice. I'm not interested in other people's secrets. I don't care who is sleeping with who. Deoxyribonucleic Acid. An acid with an urge to replicate itself. That's what life is all about. And what the hell is telephone sex?

The whole time he's delivering this increasingly urgent monologue, Hodes is trying desperately to keep Hook from falling to the floor. Completely passive, she has become the weight of aging, a fleshy, unwieldy manifestation of mortality.

Hook takes on several personae as a foil to Hodes's musings. At one point, she asks imperiously, "Has the jury reached a verdict?" When Hodes says that they have, she pronounces him "guilty of having LUST in your heart" while she beats him mercilessly around the head and shoulders. "Have you anything to say for yourself?" she demands. Cowed, hunched over in a defensive posture against her blows, Hodes pauses, and then offers the only defense he has: "A chicken is an egg's way of making another egg." This exchange leads them into a sensual, sexually charged tango, which builds toward a breathily orgasmic crescendo. Later, Hook takes Hodes's chin and firmly turns his gaze to a spot on the floor. "Fourteen years old," he remembers. "On the way to high school, a graffiti caught my eye." Hook chimes in, intoning quotation marks: "GIRLS FUCK." "I thought about it all day," Hodes continues. "I thought it was profound." Hook suddenly becomes a raging evangelical preacher, denouncing Hodes as a sinner, demanding that he look into his heart and find lust and lewdness—while simultaneously grabbing at his crotch and rubbing lasciviously against his body. These scenes between Hodes and Hook shock on a number of levels: Their audiences are not accustomed to seeing the elderly as both subjects and objects of lust. *New York Magazine* dance critic Tobi Tobias noted that Hook "treats Hodes with the spunky defiance women accord to the virile and deny the decrepit" (88). But what is so challenging—surprising, to many viewers—in "Dirty Old Man" is that Hodes is virile not in spite of his age, but because of it; his sexuality, like his humor, grows out of his years of experience. Koplowitz and Hodes make it clear that we should not mistake that experience for the stereotypical wisdom of the aged: After all, the best homily Hodes can offer is that "A person is DNA's way of making more DNA"—but that old age is an opportunity to integrate multiple, contradictory images and ideas that have accrued over a lifetime.[15]

Koplowitz seemed surprised when I asked him about the choice to deal so openly with sexuality in a piece that explicitly engages questions of aging: "I just think that's my view of sexuality. I don't think we ever stop being sexual beings. It's what makes us human." Nevertheless, in the context of societal conceptions of the elderly as asexual, this decision is radical for younger audiences—as is Koplowitz's commitment to presenting older people as fully rounded human beings, with vigor and infirmity, sexual desire and humor. One reviewer wrote of Koplowitz's use of nontraditional performers, "These people are nearly as interesting for who they are as for what they do. So even though Koplowitz announces a dance 'about relationships,' which seems like something to stay away from, he keeps his actions and insights specific—just the facts, ma'am. The meanings will take care of themselves" (Sandal 60). Specificity allows Koplowitz to venture into areas often outlined by stereotypical emotional displays or ideological posturing, without capitulating to clichés. This specificity also demarcates Koplowitz's work from Lerman's—much of the time, the performers in Lerman's dances stand for big ideas: communitarianism, faith, diversity. On the other hand, Koplowitz's dancers—whether older people, young adults, or children—represent themselves.

Koplowitz responded to my question about the possible limitations of working with older dancers with much the same attitude of bemused surprise as when I asked him about depictions of sexuality in "Dirty Old Man": "No, because you see, I really am a site-specific choreographer, and my work is people-specific, the work is based around what the performers can do and who they are."

There is one other example of concert dance performed by older adults that I will describe briefly, because it refutes both Lerman's and Koplowitz's approaches and offers a new, exciting, and potentially dangerous model. In 2000, Pina Bausch decided to restage her 1978 piece "Kontakthof" with a cast of "Ladies and Gentlemen Over 65," to quote both her newspaper ad seeking performers and the title of a 2002 documentary on the production by Lilos Mangelsdorff. Chosen from a group of 150 people who responded to the advertisement, the twenty-six participants in Bausch's experiment ranged in age from their sixties to their eighties and had never danced or acted professionally. *Damen und Herren ab 65 [Ladies and Gentlemen Over 65]* shows us scenes of auditions, rehearsals, and performances, all of which diverge dramatically from the processes and performances Lerman and Koplowitz undertake. The first incarnation of "Kontakthof" was performed by dancers within a more traditional age range, and Bausch does not significantly alter her original choreography to accommodate the older dancers; rather, she kindly but firmly expects them to find ways to inhabit her idiosyncratic, passionate movement style. The performers develop a variety of strategies for remembering long sequences and complex spatial patterns, coping with the emotional consequences of executing grueling dramatic scenes, and keeping pace during energetic unison phrases. In interviews for the film, the dancers speak about their nervousness and hesitation, and their astonishment at discovering that they could do the rigorous physical and psychological work being asked of them. It is impossible to gauge what kinds of discussions may have taken place off camera, but even in the most anxious interview subject there seems to be no indication of fear—fear of performing, of failing, of injury. It is impossible for me to imagine this kind of project taking place in the United States, where the myths Halprin describes hold such sway, and the fear of litigation would likely quell even the most avid desire to do such physically challenging work with nonprofessional populations, especially the elderly. I also suspect that the kind of state funding Bausch is able to receive in Germany is essential to developing and sustaining an effort of such length and complexity (the company trained for more than a year, and then took "Kontakthof" on a worldwide tour).

Not only would an endeavor like "Kontakthof" be difficult in the United States, but it also seems tied to a vision of dance and of aging that is particular to European Dance Theatre (*Tanztheater*).[16] However, Bausch's use of older dancers offers several possibilities for reassessing the presentation of the aging body on stage. Like work by Lerman and Koplowitz, "Kontakthof" generated a strong sense of common purpose and community among its participants. However, Bausch maintained complete choreographic authority, rather than working collaboratively with the performers to create movement phrases or textual material. The agency that the performers clearly felt within the creative process derived from the simple fact of hard work toward an artistic aim in which they had a stake: the same feelings that motivate dancers of all ages who perform choreography that is not their own. Older dancers, like their younger counterparts, can create and find meaning in movement through a group commitment to the artistic product of their work as well as through individual commitment to their own kinesthetic experiences or a feeling of ownership of movement sequences that they have helped develop. The collaborative model, embraced to differing degrees by Lerman and Koplowitz, is only one way of approaching work with younger, aged, and other nontraditional dancers.

Both Lerman and Koplowitz do work that they consider community-based, and both struggle to "negotiate professional standards with the rigorously democratic spirit of community art" (Cohen-Cruz, "Speaking" 214). Work done in nontraditional arenas, by and for nonprofessional artists, can be more easily read in terms of social and ethical value, but when choreographers utilize bodies that are older, or younger, or less trained, or differently abled from traditional professional dancers within a professional context, the frictions between artistic and social merit become intensified. Lerman dancer Celeste Miller offers one way of resolving this conflict, drawing a distinction between "community-informed and community-based art," acknowledging the "value of input from social workers, teachers, nurses, health care workers, administrators, electricians, mothers and others who work with me on projects. But there is a difference. I eat, breathe, sleep, die over this art stuff" (Cohen-Cruz, "Speaking" 214). Lerman herself argues for a "model of art planted in people's lives" (222), which in some ways resembles Isabel Marques's Freirean notion of context-based dance education. In "Dance Education in/and the Postmodern," Marques writes that "the student's context— the intersection of lived, perceived, and imagined realities—should be both the starting point and the continuation of what is to be understood, constructed, unveiled, transformed, problematized, and deconstructed in a transformative educational action" (181). However, Lerman's understanding of context is more idealistic than that of Marques: Lerman believes that "dance saves lives" (qtd. in Slaughter 32) and that her inclusion of dancers of multiple ages, races, religions, and sexual orientations can change the minds of audiences who watch them.

That idealism, while inspiring, may overestimate the potential for this type of work to engender social or political transformation. Inclusiveness is a good goal, and certainly one at which Lerman is more successful than most of her colleagues, but in and of itself it cannot bear the burden of inciting the kinds of social or political change that Lerman claims to seek. Instead, the kind of diversity Lerman's work often invokes can unintentionally reproduce dominant structures: The older people in her choreography may be portrayed in more positive terms than the elderly in the culture at large, but they remain isolated and circumscribed. Koplowitz's vital, humorous, angry, sexual, idiosyncratic depictions of older adults offer an alternative that is rooted in the individuality of his performers and gestures toward a diversity grounded in the real world, rather than in aspirations to an ideal one. "Art planted in people's lives" must look past facile celebrations of difference to elements in those lives that resist easy categorization and simple axioms. Community-based—and community-informed—dance must become truly context-based, interrogating power relationships and continually questioning our notions of diversity while at the same time opening dance's doors to the many bodies who have for so long been kept out.

Notes

1. Concert dance refers to theatrical or "art" dance presented in a public forum, as opposed to popular or social dance. Certain forms of social dance, such as salsa, can actually privilege older dancers because of their experience and expertise.
2. "Older" is a relative term; in the world of professional theatrical dance, dominated by dancers in their twenties and early thirties, forty is often considered "older," if not "old." Lerman's insistence that people can and should dance into their nineties and beyond was thus radical when she began her career, and still is today.
3. In 2006, Koplowitz was appointed as dean of the dance department at California Institute of the Arts.
4. In "The Myth of Authenticity," Gareth Griffiths examines notions of authenticity in relation to postcolonial literature and drama, but his warning is relevant for discussions of performances by other marginalized groups:

   There are real dangers in recent representations of indigenous peoples in popular discourse, and especially in the media, which stress claims to an "authentic" voice. For these claims, by overwriting the actual complexity of difference, may write out that voice as effectively as earlier oppressive discourses of reportage. In fact, it may be the same process at work, and the result may be just as crippling to the efforts of indigenous peoples to evolve an effective strategy of recuperation and resistance. (237)

5. Lerman's company is noted for large-scale projects that involve workshops and performances with community members, such as the multiyear, multicity Hallelujah Project that took place from 1998 through 2002. I touch on this project later in this chapter, but for the purposes of my inquiries into the presentation of aging and intergenerational performance, I focus on Lerman's concert work and her teaching methodology.

6. Lerman's father, who introduced his daughter to dance and insisted she see any and all the dance productions that came through their hometown of Milwaukee, went to college with Anna Halprin and did publicity work for her concerts (Lerman, "Dancing in Community" 2). Halprin wrote the introduction to Lerman's book *Teaching Dance to Senior Adults*; this biographical link further illuminates the thematic connections between their work.

7. This is a phrase that John Hodgson and Valerie Preston-Dunlop used to describe Rudolf Laban's beliefs about one of the purposes of community dance; see their book *Rudolf Laban: An Introduction to His Work and Influence*.

8. Laban Movement Analysis is a system for describing and interpreting movement that is associated with Labanotation, a symbolic system analogous to musical notation.

9. Lerman has developed a widely praised system for generating constructive feedback, her Critical Response Process. For more information, see www.danceexchange.org or http://www.communityarts.net/readingroom/archivefiles/2003/10/toward_a_proces.php.

10. It is worth noting that Lerman herself values technique, and in some of her intergenerational work seems to segregate dancers on the basis of their technical abilities as a corollary to their age groups. However, she clearly views technique as a means to an end, while in some contemporary concert dance virtuosity can be seen as an end in itself.

11. See Keller.

12. Although of course Graham herself danced well into old age, aging is a fiercely repressed undercurrent in her later performances rather than explicit content.

13. Zahra's feelings in many ways echo Susan Manning's description of taking part in one of Anna Halprin's outdoor movement rituals:

What did surprise me was the moment when I experienced the immutability of the form of the movement choir, a seemingly direct connection between its use in Nazi spectacle and in Earth dance... It was when the group gathered around the base of the tree and reached up to touch its bark that I pulled back, attempting to drag a friend along with me. The association with Nazi nature worship—all those groups of Hitler youth camping out together—seemed so direct that I couldn't remain a part of the event. I did later continue, mostly because in that moment of pulling back I had begun to meditate on exactly how mutable was the form of the movement choir. (Foster 173)

14. These pieces can in some ways be seen as an update of the movement choirs that Rudolf Laban and others undertook in Germany and central Europe in the 1910s through the 1930s. For additional information, see my essay "Mass Movement: Laban's Lay Movement Choirs."

15. See Erikson, *Identity and the Life Cycle*.

16. As its name implies, European Dance Theatre historically has emphasized theatrical values within a dance idiom, often focusing on characterization and (frequently nonlinear) narrative rather than movement for movement's sake.

Works Cited

Albright, Ann Cooper. *Choreographing Difference: The Body and Identity in Contemporary Dance*. Hanover, NH: Wesleyan UP/UP of New England, 1997.

Berson, Jessica. "Mass Movement: Laban's Lay Movement Choirs." *Community Performance: A Reader*. Ed. Petra Kuppers. London: Routledge, 2007.

Bodensteiner, Kirsten. "Input Leads to Output: Diverse and Exciting Collaborations from the Liz Lerman Troupe." *Washington Post* Jan. 22, 2001: C4.

Cohen-Cruz, Jan. *Local Acts: Community-based Performance in the United States*. New Brunswick, NJ: Rutgers UP, 2005.

———. "Motion of the Ocean: The Shifting Face of U.S. Theater for Social Change since the 1960s." *Theater* 31.3 (2001): 95–106.

———. "Speaking across Communities: The Liz Lerman Dance Exchange." *Performing Democracy: International Perspectives on Urban Community-Based Performance*. Ed. Susan C. Haedicke and Tobin Nellhaus. Ann Arbor: U of Michigan P, 2001. 213–26.

Croce, Arlene. "Discussing the Undiscussable." *The New Yorker* Dec. 26, 1994/ Jan. 2, 1995: 54–60.

Dance Exchange. <www.danceexchange.org>.

Dunning, Jennifer. "Digging up the Perfect Potato, and Other Joys." *New York Times* Aug. 22, 2002, sec. E: 5.

Erikson, Erik. *Identity and the Life Cycle*. 1959. New York: W.W. Norton, 1980.

Foster, Susan Leigh, Ed. *Choreographing History*. Bloomington: Indiana UP, 1995.

Griffiths, Gareth. "The Myth of Authenticity." *De-Scribing Empire: Post-Colonialism and Textuality*. Ed. Chris Tiffin and Alan Lawson. London: Routledge, 1994. 70–85.

Halprin, Anna. *Moving Towards Life: Five Decades of Transformational Dance.* Hanover, NH: Wesleyan UP/UP of New England, 1995.

Harding, Cathryn. "Liz Lerman: Seeking a Wider Spectrum." *Dance Magazine* 70.1 (Jan. 1996): 78–81.

Hodes, Stuart. Personal communication with the author. Bates Dance Festival, 1992.

Hodgson, John, and Valerie Preston-Dunlop. *Rudolf Laban: An Introduction to His Work and Influence.* Plymouth: Northcote House, 1990.

Keller, Evelyn Fox: *A Feeling for the Organism: The Life and Work of Barbara McClintock.* New York: W.H. Freeman, 1983.

Koplowitz, Stephan. Interview by author. Apr. 18, 2005.

———. "There Were Three Men." Videocassette. Stephan Koplowitz and Company. Recorded at Dance Theatre Workshop, New York City, 1995.

———. 'To My Anatomy." Stephan Koplowitz and Company. Recorded at Dance Theatre Workshop, New York City, 1988.

Koplowitz, Stephan, and Stuart Hodes. "Dirty Old Man." Videocassette. Recorded at Dance Theatre Workshop, New York City, 1995.

Lerman, Liz. "Dancing in Community: Its Roots in Art." Sept. 2002. <http://www.communityarts.net/readingroom/archivefiles/2002/09/dancing_in_comm.php>.

———. *Liz Lerman and the Senior Citizens.* Videocassette. Recorded in Lee, MA, July 25, 1986.

———. "Still Crossing" (1994). Videocassette. Videotaped in performance at the Cowell Theater at Fort Mason, San Francisco, 1994.

———. *Teaching Dance to Senior Adults.* Springfield, IL: Charles C. Thomas, 1984.

———. "This Is Who We Are" (1993). *Liz Lerman Dance Exchange at Bates Dance Festival.* Videocassette. Bates Dance Festival, 1996.

Liz Lerman Dance Exchange Press Packet. Liz Lerman Dance Exchange, 2004.

Mangelsdorff, Lilos, dir. *Damen und Herren ab 65* [Ladies and Gentlemen over 65]. Film. 2004. Screened at 2004 Dance on Camera Festival, Walter Reade Theatre, Lincoln Center, New York City.

Manning, Susan. "Modern Dance in the Third Reich: Six Positions and a Coda." *Choreographing History.* Ed. Susan Leigh Foster. Bloomington: Indiana UP, 1995. 165–76.

Marques, Isabel A. "Dance Education in/and the Postmodern." *Dance, Power, and Difference: Critical and Feminist Perspectives on Dance Education.* Ed. Sherry B. Shapiro. Champaign, IL: Human Kinetics Publishers, 1998. 171–86.

McCleod, Heather. "Community in Motion: An Interview with Liz Lerman." *Who Cares* (Spring 1996): 18–21.

Patrick, K.C. "Aging In and Out." *Dance Teacher Now* 12.5 (June 1990): 25–29.

Perlstein, Susan. "Arts and Creative Aging across America." Sept. 2002. <http://www.communityarts.net/readingroom/archivefiles/2002/10/arts_and_creati.php>.

Phelan, Peggy. *Unmarked: The Politics of Performance.* London: Routledge, 1993.

Sandal, Robert. "Narrative Thrust." *Dance Magazine* 61.11 (Nov. 1989): 60.

Segal, Lewis. "Lerman's Ambitious 'Hallelujah' Lost in L. A.: The Local Chapter in this Multidisciplinary Epic Overlooks Key Communities." *Los Angeles Times* Feb. 12, 2001, sec. F: 3.

Slaughter, Lynn. "It's Never Too Late: Liz Lerman Brings Dance to the Third Age." *Dance Teacher Now* 12.5 (June 1990): 31–34.

Sommers, Pamela. "Lerman; Stepping Out for 20 Years." *Washington Post* June 13, 1997, sec. N: 36.

Tomalonis, Alexandra. "Liz Lerman Dance Exchange." *Dance Magazine* Oct. 1995: 62.

Traiger, Lisa. *Making Dance that Matters: Dancer, Choreographer, Community Organizer, Public Intellectual Liz Lerman*. MFA Thesis, University of Maryland, College Park, 2004.

Young, Iris Marion. "The Ideal of Community and the Politics of Difference." *Feminism/Postmodernism*. Ed. Linda J. Nicholson. New York: Routledge, 1990. 300–23.

Zahra, Tara. "Lerman's Lockstep Healing: Disempowered at the Power Center." *The Dance Insider* Oct. 2001. <http://www.danceinsider.com/f2001/f1016_1.html>.

CHAPTER 9

AGE AND THE DANCE ARTIST

Barbara Dickinson

For performing artists in many Western dance forms, the deepening and maturing of artistry are eventually and inevitably tied to a decline in physical capabilities. Once performers pass their physical prime, de facto retirement from the stage almost always follows. What is the potential for mature artists to make important contributions as performers when they are beyond their physical prime? What cultural forces, attitudes, and other factors inhibit a decision to continue? What is the nature of virtuosity in the dance practice of mature artists? Do they possess attributes that younger performers have not yet acquired? Interviews, performance analyses, and readings on aging and ageism are the tools used to ponder these questions. In this chapter, a mature dancer is defined, somewhat arbitrarily, as one who is forty-five years or older, because few would disagree that at that age, athletic virtuosity is on the decline. The artists referenced in this chapter are regarded as outstanding in their genre. Only the Euro-American forms of modern dance and ballet as practiced in North America have been examined. Those interviewed include Tyler Walters and Julie Janus Walters, former principal dancers with the Joffrey Ballet of Chicago; Risa Steinberg, formerly with the José Limón Dance Company and an internationally known solo artist; Sara Rudner, considered one of the greatest of Twyla Tharp's dancers and the director of the Sara Rudner Performance Ensemble; David Dorfman, an internationally known dancer and choreographer and the artistic director of David Dorfman Dance; Irene Dowd, a choreographer and expert in neuromuscular training and kinesthetic anatomy; and Liz Lerman, the recipient of a MacArthur "Genius Grant" Fellowship and founding artistic director of Liz Lerman Dance Exchange, a multigenerational ensemble that is a leading force in contemporary dance.

A key question facing older performers is what they have to offer an audience when their dance athleticism has waned. The descriptor "virtu-oso," when applied to younger dancers, is linked inextricably with their physical prowess. However, when considering the nature of virtuosity in older dancers, one must ask what qualities these artists possess now that were not present in their younger selves. Risa Steinberg went straight to this core issue: "I'm no longer just an implement to be physical. I'm much more." For Sara Rudner, "You become a little bit more efficient and spe-cific and articulate. Your goals are clearer." All spoke about a maturity that comes with living life, which in turn feeds what they bring to the stage. Tyler Walters commented, "When you do a role over and over, you're always looking for something more to bring to it. You have to retrace your approach to it, and when you do that, you question the way you [performed] it [in the past].... Am I going to do that the same? What other experience do I now have to draw on?" Risa Steinberg echoed that response in a different conversation: "If we're talking about a dramatic role, the work [of preparation now] would be in having to make choices because there are so many different ways of doing something." Julie Janus Walters talked about the importance of more experienced artists serving as role models for younger dancers: "It's hard to train [younger dancers] when they don't have older dancers to learn from. You'll [find some] youthful companies don't have much depth in their artistry [because of that lack]." These artists are speaking about what fills the technical shell of the movement. A competent dancer rehearses the dance steps until she or he can perform them very well, but that is just the most basic level of preparation for performance.

What must follow is the development of an expressivity and an intent that fill the choreographed movement. For these artists, experiences over a long period of time filter into their art and nourish their ability to com-municate deeply through gesture and movement. Tyler Walters spoke of

> [p]ower, potency. The power of a gesture is related to the ability of the audience to see the internal force that's driving that [gesture]. The clarity of movement, the focus of movement, makes the audience see the force.

He noted that some writers are called virtuosic because they are able to use language in a way that communicates very powerfully. In the same way, he argued, dancers could be defined as virtuosic, not for their ath-letic technical achievements marked by high extensions or phenomenal jumps and turns, but for the impact of their movement. Does it pack an emotional punch? Is there a focused concentration in the mover that draws the observer into the moment?

An important element of potency is the achievement of a sense of immediacy in performance, an illusion of spontaneity—that one is performing the movement for the first time. However, except for improvisatory performance, choreography is usually set in time and space. Performance therefore requires a two-sided consciousness. On the one hand, the dancer is aware of and monitors what comes next (e.g., "I must remember to drop my weight fully here in preparation for the next step"). On the other hand, the dancer's performance must be completely submerged in the immediate moment of movement and image. Ruth Currier, performing legend of the José Limón Dance Company, provided a vivid example of potency during a class in her studio in the 1980s. She became annoyed that her twenty-something-year-old students (myself among them) were not performing a phrase as it should be done. Currier, who was then in her late fifties, proceeded to demonstrate the phrase in full performance mode. I thought, "Oh my God, we all need to sit down and just watch this woman dance." Her performance potency could be likened to a hatch opening somewhere in her core and a blinding light streaming out of her body. Achieving such potency is one of the more esoteric, even mystical, aspects of performance. When two dancers execute the same movements accurately and with exemplary technical skill, why is it that one draws the viewers' focus and the other does not? It has to do with what the dancer brings to the movement beyond the movement itself. Although difficult to describe, the resultant power is abundantly clear to viewers, as it was to the students watching Currier dance in class. In that small amount of time, Currier dove into the now,[1] buoyed by her immense experience, technique, and artistry.

Tyler Walters and I have been team-teaching a course at Duke University entitled "Beyond Technique: The Art of Performance," a course that includes a studio laboratory component as well as readings, discussion, and video analysis. We have found that our college-age dancers, some of them at a professional level of technical proficiency, equate dancing in the moment with the adrenaline rush of performing. They speak about performance as a time when they feel most alive. But this is an awareness of performance that involves only personal feelings. They do not yet understand the act of performance as a moment-to-moment creation of the images that lie behind the movement.

The students' performances may someday reach the potency of a work such as *Short Story*, a concentrated vignette of a long-term, personal relationship between a man and a woman, choreographed by Doug Varone. A 2002 video captures the performance by Varone and Nina Watt, then ages forty-six and fifty-one, respectively. Even in the video format, so inadequate to convey the power of a live performance, the dancing was very finely nuanced, powerful, and concentrated. Movement transitions were exquisitely crafted, shaped by the continuous thread of the emotional journey these two were taking. The smallest gesture resonated throughout the entire body, just as emotions resonate and can be sensed by an observer in daily life, even though there is no overt movement involved. Every change of direction, of movement texture, and of effort, no matter how subtle, was infused with the undercurrents of this couple's relationship. It was breathtaking. It was not an athletic tour de force, but a physical tour de force; these dancers had mastered the integration of the nuanced emotional intent in movement with its physical manifestation.

Eric Bruhn,[2] legendary twentieth-century interpreter of many seminal male roles in classical ballet, said that dancers are trained to learn the technique and the steps of a role, and perhaps to copy the way it was done by artists before them, but no real communication is possible until the dancer knows why she or he is doing the role (17). Moreover, communication is not possible until the dancer creates an idea that gives the physical work of the role a reason and a purpose (37). He spoke about playing the character of James, a man in his late teens or early twenties, the principal male role in the French Romantic ballet, La Sylphide. Bruhn said that when he was the same age as James, he could only be himself, and this limited what he could bring to the role. When he was more mature, he had more imagination about what a young man would do, which in turn brought a greater youth and vitality to his characterization of James (17). Bruhn believed younger dancers "tend to want to be busy with...steps and jumps and leaps and gestures...." Only later, he said, do you understand that you were busy with too much (41). The thrill of physicality does not always convey the subtleties of character.

Not all dances are narratively themed or driven by emotion; nevertheless, all movement has intent—of effort, direction, flow and speed, and attitude. For example, if a movement phrase requires that the dancer reach into space with a strong thrust, the internal motivation must feed the physical action. The dancer must be aware of the lines of energy flowing beyond the parameters of the physical body. A great deal of the artistry of a dancer lies in achieving the ability to integrate the intent with the physical manifestation of it. Otherwise, only a physical shell of the movement will exist. Eric Bruhn was forty when he spoke about being "infinitely more interested and more curious about the abstraction of all art" at that stage of his career (35). Although a common view is that abstract ballet is a matter of mere exercise, he believed strongly that "within that moving body there has to be a mind, and that mind expresses and guides the movement" (29).

Sara Rudner also touched on this indirectly when she spoke about having "a much different relationship [now] to the idea of what movement manipulation does. What reordering a sentence does, for instance. Reordering a phrase. What's the goal in this phrase? And it usually is a kind of statement about effort, about relationship, about the state of our society." I believe she is speaking about the tendency of those with age and experience to use a larger frame of reference, and to be sensitive to the massive changes of emphasis and focus that can occur with something as seemingly innocuous as reordering a movement phrase.

Given the hard-won artistry of older dancers, why do so few (almost no) mature artists continue performing? There are undoubtedly powerful reasons for ending a performing career—physical fatigue, injury, weariness of the fight, desire for a family, a transition to choreography as the only focus, financial needs, and marketing forces. It also is understandable that dancers do not want to perform work that casts them as weaker, more limited versions of their younger physical selves. In the current climate, all of these reasons at the very least change the nature of artists' involvement in dancing and often end it. Why do they not attempt to "retool" and develop a new performing language that may be somewhat different, but equally as rich as their former language? Are there other forces that play a part in these transitions? Perhaps if it were normal for performers to continue in other performance venues, if choreographers created work for dancers of all ages as a matter of course, if dancers could dance less than younger dancers in their physical prime and still be judged as high-level professional artists, then dancers over forty-five would not disappear so regularly from the stage. What aspects of ageism, so prevalent in every part of American life, do these questions reveal? These questions foreground the age ideology of our culture.

In *Aged by Culture*, Margaret Gullette writes,

> The meanings of age and aging are conveyed in large part through the moral and psychological implications of the narrative ideas we have been inserting into our heads, starting when we were very young.... Certainly, whichever accounts you and I find ourselves living with and seeing the world through make a fundamental difference to the quality of our lives, starting with our willingness or reluctance, at any age, to grow older. (11)

Aging narratives influence how we view the journey of our spent life. Gullette says we have been conditioned to give weight primarily to negative differences, when in fact there are many ways we have improved, and other ways in which we are very like our younger selves (6). Our hypervisual culture places unwarranted value on appearance and presentation. As the years pass and we of necessity no longer look young, we are judged as being less than we were before. This conclusion ignores that the aging process continuously enriches our inner life with a growing library of memories and experiences (10). Appearance is a mere frame to the real self-portrait. Unfortunately, the metaphor of decline "tends to stain our experiences, our views of others, our explanatory systems, and then our retrospective judgments" (11).

Consider the role of the mirror in a dancer's career. The mirror is present in almost every studio the dancer enters throughout his or her dancing life. It is used to refine and clarify positions and lines of the body, to provide instant evidence of who possesses the highest leg extension or best balance in class, and to reflect every physical change in the body. The mirror can become the virtual true image, the arbiter of perfection. As dancers age, the mirror reflects the specter of physical decline as a messenger of decline in career and artistry. Indeed, because the art of dance integrates one's emotional, spiritual, and physical selves, then exhibits them through the physical vessel, it seems an almost insurmountable task in an ageist society to create a narrative of progress (one in which age equals improvement) when dealing with the aging physicality of the dancer, yet that is what this chapter ultimately will contend can—and should—happen.

Tyler Walters, speaking about aspects of his personal narrative, said, "When people go into dance there's a whole mind-set. You know you're only going to dance until you're thirty-five or forty, or if you're lucky, forty-five. You set yourself up with that in mind." Julie Janus Walters added, "It's even more ingrained for a female.... It's a hard narrative to buck. Even Mr. Joffrey wasn't hiring any females over thirty." Yet the repertory of the Joffrey Ballet required dancers capable of giving nuanced, dramatic performances, found most readily in dancers with some maturity. Both quotations emphasize an assumption that a successful dancer must live dance, and breathe it, and eat it, until the body wears out, and then one must stop.

In order to change this firmly established, preexisting narrative for dancers, this assumption must be examined. Although older dancers cannot continue the athletic pace of their youth, their art has become more distilled. Perhaps it might be seen less frequently, but it still can be experienced intensely. Another element in the mix is nostalgia. Gullette states that age anxiety is one negative result of our age ideology. Another is what she calls the "speed-up of the life course," a feeling that time is scarce (29). Speed-up joined with the decline narrative encourages regret (31). The older performer compares himself or herself to the younger performer. What the dancer used to be able to do physically and is no longer able to do is inevitably viewed as decline. When I asked Sara Rudner about watching her younger dancing self, she said:

> In my forties I had to spend time divorcing myself—not from who I was and what the dancing was—but I had to go back and recognize what I had done, and try to understand what that was and how that is still in me. I did that through the help of some of my students who wanted to look at those old tapes. I said, "I'm not looking at any of that stuff!" But [when I did] I was able to appreciate myself, but not feel that I had to do that anymore.

Too often, older dancers stop at the point of recognizing their physical decline and judge it as the end of their potential for contributing as a performer. Unlike Rudner, they fail to pursue those gifts that are not defined by their peak physical abilities.

The separation from the younger self becomes more complex when one's physical approach to movement becomes one of the building blocks of a style of dance; in Rudner's case, her personal movement style had contributed to the physical embodiment of Twyla Tharp's style. Rudner said, "Part of the exercise [of viewing old tapes] was trying to separate my identity from Twyla's identity. I'd been so linked to that style and that performance manner." After she left the company, Rudner was able to define performance and choreographic values that were specifically hers and very different from Tharp's. For example, Rudner wanted to create work that was presented in venues other than traditional theatres. She had questions about what was age appropriate in performance. Also, for Rudner, as for many dancers, stages of life demanded new ways of being in performance: She developed arthritis. At the age of fifty, Rudner had a hip replacement. She said that exploring how to work with this change and retool became a creative revelation, which kept her very interested choreographically. When she performed again, the work involved a high element of improvisation. Rudner sums up her attitude:

> I've seen the world through this medium for sixty-two years, through movement and through having an appetite for it. And I can't imagine [stopping]. When I stop, I hurt. I have sciatic pain, I get crotchety, I'm probably a pill to be around. So…the discipline serves a life purpose. And every once in a while, the door will open, and I'll do it publicly.

Rudner found richness in new methods of choreography and performance that were true to what she always valued, yet very different from her accomplishments as a dancer in Twyla Tharp's company. She successfully avoided nostalgia because she was not trying to hold on to what she used to do.

Nostalgia also plays out through the audience members who have watched an artist over time. They hold the memory of the dancer at a younger age in his or her physical prime. How can a mental comparison of decline be avoided, especially when a dancer, such as Mikhail Baryshnikov, is known for incredible physical virtuosity? When Baryshnikov, often considered the finest male ballet dancer of his generation, was forty-two and suffering from chronic injuries that limited his physical performance, he collaborated with modern dance choreographer Mark Morris on the formation of the White Oak Project, a small touring group made up of some of the best veterans of American dance. White Oak enabled Baryshnikov to present his artistry in very different kinds of roles by a range of contemporary choreographers (Reynolds and McCormick 632, 838). When performers such as Baryshnikov continue to perform, thereby demonstrating the skills of age rather than skills of extreme physicality, audiences are given much-needed encouragement to expand their appreciation of extraordinary artistry. Because the performer is greatly acclaimed, the audience can feel confident that the dancing they see is valuable and of the highest caliber. They may be more willing to pay closer attention to the power of subtle, less explosive movement. They may begin to understand the deeper levels of messaging that dance can serve.

Risa Steinberg talked about the difficulty of finding someone to create for her now. "It's a special thing I want. It has to be so much more than what I wanted when I was younger. [The choreography] has to be so three-dimensional. I'm lucky my body is still so facile and I can jump, but I don't want that to be my only resource of communication." Just as a dancer must bring more to the choreography than well-executed steps, a mature dancer seeks choreography that will demand a deep investigation of the content in order to fully realize a role. Steinberg continued, "Last year Alan Danielson did a remarkable piece for me that [did] everything I wanted it to do. It was physical, emotional, poignant, fun. When a work allows me to fulfill all those things, then I'm not nostalgic for anything because I'm not missing anything. I'm only nostalgic for it when it's not in my life." For Steinberg, performance is a way to touch and use "all those sides" of her, all parts of her personality and humanity—in essence, to keep all parts of her alive. The Danielson piece allowed her to fulfill the gifts she has as a performer, which at her age go far beyond the achievement of movements performed in a technically proficient manner.

David Dorfman believes that the field of dance needs more people who are envisioning performances for older dancers. For example, he asks, "Can you incorporate choreography for older dancers within a signal choreographer company or a mixed program? The more people are seen in those roles, the more we will see that it's a wonderful thing." Now entering his sixth decade, Dorfman is able to create roles for himself because he is artistic director of his own company. Such choreography does not typically extend to other members of the company as they age (except perhaps for a dancing partner) or to older dancers who might wish to join the company as new members. The circular logic become exclusionary: the narratives of the members of such a company rarely embrace the idea of continuing dancing beyond the late thirties or early forties; as a result, the artistic director is seldom or never asked to consider making work that would allow his company members to continue performing past their physical prime. Moreover, what professional dancers over forty-five would assume they have any chance at all of becoming new members in the Paul Taylor Dance Company, or the José Limón Dance Company, or the New York City Ballet, or the hundred other companies one might name? Julie Janus Walters believes there is a niche that could very easily be developed for artists passing through the later stages of their careers. Dancers must "become more varied and sophisticated in how we think of our involvement in dance [onstage]. Proportions of life activities may change [as we age], but [we should] allow performance to be one of those expectations."

Aged dancers cannot deny that medically recognized, involuntary physical decline is a fact of aging. We lose muscle tissue and fast-twitch muscle fibers, aerobic power and endurance, and explosive muscle power, and the speed spectrum decreases. We sag all over; a life spent under the force of gravity takes its toll. Even so, researchers on aging are finding it extremely difficult to determine which changes are due to the physical progress of age and which are due to environmental and cultural factors. Experimental psychologists and physiological anthropologists track many physiological declines of aging, but they constantly qualify their statistics by cautioning that the results may owe as much to socioculturally influenced lifestyle patterns as to aging itself (Charness).[3] As early as 1965, G.A. Talland, in *Behavior, Aging, and the Nervous System*, wrote, "Are our aged masters freaks of nature, paragons of self-discipline, or do they but demonstrate the inadequacy of our present notions about the effects of age on human capacities?" (558). Yes, physical decline is inescapable. However, surely dance is so much more than movement performed during the years of peak physical capacity, so much more than virtuoso athleticism.

When athleticism declines, should performers retire? The audience/performer and choreographer/performer relationships play key roles in answering this question. Irene Dowd cautioned that as an older dancer,

> [e]ven with a limited palette you can be a fine artist, but you are limited. You say, "Well, I don't have that, but I have all these other things." Maybe the choreographer isn't interested in all those other things. The limits are imposed, not chosen.

The system of supply and demand in the dance world permeates, even contaminates, methods of dance training, marketing, audience development and therefore audience expectations, sponsor programming, the design of arts series, and the ways in which choreographers and artistic directors envision the nature of companies and choreography. The existing system influences to a great degree why the choreographer "isn't interested in all those other things" the mature dancer has to offer.

In terms of audience response, Dowd said,

> The audience can't help but see that our bodies are older, more fragile, literally closer to death. This reality lends poignancy to the performance event. Sometimes it is too poignant for the audience to bear; people don't want to be reminded of their mortality. As long as this culture is so "anti-death," we're going to have this reticence to seeing older dancers.

Until older dancers are frequently seen performing, this reticence will be difficult to overcome. The limited number of dance pieces written specifically to foreground aged dancers' strengths combines with audiences' reticence to view the aged performer, creating an artistic milieu in which aged dancers have few performance options. One way to increase those options is for audiences to become accustomed to seeing mature artists such as Baryshnikov, who have recognition as being first rate.

According to Risa Steinberg,

> The saddest thing about getting older in this field is that for some reason...if you don't do something as well...it's because of your age versus because you're having a bad day. "Oh she can't do it because it's an age thing." And when that starts entering into the thinking, it's very bizarre. "Oh my God, you're still doing it!" That phrase gives you a lot of information! "How much longer do you think [you'll perform]?" These are very pointed questions about one's age. Even though you don't think about it, you're very aware that other people...are [thinking about it]. It's hard to unravel the knitting of what came first, and then how it's affecting you.

As a dancer ages, there is a presumption of decline that is based on a societal model of quality that is completely invested in physical virtuosity.

As the artist moves away from using athletic virtuosity as the primary tool of performance and relies more heavily on other aspects of artistry, the audience is programmed to see that as decline, not as maturation and transformation.

David Dorfman talked about his preemptive age comments. "I find I'm saying [things] when I don't really mean it or need to, like, 'Oh, I'm still getting around.'...If you say it first before someone else says it, then you don't have to wait for that moment of, 'Are you still dancing?' I do get that a bunch. It's said in a neutral manner, but still it's a loaded question. They wouldn't be asking it if they didn't think that either the way I look or my presumed age is out of the realm." Such comments make an artist self-conscious and concerned, so much so that it is common to have a "designated driver," one who promises to tell the artist honestly when he or she has "had too much" and should stop performing. Yet the "should" is usually because she or he cannot jump as high or move as fast—the very reasons for stopping that need to be reexamined by artists, audiences, and booking agents alike.

American attitudes toward the arts complicate these issues even further. As Irene Dowd said, "Our culture doesn't support anything with the arts and certainly not dance....I don't think the opportunities are there even when [dancers] are young, [and] at [the] age where they're so fantastic they can do anything and [they] are all potential. I don't think it's a case of ageism. It's [just] really tough out there." Nevertheless, Liz Lerman, a choreographer who has been committed all her creative life to including older dancers as performers, finds that the mix of ages in her company is one of the attractions of her performances. She believes the resistance to older performers is coming from the part of the dance world that is defined by downtown New York. "It weights our sense of standards and what's working in the world....Whereas if you take all the rest of the United States...they don't necessarily buy any of that. They're thrilled to see the old people; thrilled. I can't tell you how many people have said to me, 'Now I see what I've been missing.' 'Oh, of course dance can mean this.'" The simple act of valuing the expression of dancers of all ages and of including them in performance seems to be one of the most important strategies for changing existing narratives of what dance is and who should do it. Liz Lerman is recognized as an outstanding choreographer and artist. She feels an older performer has value, and her audiences accept that belief.

Factors beyond a lack of opportunity, such as the practicalities of time, energy, and health, also inhibit a choice to continue dancing. Dowd gave an example of a young choreographer who spent two years of her life getting permission to use a public space as a venue for her performance. A dancer of fifty and a dancer of twenty-five might view very differently a project that would take two years to mount.

There is a message—sometimes clearly stated, sometimes unspoken—
that older dancers should gracefully vacate the stage and make way for the
young ones. The young dancer must be nurtured and celebrated; David
Dorfman eloquently described the rewards of doing that:

> I believe that giving [my] phrases to [dancers] who [are] younger, more
> traditionally [and] technically trained, connected to their bodies, [con-
> nected] to [the] subject material, grounded, gifted, explosive—that could
> and should be an incredible experience equal to me doing it, and perhaps
> beyond, because they have a different imagination, or their body can just
> do more than mine can.

However, nurturing younger dancers should not preclude doing the same
for older dancers who have so much to contribute, onstage as well as off.
Just as art reflects life, dance should investigate, illuminate, and com-
municate issues for all ages through all ages. Eric Bruhn made the argu-
ment that a dancer of maturity can present a more complete, complex
characterization of youth as long as he or she is able to move with the
physicality of a young person. Is the reverse possible? A colleague of mine
in her mid-fifties spoke of her delight in seeing performances by young
dancers in their twenties and thirties. "But," she asked, "who will speak
for me?" The implication was that younger performers could not comprehend, and therefore could not artistically perform, the inner life of a
fifty-year-old. She could not look to them for a reflection of herself and
her experiences.

Gullette states that practitioners in age studies work "with the knowledge that the systems producing age and aging could be different—and
that if they were, our experiences of the life course would be too" (102).
Most of the artists with whom I spoke agreed that if mature performers
were provided with systems that naturally included the option of continuing to perform, more would choose that option. Considering the age
biases in dance and in society, wholesale changes will have to be made
in the age narratives of choreographers, companies, audiences, and the
dancers themselves.

Older performers need to create new meanings by creating new stories
of their dancing lives. At present, the only sure way for artists to continue
dancing is if they create their own opportunities. Peggy Lawler,[4] fac-
ulty member and architect of the dance program at Cornell University,
choreographed a concert of solo work to celebrate reaching the age of
fifty. She packed up her costumes and sets and began a six-month car
trip traveling the country. When she arrived at a town, she would make
inquiries as to where she might perform—an assembly hall, an empty

room, perhaps even a stage—and then put up flyers announcing her free concert. She said that many places had not seen a modern dance concert, and definitely not a woman of fifty performing concert dance. Her audiences numbered from three in some towns to fifty or more in others. By means of this tour she defined her own age narrative of dance performance. Who can say what effect she had on the age narratives of those in her audiences.

Sara Rudner brought forward an important element in the logistics of performance by mature artists—that of context. She loved viewing older performers, but she felt the context had to be very clear. What were they doing, what was their choice of movement, with whom were they dancing? For example, she found it very disturbing to watch Merce Cunningham perform with his much younger company because she wanted to focus completely on him.

> If you had seen Merce in a gallery, just doing what he did on stage, it would have been unique, so special....[A]s we get older we bear even closer scrutiny. The closer we are to the audience in performance the better, because of the detail work and because of the subtlety of expression and communication that can happen. That's what I mean by context. And there's no reason why we shouldn't see these performances....That's where we are so unsophisticated. We are...caught in our American paradigm of entertainment.

Liz Lerman agreed, "Context is everything, and if you can control the context—through program notes, through discussion, through the titling, through the costuming, how we structure the events that will be around [the performance]—you can have the audience come with you on just about anything." One contextual element for Lerman was the recognition of age onstage. "Even in the early years [the 1970s], I used to tell the old people, 'Don't dye your hair....I want the audience to know you're old so that the fact that you're old builds the fabric of the life we're trying to place on stage.'"[5] Although the commercial culture and the celebrity culture exert enormous pressure for bodies to look and be a certain way, Lerman believes that the old people in her dance company can contribute to easing that pressure.

David Dorfman commented on the context of his age relationship with the other members of his company. He started a company with a group of slightly younger peers, but the age distance from his subsequent company members has increased with each change:

> It's not unnatural that the division between what I can do and what they can do is farther, even though I feel I'm still performing strongly on stage.

I'm really happy to share a stage with my company but it would be [in]
more of a character [role]. I just wouldn't be right with them [dancing] in
unison.

Unison movement for a group composed of many dancers under
thirty-five and one dancer over fifty would not reinforce a narrative that
affirms that all ages have something to contribute as dancers. Such a
unison group would only highlight the comparison of athletic physical capacities. Dorfman's choreography for himself versus for his young
company is very different. He spoke about there being little opportunity
in dance to "see someone show the 'chops' that we get by being around
so long." Dorfman seems to agree with Rudner that intimate settings for
older performers are necessary to reveal the richness of their artistry. Too
often, he said, success is based on large houses featuring large companies
in large productions. Intimate performances with small audiences do not
fulfill the criteria for success, so heavily defined by the market.

Perhaps the aging of the baby boomers will help in creating more
options for performances by mature artists. Liz Lerman believes, "[B]
oomers are always going to be about boomers. And as they get older,
they are not going to want to watch young people; they're going to
want to see themselves. Now they may want to see themselves as young,
which has proven to be true, but they want to see themselves....If
they're not up there [onstage], they're not going to come. I believe that."
There is another bright spot: Lerman says she is always looking for older
dancers.

Until mature dance artists appear frequently onstage, or perhaps until
the majority of viewers are of the age of the current boomer population,
most audiences will never be able to accept these artists as a normal and
welcome presence. The "fabric of the life...on stage" (Lerman) should
be much more complete. Just as one might look to an elder statesman for
a comprehensive perspective on current social issues, an audience member might look to an older dancer for knowledge about the physical and
emotional potency that can exist in the latter part of life. When the vitality of youth is no longer the uppermost quality, resilience and knowledge
and experience come to the fore, each quality being revealed onstage
through movement and gesture. A dance performance can illustrate how
experience can resonate expressively and subtly through the body of a
fifty-year-old or a sixty-year-old or onward through the decades of life.
Only then will viewers expand their understanding of the concepts of
beauty and physicality in performance, train their eyes to see in more
sophisticated ways, and ultimately be challenged by a progressive narrative of aging as the accumulation of experience and wisdom.

Notes

1. A performer must dance a "dance that knows dance can be, should be, and is a way of saying now" (Woodworth 15).
2. This chapter focuses on Euro-American dance forms and dancers. Eric Bruhn was born in Copenhagen and was trained by the Royal Danish Ballet. Nevertheless, he spent protracted periods guesting for American Ballet Theater as well as appearing with the New York City Ballet and Harkness Ballet. I believe his comments to be pertinent to the dance culture here in America.
3. See Chapters 7 and 9 in *Aging and Human Performance* for acknowledgement of the complexities of separating the physiological declines of aging from those caused by environmental and cultural factors.
4. Peggy Lawler (1929–1996) was professor emeritus of dance at Cornell University, Ithaca, NY. Under her leadership, dance at Cornell developed from an extracurricular activity to an academic major. For a biography, see <http://www.news.cornell.edu/Chronicle/96/12.12.96/obits.html>.
5. Interestingly, Lerman had to make another choice. "In the very beginning...I also had heavy people-very important to me. And I realized that...the audience could handle only so much difference. If I wanted to allow audiences to receive the older people, then I needed the rest of the cast to, quote, look like dancers, unquote."

Works Cited

Bruhn, Eric. "Beyond Technique." *Dance Perspectives* 36 (Winter 1968): 3–73.

Career Transition for Dancers. The Caroline & Theodore Newhouse Center for Dancers. Sept. 18, 2007. <http://www.careertransition.org>.

Charness, Neil, ed. *Aging and Human Performance*. Chichester, NY: Wiley, 1985.

Dorfman, David. Personal interview. Oct. 2–3, 2005.

Dowd, Irene. Personal interview. Sept. 29, 2005.

Gullette, Margaret Morganroth. *Aged by Culture*. Chicago: U of Chicago P, 2004.

Lerman, Liz. Personal Interview. Sept. 7, 2006.

Limón Dance Company. Videotaped in performance at the Joyce Theater, New York, NY, on Nov. 24, 2001 (matinee). Vid. Evann E. Siebens and Jonathon Beck. Ed. Mathieu Aleksandr Borysevicz. Videocassette. Limón Dance Company, the Joyce Theater Foundation, and Jerome Robbins Archive of the Recorded Moving Image, Dance Division, The New York Public Library for the Performing Arts, 2002.

Reynolds, Nancy, and Malcolm McCormick. *No Fixed Points: Dance in the Twentieth Century*. New Haven, CT: Yale UP, 2003.

Rudner, Sara. Personal interview. Sept. 30, 2005.

Steinberg, Risa. Personal interview. Sept. 28, 2005.

Talland, G.A. "Initiation of Response, and Reaction Time in Aging, and with Brain Damage." *Behavior, Aging, and the Nervous System: Biological Determinants of Speed of Behavior and Its Changes with Age*. Ed. A.T. Welford and J.E. Birren. Springfield, IL: Charles C. Thomas Publishers, 1965. 526–61.

Walters, Julie Janue, and Tyler Walters, Personal interview. Sept. 26, 2005.

Woodworth, Mark. "Opening the Eye of Nature." *Five Essays on the Dance of Erick Hawkins*. Ed. M.L. Gordon Norton. New York: Foundation for Modern Dance, 1970.

CHAPTER 10

STILL TAPPING AFTER ALL THESE YEARS: AGE AND RESPECT IN TAP DANCE

Wendy Oliver

An elegant, silver-haired gentleman in a white suit taps his feet sharply against the floor in syncopated patterns, swinging his arms front to back. His right leg bends and snaps quickly—front, back, front, across his left ankle. One moment, he's a skater gliding across the stage; the next, he's a jokester, dragging one leg behind him in an irregular limp. He pitches backward with an exuberant front hitch-kick, jumps lightly into a wide stride facing front, slides his seemingly frictionless feet together, and finishes it off with a two-footed double spin. The man is Jimmy Slyde, age seventy, performing at a tap festival in Rio de Janeiro in 1998.

Before his passing in 2002, Slyde was "one of the giants of rhythm tap, known for his great musicality, his impeccable timing and his ability to glide across the stage effortlessly" (LaRocco 1). In his late fifties and early sixties, he starred in the musical *Black and Blue*, as well as appearing in the popular Hollywood movies *Tap* and *Cotton Club*. He continued to appear at tap festivals during his seventies until declining health prevented him from doing so. Slyde is only one of many artists over the age of fifty who have graced and are gracing the stage; tap is unique as a dance form because it is well suited to the older performer.

Tap dance is a truly American dance form, with African American origins dating from the early 1800s; it has been linked to jazz music, Broadway, and Hollywood. Although its popularity has waxed and waned over the decades, tap is considered one of the predominant performance styles in the United States, along with ballet, modern, jazz,

Figure 10.1 Jimmy Slyde performing at the 55th National Folk Festival in Chattanooga, TN, 1993. Photo courtesy of the National Council for the Traditional Arts.

ballroom, and hip-hop. Tap is distinguished from those other forms because its physical demands and aesthetic qualities discriminate less against older performers. Although there are examples of older dance performers in other Western dance genres, including both modern and ballet, tap seems to have an especially large number of older performers who are not only tolerated, but embraced. The younger dancers generally revere the knowledge of the older generation, even though dance trends and styles are changing over time. According to dance writer Claudia La Rocco, "tradition, lineage, and community are highly prized among tap dancers; in interviews Mr. Glover [Savion, age thirty-five] and Mr. Slyde [eighty] described each other as being like family." Tap dance is uniquely situated as a performance genre for dancers over fifty because of its flexible physical requirements and its particular aesthetic qualities. Furthermore, the field boasts a high, positive regard for older performers, which can be traced to tap's African American roots.

In "Tap Dance: Manifestation of the African Aesthetic," dance scholar Cheryl Willis points out several qualities of tap that exhibit the African aesthetic as put forward by Africanist scholar Richard Farris Thompson. One of these qualities is "ephebism, the stronger power that comes from youth" (155) and is applicable to a dancer of any age. Thompson says,

> People in Africa, regardless of their actual age, return to strong, youthful patterning whenever they move within the streams of energy which flow from drums or other sources of percussion. They obey the implications of vitality within the music and its speed and drive. (7)

Willis notes a number of tap dancers in their sixties and seventies who connect to those "strong, youthful streams of energy" (155) as they perform. These performers may do things that seem virtuosic by the layperson's standards, such as the "shim sham" (the tap "anthem" known by the entire tap community, which has been handed down through the decades), or they may perform movements that are truly virtuosic by any standard, such as the acrobatic moves of the Nicholas Brothers, who were known for their high jumps followed by landing in splits on the floor.[1] Dancers enjoy the act of dancing and performing, thus contributing to a generally positive feeling about themselves and a sense of feeling vigorous and energetic. As one eighty-year-old tapper put it, "The secret to being old is to keep moving" (Kristofic 2). This sense of ageless power in movement stemming from the African aesthetic seems to be an intrinsic part of tap dance, creating an aura of youth.

Age studies scholar Margaret Gullette notes that people can change their body language, looks, and mannerisms to appear older or younger. While aging is usually viewed as involuntary and passive, age studies views aging as active and interactive, because we can change appearance and other outward signs of age. "We both *have* a body and...*perform* our body," Gullette observes (162). Older dancers may not be consciously performing "younger," but audiences often read them that way. Dancers may seem younger than their chronological ages due to their excellent physical fitness, energetic movements, and passion for what they do. Performers aged eighty and older may still perform with panache. What is it about tap that is particularly conducive to this phenomenon?

Tap Origins and Legacy

The origins of tap provide a road map for the interpretation of aspects of its aesthetic and attitudes toward age. The roots of tap dance are found in African American dancing, which developed from West African dance forms reshaped by the oppressive forces of slavery. For instance, according to dance scholar Lynne Fauley Emery, the use of drums was banned after a slave uprising that featured drums as a means of communication, so clapping, stomping, and beating on improvised instruments replaced the centrality of the drum (83). In addition, slaves had to give up their own religious practices, which involved dance, and convert to Christianity, which forbade dancing in church. There was a specific taboo against crossing the feet, which led to a multitude of alternatives including sliding, shuffling, and stomping (122). A large variety of dance was created during the plantation era; this served as the foundation for a related group of contemporary American dance genres, including African American vernacular dance, jazz dance, tap, and others.

One of the founders of tap, William Henry Lane, was a free African American born in 1825 who lived in the Paradise Square area of New York, a poor neighborhood where Irish immigrants and African Americans lived next to each other and learned one another's dances. He blended these two dancing styles into a new kind of jig, and became known as "Master Juba." Thus, tap resulted from a "cross-breeding" of African and Irish/Scottish/English dance emphasizing the rhythmic stomping of the feet. However, "it is appropriate that an African-American is given credit for this art form, because without the vitally important contribution of African syncopation and improvisation, there would be no tap" (Knowles 91). Syncopation, or the accenting of the off-beat or spaces between beats, made tap rhythmically distinct from the jigging of the United Kingdom. The extensive use of improvisation, which is movement created on the spot, also dominated tap but not its white correlates. From these essential ingredients, tap developed over the decades to become the form we know today.

Tap evolved in tandem with the music of the times; after World War II, the advent of complex bebop music and the decline of big bands led to a decline in the popularity of tap dance. Although the big nightclubs closed down, tap dancers managed to survive by teaching in studios and performing in smaller theatres. Fortunately, in the 1970s and 1980s, tap had a revival in Broadway shows such as *The Wiz* and *42nd Street*, and continued into the twenty-first century with shows such as *The Producers*.

Because of the ebb and flow in the popularity of tap dance, proponents often refer to it as an endangered form. In articles and documentary films, dancers discuss their concern about losing classic tap dance choreography. Brenda Bufalino[2] founded the American Tap Dance Foundation to preserve the roots of rhythm tap, a style that focuses upon hard-hitting, complex rhythms of the feet while deemphasizing movement of the torso. Bufalino's curriculum includes rhythm tap choreography that has been passed down through the decades, which she learned from old masters, including Honi Coles.[3] Bufalino notes, "[W]ithout works that can be continued on and reconstructed, tap dance is always in danger of being lost" (Rolnick 29). In the 1980 documentary *Tap Dancin'*, Maceo Anderson, of the Four Step Brothers, teaches a routine to some younger performers. One of the performers acknowledges his gratitude to Anderson for handing down his routine, saying, "Without people like you there wouldn't be people like us." Later in the same film, a member of rhythm tap group the Copasetics says, "When the old-timers go, it's going to be sad if someone doesn't try to keep it alive somehow."

Another example of this theme is embedded in the movie *Tap*, which, although fictional, uses a star-studded cast of bona fide rhythm tappers, all African American, including Gregory Hines, Bunny Briggs, Henry LeTang, Sandman, Jimmy Slyde, and many others. Part of the plot revolves around the idea that these older hoofers do not perform for a living any longer because the work has evaporated. The younger protagonist, played by Hines, serves as a symbol for the art form of rhythm tap. He has to decide whether he will follow a life of crime by working as a well-paid second-story man, or return to his tap roots, becoming a performer with a less certain financial future. The older hoofers, who are his mentors, want to see him "make the right choice" not only to keep him away from crime, but also to further the cause of rhythm tap, which they fear will die when they do. In the end, he does choose tap, both preserving its traditional style and moving it forward by tapping to rock music and African conga drumming. As a member of the younger generation, Hines picks up the mantle of the rhythm tap legacy and makes it his own.

In her analysis of tap dancing, scholar Brenda Dixon Gottschild notes that both Hines and Savion Glover have honored their predecessors. "Like Hines, Glover pays glowing tribute to his mentors, acknowledging that he is building on their superb lead. These hoofers and troupers developed tap culture and spirit...They passed the legacy on to him and encouraged him to build upon it" (121). This idea of legacy and history is prominent in classes and courses based on rhythm tap; the American Tap Dance Foundation created an educational show based on tap history in New York that has been touring area schools through the Young Audiences program (Rolnick 32).

The importance of tap dance history and legacy can be viewed as a way of counteracting the fear that tap could die out without adequate support. Because of this mind-set, many tap dance teachers are taking care to instill in their youth a respect for the elder statesmen and women of tap. This kind of respect for older, experienced artists makes the survival of tap much more likely, since youth admire the artistry of their elders and want to keep it alive. Master teacher Dianne "Lady Di" Walker says, "You have to know the history. You have to have an understanding of what it all is, the spirit about the dance. It's more than just steps. The young tap dancers coming out of the festivals today are also repositories for people of my generation and everything we brought with us and inherited" (Goldberg 1). As time marches on and many of the old masters pass away, Walker's admonitions become ever more pertinent.

Tap is an intergenerational form that continues to be handed down from older, experienced dancers to younger ones. In many cases, dancers of very different ages perform side by side onstage, as Dianne Walker (age fifty-eight) and acclaimed New Yorker Michelle Dorrance (age twenty-nine) did at the Massachusetts Museum of Contemporary Art tap residency in 2008 (Liberatore 1). Dorrance's website lists some of the older "greats" with whom she has performed, including the late Fayard Nicholas, who was sixty-six years her senior! As evidenced in these examples and many others, old, middle-aged, and young tap dancers may all take the stage together, united through the artistic expression of their feet. It is interesting to contemplate what aspects of tap make it physically possible for such a wide range of ages.[4]

Physical Demands of Tap

There are many different styles of tap, some of which are more strenuous than others. The flash acts of the Nicholas Brothers involved tapping interspersed with acrobatics; Fred Astaire's style was fluid and balletic;

rhythm tap has a focus on the feet, which hit the floor hard to create distinctive sounds. Clearly, acrobatic feats become more difficult as bodies age and lose flexibility, although the Nicholas Brothers continued such moves well into their sixties (Hill 258). However, most kinds of tap do not require extreme flexibility of the joints, since the high kicks, back bends, and soaring leaps of other dance forms are not essential parts of the tap movement vocabulary.

Tap requires extremely refined control of the feet; it appears that once this skill has been inculcated, it diminishes little until very old age. Also, since rhythm tap involves improvisation, dancers are free to show off their individual strengths and omit movements that are problematic. When Fayard Nicholas developed arthritis in his late sixties, his brother Harold said, "Don't do the splits, just let me do it. Just use your hands" (Hill 258). They adapted their act to accommodate Fayard's arthritis and continued performing successfully for many years afterward. Even non-improvisational forms of tap showcase the talents of older dancers appropriately, since the dancers themselves usually choreograph them, either collectively or individually.

Moreover, tap dancers are not as likely as other kinds of dancers to be judged by traditional standards of beauty; women and men of various shapes and sizes are welcomed onstage, as is clear from performances and films I have seen. Tap dance emphasizes the motions of the feet rather than the shape or line of the body. There is no perfect height or weight for a tap dancer, because the requirements are more focused around rhythmic ability, precision, dexterity of the feet, and individual style, which come in bodies of many shapes, sizes, and ages. Another feature of tap is that extended high-energy stints requiring an athletic aerobic capacity are optional, allowing performers or students to use a slower, smooth style if desired. Tap teacher Elaine Colaneri (age seventy) says, "I have three students who are in their seventies. You *can* tap when you're older. The Shim Sham, instead of doing it shuffle step, shuffle step, you keep it close and just slide…" (2). Although tap can be modified to suit varied physical states, most over-fifty performers that I have seen excel both technically and artistically.

In the keynote address at the Women in Tap Festival in 2008, dance historian Sali Ann Kriegsman notes, "You can be technically brilliant, but there is more to being an artist. We see it in the older dancers. Most ballet and modern dancers mature artistically just when their bodies begin to give out. Tap dancers can look forward to a long dancing life, one that will become more about your interior life than your outward flash" (5). In tap, a focus upon elements such as syncopation, musicality, precision, clarity, and improvisation make it possible for mature performers to shine. These older artists are revered within the tap community and intermingle freely with younger performers; however, this is not the norm in American society. Age studies research shows a distinct segregation in American society between the young and old.

Aging and Tap

According to many age studies scholars (e.g., Cuddy and Fisher; Greenberg, Schmid, and Martens; Cruikshank; Gullette), old people evoke fear in younger people because aging faces remind the young and middle-aged of their own mortality. Encounters with elders' wrinkled faces reflect their own images twenty, thirty, or forty years from now. Additionally, in their article "Doddering but Dear: Process, Content, and Function in Stereotyping of Older Persons," Amy Cuddy and Susan Fisher note that age is a marker for how to treat others, and invites stereotyping. They posit that stereotyping requires an "in group" and an "out group," in this case, "not old" versus "old." Stereotyping is a shortcut that quickly allows us to decide how to treat people whom we do not know personally.

Researchers have identified three common stereotypes of "out groups": (1) warm and incompetent, (2) competent and cold, and (3) incompetent and cold. Only the "in group" can be both competent and warm, where warm is defined as "affectionate, friendly, good-natured, kind and trustworthy," and cold is the lack of those qualities (Cuddy and Fisher 11). Cuddy and Fisher note that old people are often victims of a paternalistic prejudice, in which they are pitied but not respected. For instance, during the 2000 presidential election, the media portrayed Florida's older voters as incompetent—that is, not knowing proper voting procedures (17). Typically in the United States, the elderly fall under the first stereotype of "warm and incompetent." An older tap dancer may confound stereotyping by being both competent and warm, since a good tap dancer, regardless of age, often exhibits the characteristics of being friendly and good-natured as well as physically agile.

Stereotyping—whether around race, gender, religion, or age—can lead to discrimination. In "Ageism: Denying the Face of the Future," Jeff Greenberg, Jeff Schmid, and Andy Martens discuss age discrimination in hiring and forced retirement, asserting that this problem stems from "terror management." This is Ernest Becker's term for how awareness of our own mortality creates anxiety. We manage this fear by denying death; we deny death by avoiding contact with the elderly, who remind us of death. However, the researchers state that the elderly who appear very healthy physically and/or psychologically can have a moderating effect on the younger person's fear of death. This effect is at play while younger people watch older dance performers; younger audiences see that these dancers are apparently physically and mentally extremely healthy, and so anxiety about old age and death recedes.

As in the earlier stereotype above in which the elderly are assumed to be warm but incompetent, Becca Levy and Mahzarin Banaji state that older adults are assumed to be less competent than younger adults. They note that although it is true that some capabilities may decline with age, it is wrong to assume, for instance, that all elderly have poor memories. In fact, several experiments have found a strong psychological component to performing tasks capably. These researchers have demonstrated that older subjects perform more poorly on tasks when they are primed with negative age stereotypes than when they are primed with positive age stereotypes (57–63). This shows that people are actually biased against themselves when they think of themselves as "old" in a negative way (58). However, people are willing to put aside negative stereotypes once presented with evidence to the contrary (68). When older adults tap, they are refuting negative stereotypes of age, replacing them with more positive images of aging. The authors suggest that by limiting exposure to negative stereotyping and by increasing exposure to positive images of aging—as happens when audiences watch older dancers performing competently—striking temporary changes in attitude result, and those results can be longer lasting (69).

The research in these articles presents a viewpoint on ageism that involves the negative stereotyping of old people, and each shows that this stereotyping is harmful and problematic for society, but can be mitigated by actions and experiences such as seeing older adults performing competently in various situations, including onstage. Although not explicitly stated, it is likely that most studies cited in these articles involved primarily white people rather than minorities. Because society remarks on such classifications as race, gender, class, or age only when they differ from what is designated as the norm, the lack of "marking" of race in most studies implies that they were undertaken on the racial majority. In order to understand differences between the "norm" in these studies and in those involving African Americans, it is important to investigate the literature written specifically about African Americans in order to make the link among tap, African American traditions, and aging.

African American Aging

Race (as well as class, gender, ability, and sexual orientation) plays a role in determining the nature of our experience as older adults. Research shows that the experience of aging as an African American is significantly different from that of a white person in the United States. Since tap was created primarily by African Americans, understanding the nature of aging in this culture may offer insights into how and why older tap dancers are often treated in a positive manner within the tap community. Tap studies can draw upon the significant scholarship about aging within African American culture, starting from the slavery era.

H.C. Covey and P.T. Lockman reviewed 2,200 ex-slave narratives collected in the 1930s, along with other historical documents, to discover how older African Americans lived during the time of slavery. Research showed that although aging slaves were less valued by whites than their younger counterparts were, they were valued and respected within their African American communities (1). The narratives showed that grandparents played a large part in raising children, as well as passing on "folk wisdom, mother wit, and cultural traditions to the young in early America" (4). In addition, instruction in reading, writing, religion, and folk medicine was passed on through the elders. The authors conclude that this same pattern of honoring elders "may be mirrored in contemporary society by the African American community and the roles of its older members" (9). The authors also discovered a sense of family among the different generations, even in the difficult conditions of slavery, in which biological families were often broken apart.

Nellie Tate's article "The Black Aging Experience" points out that blacks and whites adjust to aging differently because of basic inequalities in society. Her article reviews a number of different studies, some of which examine satisfaction in old age comparing blacks and whites. Tate describes a 1981 study that showed that blacks between the ages of eighteen and sixty-four had more positive attitudes toward the elderly than did whites:

> Many values associated with Afro-American life are rooted in West African cultures, which tend to espouse a view of humanity living in harmony with nature. Values associated with this philosophical perspective underscore the importance of mutual cooperation, interdependence, and the collective rather than individual good. (98–99)

One example of this philosophy is "absorption of the young," meaning that older black adults may take in children, grandchildren, or other younger relatives. These younger relatives are more likely than young whites to "accept their aged who become functionally impaired as a result of debilitating chronic conditions. Consequently, absorbed relatives may reciprocate important emotional and other care-giving benefits..." (99). Also, older blacks often have close relationships with "fictive kin" (people who are not related by blood, but are nonetheless accepted as family members), while most whites do not. "For blacks, the system of extended kinship, allowing flexibility in family boundaries and roles, has been an important coping mechanism helping family members survive hardships imposed by slavery, Jim Crow laws, and economic bust periods" (Tate 102).

Similarly, tap artists often speak of fellow dancers as family, as Dianne Walker did in a 2009 interview. Many years ago, she performed with the eleven-year-old Glover for an extended run in Paris: "He was at my hip...We forged a relationship. I consider him my son. He had such enthusiasm for tap...We were quite a match. We were very close" (Liberatore 2). The importance of supportive relationships among people of different generations outside the traditional family structure is apparent within both the tap and African American communities.

In a related vein, Tate cites a study by Linn (100), which found that 73 percent of older whites and 43 percent of older blacks viewed themselves as younger than their actual ages. This difference suggests that the stigma for being older is greater for whites than for blacks. As a corollary, it appears that black elders have more prestige than white elders within their own racial group (101), as evidenced by attitudes toward issues such as elderly caregiving. Scharlach, Kellem, Ong, Baskin, Goldstein, and Fox found that "minority caregivers tend to use formal support services substantially less than their non-Hispanic white counterparts" (134). One African American caregiver said, "Minority groups have more cultural emphasis on caring for their own people. It provides stronger family ties, and that's what allows me to do it, as part of the community, part of the culture" (140). Other African Americans concurred that family are expected to take care of their older members, but rather than thinking of it as a burden, most thought of it as a positive experience.

Other studies on caring for African American elders show similar results: African Americans are more likely than whites to take on eldercare within their extended families and derive a sense of personal fulfillment from it (White, Townsend, and Stephens; Stewart). Regarding respect for elders, a 2008 Yankelovich survey showed that among the thirty-nine million African Americans in the United States, 88 percent of respondents, including 84 percent of teenagers, have a great respect for their elders (Jones, "Radio One"). With this in mind, it seems logical that an African American dance form, although practiced by whites as well as blacks, would mirror many of its originators' cultural attitudes, including those concerning family and the elderly. Multigenerational kinship networks and respect for elders are values held dear by the tap community.

These values were particularly apparent during the 1970s and 1980s, when a number of women, white and black, sought out the "old masters" of tap and brought them back into the limelight. The masters, mainly African American men, had been through the tap heydays of the 1930s and 1940s, and then endured a lengthy hiatus when tap was no longer popular. Women such as Brenda Bufalino, Lynn Dally, and Dianne Walker were responsible for bringing renewed energy and respect to the art of tap by hosting tap festivals and performances, opening schools, and creating tap companies that paid tribute to their elder statesmen. Sali Ann Kriegsman, another sponsor of the tap renaissance, asked of the tap community, "Are we taking the gifts we have received from our elders and contemporaries and passing them on with attribution and credit to those coming up now? Are we working to include rather than exclude? And are we practicing and inspiring in others high standards of craft and artistic practices and professional behavior?" (5). This quotation sums up the values that are so important to the tap community: respect for elders, working intergenerationally, appropriate attribution, inclusiveness, and holding high standards.

An Audience Member's Perspective

Scholar Anne Davis Basting discusses several senior-aged performance groups in her book *The Stages of Age*, including the Grandparents Living Theatre, Roots & Branches, Suzanne Lacy's *Crystal Quilt*, and Kazuo Ohno's *Water Lilies*. One group, the Geritol Frolics of Minnesota, performs a musical review with singing, dancing, and several costume changes. Basting points out that although the version of "old age" that is performed in each group is different, "they share a common attempt to ease the fears of old age by demonstrating the ability of older adults to represent and perform themselves even at the farthest reaches of the life course" (184). Basting believes that these performing groups construct age in a way that makes it impossible to generalize about being old, which is also a way to prevent elders from becoming "the other."

My viewing experiences corroborate Basting's insight about watching older performers. I have seen live performances of the Copasetics (in their eighties) and Brenda Bufalino (in her seventies), both of which amazed and delighted me. Perhaps my amazement was ageist—as a middle-aged person, I probably automatically underestimated what people of that age can do onstage, and thus was surprised when their technical proficiency was so outstanding and their energy level so high. It is impossible to separate the perceived age of the performer from his or her persona onstage, so it is difficult to know how much the knowledge of a dancer's age colors one's enjoyment of the show. I suspect it does add an extra positive ingredient, since the viewer is relating to the performer and thinking, "If she can do that at her age, then I may also be equally energetic when I'm in my seventies." As Basting has pointed out, simply replacing negative images of aging with positive ones does not solve the problems of ageism or of failing health (14). However, it does underline the need to view aging as a multidimensional process that is neither totally joyful nor totally depressing. When I viewed Bufalino and the Copasetics onstage, they changed my perception of what it means to be in one's seventies or eighties, and as a result, it was impossible to hold on to a particular stereotype of old age.

A Meaningful Passion

Simone de Beauvoir's extensive treatise *The Coming of Age*, concludes:

> There is only one solution if old age is not to be an absurd parody of our former life, and that is to go on pursuing ends that give our existence a meaning—devotion to individuals, to groups or to causes, social, political, intellectual or creative work...in old age we should wish still to have passions strong enough to prevent us turning in upon ourselves. (540)

Veteran tap performers have this meaningful passion; they have devoted themselves to creative work as well as to the honing of the technical skills and expressive qualities that accompany it. Many of them also are devoted to groups of like-minded dancers and to the cause of preserving tap.

Proponents of rhythm tap in particular are passionate about proclaiming and preserving its African American heritage. One reason for this attention to heritage is the past history of cultural appropriation of black art forms by whites, where whites adopt and adapt music, dance, and visual art originating in black culture without giving credit to their sources.[5] Tap dancers who respect and credit their tap heritage counteract this tendency. Reverence for heritage is also related to the African American experience of aging, which is significantly different from that of white America. African Americans generally show greater respect for elders and view aging in a more positive light than do their white counterparts. Tap dancers (whether black or white) reflect these values by revering older "dance heroes" and passing on their legacies to the next generation.

Aside from cultural values that promote longevity in performers, tap is also physically well suited to older performers. Although tap dance can be extremely athletic, it does not need to be. It requires rhythmic precision and style, but not extreme flexibility, acrobatic moves, or extensive turn-ing, features that are typically present in other Western dance forms, from which performers typically retire by about forty years of age. Tap is per-haps the most musical North American dance form, since the performer is actually creating music with the feet, and in the case of rhythm tap, may be "conversing" with live musicians onstage. This musical ability is clearly on view in performances of the "old masters," male and female.

Both the practice and performance of tap by dancers over the age of fifty is a way of destabilizing age-based stereotypes and creating positive images of aging. The power of dancers' "meaningful passions" creates a space for audiences to reenvision themselves as fully engaged members of society all the way into old age. Nowhere is this more evident than in the Shim Sham, the short dance learned by tappers of all ages. Commonly, at a tap performance where many different groups or individuals are par-ticipating, the show ends with everyone performing this delightful piece. The Shim Sham is a lively metaphor for the tap community: an inclusive, multigenerational place that treasures its "old masters" and their legacy.

Notes

1. The Nicholas Brothers, then 22- and 15-years-old, premiered in the Zigfield Follies of 1936; in 1996, they were the Ruth Page Visiting Artists in Dance at Harvard and Radcliffe.

2. Brenda Bufalino is one of the white women responsible for the revival of rhythm tap in the 1980s and 1990s. Now in her seventies, she continues to create new work and tour with her company, and is a popular figure at tap festivals around the world. She works with text and film as well as live music, creating new blends of varied art forms. In a 2009 postperformance discussion in Rhode Island, one of her dancers described Bufalino's studio as the "mecca for tap dance" in New York.

3. Honi Coles (1911–1992), an African American, worked in New York night-clubs during his youth, then toured with big bands such as Duke Ellington's and Louis Armstrong's. At age 65, he performed in the musical *Bubbling Brown Sugar*, both on Broadway and touring through Holland. At seventy-three, he was starring in *My One and Only* on Broadway, winning awards for best featured actor in a musical. Coles also worked with Brenda Bufalino and her company, the American Tap Dance Orchestra, in his seventies (Fraser 1).

4. The strong presence of tappers who dance in their older years is exempli-fied in the amateur as well as the professional tap community. Some of the hundreds of groups listed online are the Toe Tappers (Philadelphia), the Twilight Tappers (New Haven, CT), Golden Tappers (Melbourne, Australia), and the St. Louis Strutters (St. Louis, MO). These almost entirely female companies boast busy schedules. The St. Louis Strutters, for example, are booked over six months in advance for approximately five

shows per month. Their ages are fifty to seventy-five, and they donate all their earnings to charitable organizations.

5. For an extensive discussion on this issue, see Brenda Dixon Gottschild's *Black Dancing Body. A Geography from Coon to Cool* (21 26; 167 68).

Works Cited

Basting, Anne Davis. *The Stages of Age: Performing Age in Contemporary American Culture.* Ann Arbor: U of Michigan P, 1998.

Black and Blue. Dir. Claudio Segovia and Hector Orzzoli. Chor. Cholly Atkins, Henry Le Tang, Frankie Manning, Fayard Nicholas. Minskoff Theatre, New York. 1989–1991.

Colaneri, Elaine. Personal interview. Apr. 14, 2009.

Cotton Club. Dir. Francis Ford Coppola. Perf. Richard Gere, Gregory Hines, Diane Lane. 1984.

Covey, H.C., and P.T. Lockman. "Narrative References to Older African Americans Living under Slavery." *Social Science Journal* 33 (1996): 23–38.

Cruikshank, Margaret. *Learning to Be Old: Gender, Culture, and Aging.* Lanham, MD: Rowman and Littlefield, 2003.

Cuddy, Amy, and Susan Fisher. "Doddering but Dear: Process, Content, and Function in Stereotyping of Older Persons." *Ageism: Stereotyping and Prejudice against Older Persons.* Ed. Todd D. Nelson. Cambridge, MA: MIT Press, 2002, 3–26.

DeBeauvoir, Simone. *The Coming of Age.* New York: G.P. Putnam's Sons, 1972.

Dilworth-Anderson, Peggye, Ishan Canty Williams, and Sharon Wallace Williams. "Urban Elderly African Americans." *Age through Ethnic Lenses: Caring for the Elderly in a Multicultural Society.* Ed. Laura Katz Olson. Lanham, MD: Rowman and Littlefield, 2001, 95–102.

Dorrance, Michelle. "Biography." Michelle Dorrance's Web site. Aug. 28, 2009. <http://www.michelledorrance.com/bio.html>.

Emery, Lynne Fauley. *Black Dance from 1619 to Today, 2nd ed.* Pennington, NJ: Princeton Book, 1988.

Forty-Second Street. Book, Michael Steward and Mark Bramble. Lyrics, Al Dubin. Music, Harry Warren. New York, 1933 and 1980.

Fraser, Gerald. "Honi Coles: Recalling 50 Years of Tap." *New York Times.* July 17, 1984. July 8, 2009. <http://www.nytimes.com/1984/07/17/arts/honi-coles-recalling-50-years-of-tap.html>.

Goldberg, Jane. "Dianne Walker: Teacher's Wisdom." *Dance Magazine* Feb. 2005. June 15, 2009. <http://findarticles.com/p/articles/mi_m1083/is_2_79/ai_n8707433/>.

Gottschild, Brenda Dixon. *The Black Dancing Body: A Geography from Coon to Cool.* New York: Palgrave Macmillan, 2003.

Greenberg, Jeff, Jeff Schmid, and Andy Martens. "Ageism: Denying the Face of the Future." *Ageism: Stereotyping and Prejudice against Older Persons.* Ed. Todd D. Nelson. Cambridge, MA: MIT Press, 2002, 27–48.

Gullette, Margaret Morganroth. *Aged by Culture*. Chicago: U of Chicago P, 2004.

Hill, Constance Valis. *Brotherhood in Rhythm: The Jazz Tap Dancing of the Nicholas Brothers*. New York: Oxford UP, 2000.

Jimenez, Jillian. "The History of Grandmothers in the African-American Community." *Social Service Review* (Dec. 2002): 523–51.

Jones, Charisse. "Sweeping Study Finds Blacks in U.S. Divers, Optimistic." *USA Today* June 27, 2008. June 23, 2009. <http://0web.ebscohost.com.helin.uri. edu/ehost/delivery?vid=9&hid=102&sid=8bede81d-8...>.

Knowles, Mark. *Tap Roots: The Early History of Tap Dancing*. Jefferson, NC: MacFarland, 2002.

Kriegsman, Sali Ann. "Can You Hear Us Now?" Keynote speech, Women in Tap conference, 2008. June 12, 2009. <http://blog.solestories.org/?page_id=902>.

Kristofic, Christina. "Toe Tappers Are Still Going Strong." *The Intelligencer* (Philadelphia) June 15, 2009. <http://www.phillyburbs.com/news/local/the_intelligencer/the_intelligencer_news_details/a...>.

La Rocco, Claudia. "Jimmy Slyde, Dancer and a Giant of Rhythm Tap, Dies at 80." *New York Times* May 17, 2008. July 8, 2009. <http://www.nytimes.com/2008/05/17/arts/dance/17slyde.html?r=1&scp=1&sq=jimmy%20...>.

Levy, Becca, and Mahzarin Banaji. "Implicit Ageism." *Ageism: Stereotyping and Prejudice against Older Persons*. Ed. Todd D. Nelson. Cambridge, MA: MIT Press, 2002, 49–76.

Liberatore, Wendy. "Lady Di Pleased with State of Tap." *Daily Gazette.com*. Schenectady, NY. Feb. 23, 2008. June 15, 2009. <http://www.dailygazette.com/new/2008/feb/23/0223_Diannewalker/>.

Linn, M.W., and K. Hunter. "Perceptions of Age in the Elderly." *Journal of Gerontology* 34.1 (1979): 46–52.

The Producers. Adapted from film by Mel Brooks and Thomas Meehan. Dir. Mike Ockrent. Choreographer Susan Stroman. New York, 2001.

"Radio One Releases Largest National Survey Conducted on African-Americans." *Target Market News: The Black Consumer Market Authority*. June 25, 2009. <http://www.targetmarketnews.com/storyid06270801.htm>.

Register, J.C. "Aging and Race: A Black/White Comparative Analysis." *Gerontologist* 21.4 (1981): 438–43.

Rolnick, Katie. "A New Take on New York Tap." *Dance Teacher* (May 2009): 28–34.

Scharlach, Andrew, Roxanne Kellem, Natasha Ong, Aeran Baskin, Cara Goldstein, and Patrick Fox. "Cultural Attitudes and Caregiver Service Use: Lessons from Focus Groups with Racially and Ethnically Diverse Family Caregivers." *Journal of Gerontological Social Work* 47.1/2 (2006): 133–56.

Slyde, Jimmy. "Here's That Rainy Day." Tap performance in Rio de Janeiro. 1998. Aug. 30, 2009. <http://www.youtube.com/watch?v—Z7b1vcchMck>.

Stewart, Pearl. "Care Provision for African American Elders: Family Attitudes and Strategies." *Journal of Intergenerational Relationships* 6.1 (2008): 61–80.

Tap. Dir. Nick Castle. Perf. Gregory Hines, Bunny Briggs, Henry LeTang, Jimmy Slyde, Sandman, Sammy Davis, Jr. Sony Pictures, 1989.

TapDancin'. Dir. Christian Blackwood. Perf. Harold & Fayard Nicholas, Honi Coles, Copasetics. Michael Blackwood Productions, 1980.

Tate, Nellie. "The Black Aging Experience." *Aging in Minority Groups.* Ed. R.L. McNeely and John Colen. Beverly Hills, CA: Sage Publications, 1983, 95–107.

Thompson, Robert Farris. *African Art in Motion: Icon and Act.* Los Angeles: University of California, 1974.

White, Tracela, Aloen Townsend, and Mary Ann Parris Stephens. "Comparisons of African American and White Women in the Parent Care Role." *Gerontologist* 40.6 (2000): 718–28.

Willis, Cheryl. "Tap Dance: Manifestation of the African Aesthetic." *African Dance: An Artistic, Historical and Philosophical Inquiry.* Ed. Kariamu Welsh Asante. Trenton, NJ: Africa World Press, 1994, 145–59.

The Wiz. Dir. Geoffrey Holder. Perf. Stephanie Mills. New York, 1975–1979.

NOTES ON CONTRIBUTORS

Heather Addison is an associate professor of film studies at Western Michigan University. Her primary research area is Hollywood's relationship to American culture, though she has recently begun writing about international cinema. Her books include *Hollywood and the Rise of Physical Culture* (Routledge, 2003) and *Motherhood Misconceived*, a collection of essays coedited with Elaine Roth and Mary Kate Goodwin-Kelly (forthcoming from SUNY UP).

Anne Basting is the director of the Center on Age & Community and an associate professor in the department of theatre at the Peck School of the Arts, University of Wisconsin–Milwaukee. Basting has written extensively on issues of aging and representation, including two books, *Forget Memory: Creating Better Lives for People with Dementia* (2009) and *The Stages of Age: Performing Age in Contemporary American Culture* (1998). Basting is the recipient of a Rockefeller Fellowship, a Brookdale National Fellowship, and numerous major grants for her scholarly and creative endeavors. Her creative work includes nearly a dozen plays and public performances. Basting received a PhD in theatre arts from the University of Minnesota. She continues to direct the TimeSlips Creative Storytelling Project, which she founded in 1998.

Jessica Berson is lecturer in drama at the University of Exeter in the United Kingdom, where she teaches dance and performance studies. She received a PhD in theatre from the University of Wisconsin–Madison in 2005, under the direction of Sally Banes. Publications include a recent article in *TDR/The Drama Review* and essays in the collections *Bodies in Commotion: Disability and Performance*, *The Community Performance Reader*, and *Dance and Culture: History, Criticism, and Recent Trends*. Certified in Laban Movement Analysis and Pilates, Berson has choreographed a number of works for intergenerational dance groups, including Kaleidoscope and B.O.L.D. (Beautiful Old Ladies Dancing).

Barbara Dickinson, professor of the practice of dance at Duke University, was director of the dance program for eighteen years before stepping

down in 2007. Dickinson has created many large-scale, full-evening collaborative choreographic works, including *Walking Miracles*, an original
dance/theater production based on the stories of six survivors of child
sexual abuse, and *Contents Under Pressure*, an exploration of the many faces
of bias in society, co-choreographed with Ava LaVonne Vinesett. She
was artistic director of the Ways and Means Dance Company from 1986
through 2002, and of Three for All, a company composed of a dancer, a
poet, and a pianist, from 1981 through 1987. She is a founding member,
actress, and choreographer for Manbites Dog Theater. A Phi Beta Kappa
scholar, she holds a bachelor's degree in classics and anthropology from
the University of California, Riverside, and a master's degree in performing arts–dance from the American University.

Janet Hill is professor emeritus in the English department at Saint Mary's
University, Halifax, Nova Scotia, where she taught the history of drama.
Among her courses were "Shakespeare: Text and Performance," in which
students attended the Shakespeare Centre in Stratford-upon-Avon and
the New Globe in London, and "Contemporary Plays by Women," a
course focusing on new women playwrights. She is the author of *Stages
and Playgoers: Guild Plays to Shakespeare* (McGill-Queen's Press, 2002).

E. Ann Kaplan, a distinguished professor of English and comparative
literary and cultural studies at Stony Brook University, also founded and
directs the Humanities Institute there. She is currently past president of
the Society for Cinema and Media Studies. Kaplan has written many
books and articles on topics in cultural studies, media, and women's
studies, from diverse theoretical perspectives including psychoanalysis,
feminism, postmodernism, and postcolonialism. She has given lectures
all over the world, and her work has been translated into six languages.
Her most recent books are *Feminism and Film* (Oxford UP, 2000), *Trauma
and Cinema: Cross-Cultural Explorations* (coedited with Ban Wang) (Hong
Kong UP, 2004), and *Trauma Culture: The Politics of Terror and Loss in
Media and Literature* (Rutgers UP, 2005). She is working on two projects, *Public Feelings, Memory, and Affective Difference in Visual Culture*, and
Screening Older Women: Desire, Shame, and the Body.

Jeanne Klein is an associate professor in the department of theatre
at the University of Kansas, where she teaches courses in theatre for
young audiences (TYA), children's drama, and media psychology. Her
national-award-winning young audience studies illuminate how children
interpret and evaluate theatre performances. She has published numerous
articles in the *Youth Theatre Journal*, *TYA Today*, *Journal of Dramatic Theory
and Criticism*, *Journal of Aesthetic Education*, *Theatre Research in Canada*, and
Canadian Children's Literature, among others.

Neal King is an associate professor of sociology at Virginia Tech. His research interests include film genres, media violence, aging, inequality, and violent crime. He is the author of *Heroes in Hard Times: Cop Action Movies in the U.S.* (Temple UP, 1999), and coeditor of *Reel Knockouts: Violent Women in the Movies* (University of Texas Press, 2001). His articles have been published in such journals as the *Journal of Film and Video, Gender & Society, Men and Masculinities,* and *NWSA Journal,* as well as in books on aging and popular culture. He earned a PhD in sociology at the University of California at Santa Barbara (1996).

Valerie Barnes Lipscomb teaches literature and directs the Writing Resource Center at the University of South Florida Sarasota-Manatee. Her articles on the performance of age in drama have appeared in such journals as *Shaw: The Annual of Bernard Shaw Studies* and the *Journal of Aging and Identity.* She has presented papers at conferences of organizations such as the Modern Language Association and the Association for Theatre in Higher Education. A PEO Scholar Award recipient, Lipscomb holds a PhD in English with a concentration in twentieth-century literature, as well as a master's degree in humanities and a bachelor's in English. Prior to pursuing an academic career, she was a professional writer and editor.

Leni Marshall's research focuses on multicultural U.S. literatures and critical understandings of aging, ageism, and old age; her current project explores aging via literary, feminist, and cultural studies, arguing that age should be a category of analysis just as other identity categories are. Marshall's work has appeared in venues such as the *Journal of Aging, Humanities, and the Arts; Transformations: The Journal of Inclusive Scholarship and Pedagogy;* and *The Women's Review of Books.* For the *National Women's Studies Association Journal,* she guest edited a special issue on interdisciplinary aging studies. Marshall serves on the MLA Age Studies Discussion Group's executive council, the advisory board for the Network of Aging Studies in Europe, and the editorial board of the *Aging Studies in Europe* book series. Before entering academia, she worked for home health-care agencies, senior care homes, and a managed health-care consulting firm, and Marshall is now an assistant professor of literature at the University of Wisconsin–Stout.

Wendy Oliver is a professor at Providence College, with an MFA in dance from Temple University and an EdD in dance education from Columbia University. She is the coeditor and a contributing author for the book *Women Making Art: Women in the Visual, Literary, and Performing Arts since 1960* (Peter Lang Publishing, 2001). In addition to choreographing for the Providence College Dance Company, Oliver has published articles in *Journal of Dance Education*; *Dance Research Journal*; *Journal of Physical Education, Recreation and Dance*; and others. Her book *Writing about Dance* will be published by Human Kinetics in 2010.

Ruth Pe Palileo received her PhD from the Samuel Beckett Centre School of Drama at Trinity College Dublin, Ireland. She also holds a master's degree from University of Detroit–Mercy. She writes screenplays (including *The Good Deed*) for Iclosada Films in Las Vegas, as well as plays (including *High Stakes*) for the Pintig Cultural Group in Chicago. Sometimes she writes poetry (most recently for Deep Bowl Press's anthology *Yellow as Turmeric, Fragrant as Cloves*). She also directs for Pintig and for Las Vegas Little Theatre in Las Vegas.

Allen Wood is a professor of French and chair of the French section at Purdue University. His research interests include seventeenth-century literature, Molière, La Fontaine, and business French writing. Wood's publications include authoring *Literary Satire and Theory: A Study of Horace, Boileau, and Pope* and editing *Les Hippolyte français du dix-septième siècle*, as well as about thirty other articles on French seventeenth-century literature and business French. Wood has been the coeditor of the *Global Business Languages* journal since 1996. This article combines his specialty with his wife's; she is the executive director of the local Area Agency on Aging. He has a PhD from the University of Michigan.

INDEX